Spaces and Significations

Critic of Institutions

Roberta Kevelson
General Editor

Vol. 10

PETER LANG
New York • Washington, D.C./Baltimore
Bern • Frankfurt am Main • Berlin • Vienna • Paris

Spaces and Significations

Edited by
Roberta Kevelson

PETER LANG
New York • Washington, D.C./Baltimore
Bern • Frankfurt am Main • Berlin • Vienna • Paris

Library of Congress Cataloging-in-Publication Data

Spaces and significations/
edited by Roberta Kevelson.
p. cm. — (Critic of institutions; vol. 10)
Includes bibliographical references and index.
1. Semiotics (Law). 2. Jurisprudence. 3. Law—Philosophy.
I. Kevelson, Roberta. II. Series.
K213.S66 95-45393
ISBN 0-8204-3017-X
ISSN 1068-4689

Die Deutsche Bibliothek-CIP-Einheitsaufnahme

Kevelson, Roberta:
Spaces and significations/
edited by Roberta Kevelson.
- New York; Washington, D.C./Baltimore; Bern;
Frankfurt am Main; Berlin; Vienna; Paris: Lang.
(Critic of institutions; Vol. 10)
ISBN 0-8204-3017-X
NE: GT

The paper in this book meets the guidelines for permanence and durability
of the Committee on Production Guidelines for Book Longevity
of the Council of Library Resources.

Printed in the United States of America.

ACKNOWLEDGMENTS

We express our appreciation to Penn State, to its several offices and divisions that have continued to endorse and support the Center for Semiotic Research in Law, Government and Economics which has provided the necessary resources to prepare this volume for publication. Again, our deepest thanks to the Xerox Foundation for its contribution to the work of the Center. Especially I thank Cindy Palecek for once more bringing a manuscript into publishable shape. Not least, it must be said that a collection of papers by scholars representing so wide a range of academic disciplines and so varied personal and cultural referents is nothing short of a realization of Peirce's ideal of a community of inquirers. Each member of the community which this book represents has been exceptionally sensitive to the demands of such relational roles, and has stepped forward to be counted, to share. It is an uncommon act to freely bind oneself into such a community as the covers of a book-collection signifies. And so I acknowledge, with thanks.

CONTENTS

Part IV

PART I

Chapter One

DESIGN as HUMANIZED SPACE

Roberta Kevelson

I
Introduction

It has been my custom to choose the most neutral manner of organizing collections of papers in books such as this which is to present contributed papers according to the alphabetical order of the authors" last names. There is always at least one reader who expresses the opinion that the chapters would be better grouped together according to some dominant commonality. But this has seemed to me an updated instinct, not so much to socialization, as to a nearly universal tendency to distinguish between "me" and "you" and by extension "us" and "them." This tendency to interpret the world according to the two major classes of us and not-us may be one of the few shared human tendencies that we may loosely rank as near-universal. It is a spatial concept, since the distinction is most elementally depicted as an "us," equivalent to inner space, and a "them," as equivalent to an outer space. It is this primitive notion which tacitly assumes such boundaries; such boundaries do in fact carry forward in the idea of legal property, of private property, of cultural and intellectual property, and of inalienable possessions translated into moral equivalents of character-attributes and personal "properties."

Inasmuch as I find little or nothing more powerful in maintaining civility, turn-taking, procedures for exchange and transaction of goods and values of all manner among people, I hold onto this idea of private property as that artifice which works better than others, in the actual world of human societies. But I like to break up this order when I have the privilege, as I do here, of bringing together a wonderfully complex and free "community of inquirers" who do not in any way fit into an editorial grid except in *provisional* manner, or in a short-lived, benign, and respectful procrustean squeeze. What I previously rejected, I do now: I am compromising my principles to be categorically neutral and will attempt to justify the "order of significance" in this book, *Spaces and Significations*.

Thus I place my principles here in the name of Design: I understand that Design is always based on the artifice of a whole universe of thought, one which has limits, definition, circumscription, frame. As a good Peircean semiotician I know that such an idea of Design is analogous with the idea of a calendar or clock, or a sentence, or larger bounded pieces in natural language, or of a lifetime as measured between womb and tomb. Design, as a plot of ground or scheme of a story, presumes an invisible wall to exist, a fence to set it apart from other grids and places. To compose, to design, to impose one's editorship upon the montage of book, as its blueprint for unfolding, is a fundamental art of using space as medium. It is a problem ...

Space is of the contextual, the contiguous, the surface at which worlds meet. It is of configurations which seem to us who live on the face of this earth like modalities of the probable and the possible replicated, interpreted in countless ways, in media of all kinds. So we make metaphors-as-connections between the various worlds by means of these modalities and their *verisimilitudes*. A verisimilitude, in Peirce, is a representation, or Sign.

It is only by the argument of Design that I attempt to present an order of chapters, non-alphabetically, yet according to arbitrary but momentarily persuasive lines of intellectual kinship that may be drawn to link several authors together, as a manifold, a cluster. But as will become immediately apparent this is the quintessential Kleenex cluster, since it is disposable, may be recyclable, but as provisional as is Peirce's "legisign": a lawlike referent rule of order.

One of the most important considerations we may bring to any logical analysis of an idea is whether it presumes that the world is finite or infinite. If the universe is presumed to be limited and finite then a clear, undoubted assumption follows, that we may be able to discover this world in its totality and to depict it in veritable manner. But if, in contrast, we assume that the universe is infinite, open, continuously evolving, then all we are able to do is take what we find as a "pattern" as we are able to perceive such an order or configuration; and then we may attempt to find repetitions all over the place. In fact, we will try so hard to locate such patterns that we run the risk of seeing them in ellipses, in parts and pieces, or to see even what we wish to see whether or not it is out there in actuality.

But since semiotics holds that there is no finite universe, and there is no There out there in replicable design, we may never see a whole picture except imaginatively, by the artifice of representation or Sign. *If* one holds as did Peirce (CP 6.421ff) and so do I, then the actual universe has no "character." In this sense no program is inscribed like a template in a homing-bird's brain, or a patterned cylinder in a player-piano or Jacquard loom. Then whatever we want to call the character of the world, or the nature of the human being, is what we choose to impose, *to mask*, as it were, the actual *as* the real.

It is especially at the level of Space that representations of imagined, interpreted, or imposed Designs occur. At the same time, it is at the spatial or syntactical level of thought that classification, categorization, and order begins. The authors of the papers in this volume are variously concerned with locating levels of meaning prior to that which becomes habitualized in symbol, and prior also to that which becomes conflictual and interactional in Index. With virtual radical intent the papers presented here are looking at the level of space—at the syntactic level of signs, or the Iconicity of meaning—which is *proto*, but not temporally *prior*. In some important sense, spatial concerns have less to do with earlier and later, in historical time, as much as with more elemental. In other words the spatial is not its own measure.

Each of the authors presenting here is especially expert in crossing disciplinary lines, since it is the interdisciplinary scope of semiotics investigations which attracts those who seek for and see connections between allegedly discrete discourses. Therefore it is particularly presumptuous for an editor to attempt to impose an order, a grid invented for the purpose at hand. It is almost as presumptuous as reshuffling the frames of a comic strip, or of splicing filmic frames into sequences that fantastically parallel, at best, the referent sequence shot. To play with the presumption further, establishing by editorial fiat an order of things is like penning authors into fields, into carved-portions of conceivable space.

But since this book has largely to do with spatial confinements, prison-houses of language, and indeed with pens of several kinds, I will meddle with syntax forewarned: It is such a risk that poets dare take, such as e.e. Cummings and other great code-breakers. And design, from a semiotics position, is not only a reassignment of order into chaos, but is also a grounding of one's ideas upon a place, a site, a plot. *Here and now* is the name of the game.

II
Who's Who in Volume Two: the Works

Most but not all the papers included here were presented at the 1994 International Association for Semiotic Studies meeting held at Berkeley. Most of these papers, but not all, were presented in the sessions on legal semiotics. However they first appeared is of less importance than that they now offer such a compatible fit, with surprising interlockings and dovetailing. Still, it is not like arranging papers in groups which correspond with key topics. Nor is it like arranging papers as if in a suit, or by a run, or in pairs. There are no rules for melds, as in a game of pinochle, or for royal flushes in other bluffing, *psychotychistic* sport. The grouping of these papers is, by contrast, an exercise in improvisation and hopefully will be seen as such.

The initial grouping, in my opinion, provides an entry into one of the most basic assumptions of Space by semiotics; it consists of several papers where each attempts to span time and culture through historical perspectives. They create, thereby, a *mediating* historiography. The second group also mediates, and bridges empirical observables in the public sphere with the interpretation of skilled semioticians. This cluster focuses on actual events and configurations which take place in designated spaces of the law. The last group centers in a sphere so defined as legal theory, the theory of signs, and the yet-to-be-formed theories of Peirce as pioneer in semiotics.

While I do not subdivide these three groupings into distinct sections, this tentative ordering should not be understood as a lineal ordering. Neither should the triadicity of the arrangement be seen to tie too closely with the Peircean Icon, index, Symbol with the respective characteristics of each sign-function. At most, the first four papers show that so little of what we hold as a constant referent is firmly in place. On the contrary, technology, rhetorical manipulation, cultural-historical shifts of power, and the tenuous walls of institutional information-vaults effect what we may discover as evidence, as facts, as material for making values by legal and extralegal means.

In the five papers that follow, as mentioned earlier, I find that the authors" ideas are related to, in each case, a specific event in law and legal theory, or to a special way of observing a predominantly spatial sign in the law. I will speak more of these papers, in turn, in a later part of this introduction.

The last section, consisting of four papers, focuses on contradiction, paradox, some level of obscurity and unintelligibility in jurisprudence which suggests there is yet a level unexplored, a space below the surface, a kind of protoconsciousness in legal semiotics in particular, and in Peirce's work especially, which asks to be brought into open relationship.

Each of the papers in all three sections deal with precarious tightropes of systems of thinking which touch, at the edge, other systems of thought. The authors walk these tightropes stretched across established conceptual space, and they comment as they make their way on the experience of the venture, the tenseness and the lay of the land, as it were, on the ideational space passed over.

To begin, Marcel Danesi opens his paper, "The Law as Metaphorical Gestalt: A Vichian Perspective," by profoundly developing connections between Vico and Peirce, following the early groundwork of Max Fish in 1969 (1986). Danesi brings Vico forward in this essay into the realm of a poetic logic, in tandem with the Vichean notion of *fantasia*. The *poetic gestalten,* in connection with the making of legal norms, is based on the idea of projecting a spatial "whole" place, and then configuring upon it emergent codes, norms becoming formed. This opening paper links with the closing paper of the volume, with Vincent Colapietro's study of a Peircean unconscious, as we will see. I do not suggest that the book comes "full circle," since such a figure of speech would belie the notion of ideas-as-signs *evolving*. But beginning and closing do cross and re-cross; in the book as a gestalt, beginning and end are cross-referential.

In a similar fashion, inner and outer are not exclusionary, but in the special spatial frame of semiotic investigations are cross-referential also. Here we look at Joseph Brent's representation of his odyssey in attempting to design a biography of Peirce's life. The chapter is appropriately irreverent, and recalls for the reader that authorial footings never go deeper than sand. Brent's paper is often painful to read. But, especially, the reader is confronted with vague demarcations between private space of gifted persons and the public space their lives demand, on behalf of both larger and smaller communities whose properties they do become.

Bill Scott explores problems of access to information in our electronic age: The media of technology and the media of tradition put two mediational instruments into conflict. Scott raises questions regarding the kinds of values which are created by each respective medium and, conversely, destroyed or evolved into insignificance. The nature of semiotic manipulation and the manipulation of the spatial components by which all media effect and interpret is central to Scott's quest. The paper asks whether technology, as awesome adversary of traditional media, may not undermine and place itself outside the very space of law's domain. To what extent may law account for that which lies outside the space of law?

In this "environment" Bill Pencak's paper on the Icelandic Sagas presents a very different picture of legal space: the *Althing*. The place where the business of the Law is done, remains. But the powers behind the law change. Pencak sees the law at the very core of Icelandic culture, and the transition between competing authorial forces represents transformations of social values in Icelandic society. The line drawn on the legal place is fine between legend and history, even as distinctions between legality and legitimacy, or "felt Justice," remain sharp.

The "medial" section of this book opens with a very different, updated bond between cultures: Ingo Hueck discusses the complexity of legal significance in the pending Eurostate. He examines these aspects of international law with respect to the Treaty of Maastricht. Hueck brings us back to law and semiotics as living, evolving experience.

In a similar fashion Norma Procopiow frames a recent controversy between cultures, that takes place on the legal stage, focused on the question of appropriateness of legal counsel's wearing of African Kente cloth in the Court rather than the more traditional western-style suit. The costume is examined as a special sign-bearer of cultural values, in the context of legal discourse. The appropriateness of the Kente cloth stole raises questions about the equivalence between appropriateness as correct conduct in human affairs and the notion of Normative Ethics, in Peirce's theory of signs, that gives account of appropriate human conduct. In this paper, as in the other papers of this volume, we are brought face to face with currencies of values set on edge, and spinning...

From quite a different perspective, but centered also on current medical and legal ethical practice, Robert Moffat raises the question of the meaning of "harm" for people who have no reasonable hope of recovering from illness to lead restored, and meaningful lives. The case concerning the right to die raises questions also about who possesses people's lives, and who or what decides on the disposition of human lives. Moffat explores various facets of significance that cling to the Hippocratic *do no harm* commitment of physicians. He asks what the role of law must be when harm, however interpreted, is tolerated, if not sanctioned, by law.

As I remarked earlier the legal concept becomes a prison-house of language, and of thought in general. We know that word-play as slang, pun, and other linguistic interludes are ways of escape from the tendency for official notions to ossify. Mariana Net, from a different point of view, looks at the space of the political prison as a play space: prisoners employ a mode of ludic creativity in order to be able to live as full human beings, enclosed and constrained by prison walls, but not unfree.

When she presented her paper at Berkeley, I as others in the audience were powerfully moved by Net's presentation. Its force is not lost in print. Here Net looks at various ways that prisoners recreate their jails into play spaces, play-pens, and thereby transform the actual into that which is more "real" than actual. Further, she contrasts the conventionality of concepts inside the prison with conventions outside the prison; and she finds that the free and the unfree are strangely kin since their common bond is conventionality: a made and circumscribing significance. Net weaves into her insights on the transformation of the prison space her careful research into recent work on this topic.

A splendid juxtaposition with Net's paper is John Brigham's rich discussion on "Signs in the Attic ..." Here Brigham takes us to close inspection of the Greek/Attic architectural pediment of the Courthouse in America. He traces its historical and semiotical passage in American law. This triadic shape does not share, as presented, with any of the triadic semiotic functions set forth by Charles Peirce. Nor need it do so. The examination of this pediment shape, as marking the space it occupies with legal insignia, is drawn with sensitivity and erudition. The reader may or may not connect it to Peirce, but it is open to such linkage. Brigham suggests that just as architecture is the most useful of arts, law is the most poetic of human practices. We find this link implied in several of the papers here, (Kevelson, 1992; 1993 on law and esthetics).

Brigham's paper is followed by Kevelson's "Law at the Border." Kevelson calls attention to a special, unique kind of problem in the modern world: the opportunity, as in post-communist Russian, of *choosing* a legal system. It is rare that a vacuum in the space once occupied by law is ever created to leave a country confused between possible options in law. Which legal system? It is a particularly complex decision, since the choice of legal system usually depends on implied or covert sets of principles and values. Values are presumed to come before legal systems. But in the world of our actual experience, our world, that is not the situation. The choice of law must bring with it a set of values to place in substratum position *after* the legal institution is established. This is somewhat like trying to put footings in place after the roof is nailed onto the house.

Kevelson's paper points up the need to understand semiotics as a logic which "lawfully" may violate the laws of thought of traditional logics: In brief, two things may occupy the same space. In the actual world people do indeed live and grow wise by such "perspectives by incongruity."

In the next paper Joel Levin deals precisely with the problem of "The Paradox of Jurisprudence." Levin regards legal theory as an instrument. Legal theory is a social instrument, but one which cuts two ways. Unless legal theory comes to be regarded as evolving—as plastic, protean and paradoxical in an honorific sense—it will fail to represent even those aspects of current legal practice which has been generated of itself. Levin is asking whether we might need to understand a paradox of jurisprudence, not as a flaw, but as a useable (however fallible) legal instrument.

José Brito's paper on relationships between law, justice, and reason looks at shifts in the relationship between law and justice. He asks whether this shift was not brought about precisely through a change in the idea of legal reasoning. From a traditional viewpoint law and justice were coupled, Brito reminds us: they were, in fact, linked by reason. But in contemporary legal theory law and justice are often regarded as not only dissociated, but even as discrete discourses. Brito traces the development of this cleavage in the ideas of Hume, Bentham, Kelsen and Dworkin. Different aspects of law/justice relations are, it is suggested, to be contextually sensitive to the spaces, or conceptual contexts, which produce them.

As promised early in this brief introduction, the collection concludes with Vincent Colapietro's paper, "Notes for a Sketch of a Peircean Theory of the Unconscious." The large question Colapietro raises is, how do ideas get from the preconscious or unconscious or protoconscious to that space we call *consciousness*? Peirce, we recall, says that pragmatism, the method of his theory of signs, is concerned with concepts of which we are conscious. But Peirce develops his great idea—which is the logic of possibility—of that which is conceivable but not yet existent. From this point of view, in the reading of Colapietro's provocative and illuminating study, I wonder if there is not some closer connection between Peirce's "logical possibility" and that which is coming into consciousness but is not yet conscious. Colapietro suggests that we may yet discover in Peirce some model of consciousness which may be as productive in this area of inquiry as other models produced by such as Freud, Lacan, Jung. Each has invented a spatial design capable of depicting the complexities of the realm of conscious ideas, that is, of signs. Perhaps Peirce's spatial model is a kind of map, or a montage in film, or a strip of cels pulled by cog (as he describes his Existential Graphs). The applicable laws, I suspect, are those that concern intellectual property, and even the crossing of state (static) lines.

In a few cases the authors who contribute to this volume will meet one another for the first time in this special place. Each of them has assured me that inquiries and discussion are welcomed. Following the last paper in this collection I have included a small introduction to the authors. I hope that this meeting will produce, in its time and place, continued dialogue, collegiality, and even friendship among this vast and nonfinite group Peirce would have referred to as a "community of inquirers."

I am reminded of a discussion by Peirce on Space and Law which was written just at the turn of the century, a hundred years ago. Peirce asks

> Would not the human race, supposing that it could survive the shock at all, be pretty sure to develop a new form of intuition in which the things that now appear near would appear far? For what is the real truth of nearness? Who is my neighbor? Is it not he with whom I intimately react? In short, the suggested explanation is that space is that form of intuition in which is presented the law of the mutual reaction of those objects whose mode of existence consists in mutually reacting. (CP 6.82)

PART II

Chapter Two

THE LAW as METAPHORICAL GESTALT: a VICHIAN PERSPECTIVE

Marcel Danesi

I
Introduction

What is the *law*? This is a question, needless to say, that can be approached from various angles. In my view, any meaningful consideration of this question will have to start by considering how the law reflects *metaphorically-based* ways of conceptualizing. The purpose of this paper is to argue that the kinds of abstract concepts that undergird modern legal systems are the result of a metaphorical process that transforms the mental realm grounded in perceptual gestalten into one of conceptualization. In other words, while the law has evolved in modern cultures to encode various abstract concepts of social organization and justice, it started out as an "expression" of something much more fundamental. This was, in fact, the view put forward by the Neapolitan philosopher, Giambattista Vico (1668-1744) in his masterful treatise of 1725, the *New Science* (translated by Bergin and Fisch in 1984). Vico insisted that in order to understand human institutions one must seek their origins in a more rudimentary form of mentality, which he called *poetic*. Vico's message to all those who study the human mind is that when we strip it of its communally-rationalized symbols and codes we are left with a form of thought and memory that is grounded in poetic gestalten. This concrete mode of knowing was the essence of the primordial mind; but it continues to reverberate in the corners of the modern mind. As Verene (1981:123) has observed, the primordial mind thought poetically. Thunder, for instance, must have made a traumatic effect on the emerging consciousness of our hominid ancestors. That effect is being "sounded" over and over in the deepest layers of our modern minds. This is why James Joyce associated Finnegan's fall to the sound of thunder on the first page of his novel *Finnegans Wake*. Joyce was obviously struck by Vico's simple, but profound, insight.

The term *poetic*, as used by Vico, encompasses all forms of thinking that are proximate to the ways in which we first come to perceive sensations, stimuli, and affective states; these come under the domain of the meaning-making operations of the human *imagination*—literally the ability to make and remake *images* and the feelings they evoke in the mind. The *fantasia*, as Vico called it, is the form of mentality that we inherit by virtue of the fact that we have a body, a brain, and a soul. It undergirds universal, or *common*, sense-making in our species. The rational, conceptual level, on the other hand, is anchored in symbolic thought. This state of knowing and thinking, which is grounded in *communal* sense-making, is not inherited biologically by subsequent generations, but must be "transmitted" to them in some culturally-specific context and form. As Solomon (1988:10) aptly remarks, it is imperative when talking about concepts and sense-making not to confuse *common* sense with *communal* sense, that is, "the habitual opinions and perspectives of the tribe."

As Bosmajian (1992) has recently shown, approaching the law through metaphorical analysis, is not as farfetched as might at first seem, given that many of the legal profession's conceptions of the law are grounded in metaphorical thinking. Bosmajian's analysis of the law as metaphor is a convincing one. He shows that many figures of speech that appear originally in judicial opinions reappear later as legal principles. However, what Bosmajian and other analysts of legal discourse should know (for example, Atkinson and Drew 1979; Danet, Hoffman, Kermish, and Rahn 1980; O'Barr 1982; Bhatia 1983; Kurzon 1984; Mead 1984; Phillips, 1984; Hoey 1984; Goodrich 1987), is that the view of the law as culture-specific discourse was put forward more than two and a half centuries ago by Vico. For Vico, the law starts out as a common-sensical response to human and divine actions, gradually developing into a communally-shaped code that ends up regulating these same actions. The semiosic link between these two dimensions is *metaphor*. (A good collection of studies on Vico's conception of the law can be found in Black 1985). The law, as Kevelson (1977, 1985, 1988, 1993) has perceptively shown in a series of pioneering studies on legal semiotics, constitutes a semiosic system based on sense-making agreements. (For various semiotic perspectives on the law see also Jackson 1985, 1988; Fish 1989; and Scott 1991). Vico's views lead to a consideration of the origins of this system.

II
Poetic Thinking

A common view of the law is that it is based upon reason and rational thought processes, not upon ordinary or common-sense thinking. A reading of Vico would demystify this conception. Vico alluded to two types of thinking modes grounded in two kinds of wisdom—*poetic* and *logical*. The former generates common sense: that is, the universal, or common, capacity in all humans to understand and model the external and internal worlds in terms of the categories of sensory and affective experience. The latter emerges at a later phylogenetic stage in the context of communal sense-making—that is, as a kind of "meaning agreement" made by members of a specific group.

Common sense is the ability to register commonly-shared patterns of perception and feeling. Vico referred to it as *poetic logic*, from Greek *poieein* "to make." It is a form of thought that derives from bodily experience: "the human mind is naturally inclined to see itself externally in the body, and only with great difficulty does it come to understand itself by means of reflection" (Bergin and Fisch 1984: par. 236). The idea that sense-making is an extension of bodily experience, which is starting to receive serious and widespread attention in the human sciences, is the unifying principle that Vico utilized to tie together all the thematic threads that he interspersed throughout the *New Science*. Common sense, for Vico, was essentially bodily-based *sensus*.

Vico located the ability to extend the body into the mind in the *fantasia* "imagination"—the neurobiological ability to form memorable images of life experiences and to transform them internally into meaningful gestalten. The *fantasia* made possible the structural and transformational relations which inhere in the fully-developed mind among feeling, metaphor, affect, sense, imagery, symbol-formation, and narrative discourse—all of which hold up the intricate "architecture" of rational cognition, to use Anderson's (1983) appropriate figure of speech. For most of the twentieth century the systematic study of the mind has concentrated on the ways in which the rational part carries out its computational tasks—deduction, inference, problem-solving, etc. Vico's approach, on the other hand, focused on how this rational part was built, *originally*, by the workings of the imagination.

Vico sought access to the *fantasia* not by means of cartesian-type methods of analysis, but through an etymological study of its creative products—especially the first myths and the original meanings of words.

He wanted to establish the "natural laws" which governed human thought by reconstructing, in the tradition of Plato and Bacon, the poetic mind-world of the first sentient and reflective humans. Only in this way, Vico claimed, would it be possible to gain some really significant insights into the true nature of human mentality and of social institutions.

Where does the *fantasia* come from? Is it tied to a human *spirit*? Vico did not ignore or dismiss this fundamental question. He did not, however, tackle it head on, for he claimed that we could only come to understand what we ourselves have made (in Bergin and Fisch 1984: par. 331). This is known as the *verum-factum* principle, or the "truth is made" principle. We can systematically study history, language, and culture, because they are products of our own minds. But we can never know what is for *certain*. *Il certo*, as Vico called it, forms an inexplicable given. We can, of course, develop religious philosophies, mythical narratives, scientific theories, and legal systems to explain *il certo*. But these are of our own making.

Vico breaks down the workings of poetic logic into the *fantasia* proper, the *ingegno*, and the *memoria*. Strictly defined, the *fantasia* inheres in the mind's ability to evoke and reflect on stimuli not present in the immediate environment. It endows humans with the capacity to transform the non-reflective form of consciousness that they share with the other animals—the physically-bound type that reacts instinctively to urges and changes in the continuum of perceived events—into a reflective one. The distinguishing feature of human consciousness is that it allows us literally to "imagine" stimuli that are no longer present for the sensory system to react to in its biologically- programmed way. As Verene (1981:101) puts it, the *fantasia* allows humans "to know from the inside" by extending "what is made to appear from sensation beyond the unit of its appearance and to have it enter into connection with all else that is made by the mind from sensation." The *fantasia* has also endowed humans with the capacity to imagine fictional (context-free) beings, objects, and events. It thus liberates human beings from the constraints imposed on them by biology and by communal sense-making.

The *ingegno*, "ingenuity, invention," is the faculty of the conscious mind that makes something meaningful out of the images produced by the *fantasia*. "Making sense" is a result of the *ingegno* imposing pattern onto the images that the *fantasia* generates. The brains of all animals have the capacity to form memorable images. This is probably a survival function. But animals would seem to lack the ability to transform their images into meaning-making "expressions." This ability inheres in the agreements or resemblances that the human mind alone is capable of making (inventing) between the images produced by the brain and their corresponding sensory units as registered by the body.

Finally, the *memoria* is the neurological system that keeps for future utilization the thought patterns forged by the *fantasia* and the *ingegno*. These are stored in the form of image schemas or feeling gestalten that underlie our models of, and reactions to, space, time, emotions, etc.

To see how the poetic part of the mind works, let us take as an example the notion of "sex." At a fundamental imaginative level, humans the world over can literally "sense" and "model" imagistically and affectively the essence of "maleness" and "femaleness": that is, humans, like other animals, can sense and feel differences in sex. These are due to the biological system reacting to signals, urges, and affective stimuli. To use Langer's (1942) appropriate designation, they are first "presented" to the inner world of the organism, where they are subsequently "represented" as perceptual gestalten in the brain. When these intuitively-perceived representations of maleness and femaleness are transformed further, through communal sense-making, "cognitive" models of sexuality—"masculinity" and "femininity" respectively—are forged and rationalized. These will, of course, vary from culture to culture because of differences in communal sense-making patterns. So, what started out as ***sensus*** *vis-à-vis* sex ends up as ***consensus*** *vis-à-vis* sexuality.

Legal systems, according to Vico, started out as poetic expressions of what early humans felt to be appropriate. In their origins, they were poetic because they were literally "made" by the human capacity to imagine situations and events in relation to bodily and affective states. Since primitive humans believed that gods, or divine beings, guided human affairs, and that they were to be feared for their awesome power, they fashioned the first legal systems according to the "will of the gods" (Bergin and Fisch 1984: par. 938). This is why legal and religious institutions have a common origin for Vico. They are poetic expressions of our needs, feelings, and fears. And this is why the first laws of a culture are also its religious laws, and why the first lawmakers are also the religious leaders of the culture.

III
Conceptual Thinking

When poetically-forged gestalten are connected to each other through the medium of metaphor, a new form of mind crystallizes. This is the key insight of the *New Science*. The particular characteristics of this metaphorically-fabricated mental universe constitute the source of differences among persons and among cultures. Although it evolved out of the poetic, or sense-making, level, it has come to be the dominant form of cognition.

To see how conceptual thinking is forged by metaphor, it is useful to portray the mind in terms of two layers or levels—a deep and a surface one (Danesi 1993). The deep level is the level of poetic logic. Thomas Sebeok (1987) characterizes the operation of this fundamental part of mind appropriately as an "affective modeler" of feelings, sensations, intuitions, and urges. Although all species participate in the instinctual and experiential worlds, only humans (and perhaps some higher primates) are endowed with the capacity to "model" these worlds *ex tempore* and to represent them in the form of signs. This level corresponds to Peirce's level of Firstness (CP 2.278ff); it is a level of mind where the universality of bodily structure and sensory perception make reflective thinking concrete and sense-based the world over. At this level, semiosis is anchored in a universal common sense or feeling for the structure of the world. Differences in representation occur at a later stage when they become remodeled by consensus within specific cultural contexts. At this Thirdness level, the communal sense of the tribe constrains the representational process, gradually refining and tailoring it to convey specific kinds of conceptual distinctions—those deemed to be significant by the social group.

Metaphor results from the *fantasia* and *ingegno* working in tandem; it allows the mind to impose a connectivity structure on perception. The instant that the metaphorical capacity interconnects perceptual gestalten, it creates completely new units of thought that have no immediate relation to perceptual processes. Metaphorical creations do not occur between the body and the mind, but between units within the mind. From a phylogenetic perspective, metaphor generated the surface level of cognition by producing the first *concepts* out of the connections it had made in the deep level. A *concept* can thus be defined as a context-free thought unit resulting from a metaphorical connection between percepts

(A is B, C is D, etc.). The connectivity function of metaphor gave primordial poetic thinking a specific configuration. In so doing, it generated abstract thought. *Abstraction*, as the etymology of the term suggests, is the ability to draw out essences from connections. Understanding the concept of "threeness," for instance, implies the ability to draw out an essence from groupings of "three things." This is possible only because we connect "threeness" concretely to such real-life referents as "three cats," "three dogs," etc. This "connectivity capacity" is at the core of the abstraction process.

Communal sense crystallizes from the abstract concepts generated by metaphorical connections. It constitutes a "logical," or language-based, form of *signification* shared by the members of a specific group or culture. It allows humans who inhabit the same cultural space to make agreed-upon connections and abstractions *vis-à-vis* life experiences.

Vico defined metaphor as a "fable-making" capacity, springing from the poetic faculty, and searching for pattern and connectivity in the world of experience. Its early products—myth, fables, etc.—created new scenarios and new mind-worlds. At this new level of cognition even inanimate bodies could be "brought to life":

> All the first tropes are corollaries of this poetic logic. The most luminous and therefore the most necessary and frequent is metaphor. It is most praised when it gives sense and passion to insensate things, in accordance with the metaphysics above discussed, by which the first poets attributed to bodies the being of animate substances, with capacities measured by their own, namely sense and passion, and in this way made fables of them. This every metaphor so formed is a fable in brief (Bergin and Fisch 1984: par. 404).

Communal, or logical, sense crystallizes from metaphorically- forged conceptual structures at the surface level of mind. To adopt Parisi's (1983) suggestion, from a phylogenetic standpoint this new conceptual level developed *on its own* a form of organization, which we commonly call *syntax*, in order to achieve stability and coherence. *Syntax* is definable, therefore, as a surface-level system that arranges and organizes the increasingly complex conceptual structures that this level of mind generates. Free from sensory control, the syntactic mode of thinking is a truly powerful one. It can be projected onto the external world of reality to organize it, classify it, and explain it *on its own terms*. These projections have produced our symbolic and cultural systems, and they underlie communal sense-making.

The error of equating common sense with communal sense occurs at the surface level of mind where *logic = truth*. Indeed, if we were to present an argument or a story which we knew to be false, all we would have to do to persuade our interlocutors that it is true is simply to arrange it in a logical form. So natural is the connection that our rational minds make between logic and truth that if the "truth" did not meet the requirements of logic, then it would likely be rejected as fallacious. The whole modern legal system of trial and jury operates on the making of "logical sense."

I have been using the term *metaphor* here, obviously, as a feature of mind, not of language. It does, of course, surface constantly in discourse in the form of verbal metaphors and other verbal tropes (Pollio, Barlow, Fine, and Pollio 1977; Lakoff and Johnson 1980; Kvecses 1986, 1988, 1990; Lakoff 1987; Johnson 1987; Lakoff and Turner 1989); but it can also manifest itself in other ways, such as in visual representational media (Hausman 1989).

Although interest in metaphor is as old as Aristotle, the experimental study of its relation to cognition and communication is a relatively recent phenomenon. Since the seventies interest in metaphor on the part of behavioral, social, and cognitive scientists has become so intense that it is virtually impossible to skim even the surface of the facts and theories it has generated. Metaphor has become a much discussed topic indeed in the human sciences. What stands out most from this research domain is that metaphor is an intrinsic feature of language and cognition (Nuessel 1991 for a good summary of the relevant findings and theories).

The model that has become the basic schema with which to discuss metaphor is the *topic-vehicle-ground* model put forward by Richards in 1936, and then refined by Wheelwright 1954; Black 1962; and Perrine (1971). After Black, this model has come to be known as the "interactional" model. The *topic* is what is talked about in the metaphor (also known as the *A-referent*); the *vehicle* is that part which makes a comment on the topic (the *B-referent*); the *ground* is the meaning that is generated by the semantic "interaction" between topic and vehicle. Thus, in the metaphor *Time is money*, "time" is the topic, "money" the vehicle, and the meaning—which would obviously require an extensive paraphrase—is the *ground*. This model has been recently extended to cover concept-formation. For instance, the abstract concept of "threeness" discussed above, would be considered to be a topic which is concretized through vehicles such as "three cats," "three dogs," etc. The process of abstraction coincides with the ground that is established by the mind between these two domains. Metaphor works at various levels and in various domains of cognition, not just in language or in analogical thinking. This is the significant finding of the recent research on metaphor (Lakoff 1987).

Research on metaphor has also shown many other intriguing things about this phenomenon. It has shown, for instance, that literal paraphrases never quite encompass the metaphorical ground, that abstract conceptualization is embedded in metaphor, that children produce metaphors regularly in order to express a physical resemblance between objects, that most of discourse is based on metaphorical and related concepts. The catalogue of findings on metaphor has become an extensive one indeed. Suffice it to say here that, when considered cumulatively, the research seems to suggest that the human mind is "programmed" to think metaphorically most of the time.

At the surface level of mind, metaphor continually produces new abstract structures, as it scans the world of mind to make new connections among different concepts and to understand new input or new experiences. The concepts forged through metaphor at the deep level can be called *first-order* concepts. Subsequent metaphorical connections among first-order concepts at the surface level can, therefore, be called *second-order* concepts. If a first-order concept has the structure A is B, and another D is F, then a second-order concept will have the underlying structure [A is B] *is* [D is F]. This process can, in theory, go on indefinitely; it constitutes the "blueprint" for the "architecture" of abstract cognition, and hence for its propositional or computational configuration: [A is B] *is* [D is F] can easily be restructured in the surface level of mind as *if* [A is B], *then* [D is F] and as other logical formations.

To complete this model of mind, it is to be noted that the surface cognitive level has its own form of memory—*conceptual memory*. The neuroscientific research on memory has, in fact, shown that there are two forms of memory in the brain, the spatial and the verbal, stored separately in the right and left hemispheres respectively (Bogen 1975), and that the spatial is a much older form of memory from a phylogenetic perspective. So, the spatial form corresponds to the deep-level memory system (Vico's *memoria*), and the verbal to the surface-level conceptual one. Access to the *memoria* is through what psychologists call episodic recollection; access to conceptual memory is, instead, through a semantically-based mode of recall (Tulving 1972).

As concepts become more and more removed from their deep-level origins, settling into their new memory system, they generate highly abstract structures *on their own.* These gradually come to dominate purposeful thinking. But the world of surface-level cognition is not a "creative" one; it is a "representational" one. In order to create new concepts, the mind must resort to poetic logic and primordial metaphorizing. In an analysis of scientific theorizing, Hoffman (1980), for instance, has shown how scientists continually rely on metaphor to create theories of the world and of the mind. Likewise, Black's, (1962), classic examination of the relation between model-making and metaphor revealed how dominant and pervasive the metaphorical capacity continues to be for science-making.

It is interesting to note that even before the current wave of fascination with metaphor within cognitive science, the writer Susan Sontag wrote a compelling book in 1978, *Illness as Metaphor*, that has become a classic study of how metaphor shapes our conceptualizations of disease. A decade later, after the advent of AIDS, Sontag (1989), followed this up with a sequel study on the metaphors we commonly use to conceptualize AIDS. The main point made by Sontag in these two books is that illness is not a metaphor, but that cultures invariably think of diseases in metaphorical ways. Using the example of cancer, Sontag (1979), points out that in the not-too-distant past the very word *cancer* was said to have killed some patients who would not have necessarily succumbed to the malignancy from which they suffered: "As long as a particular disease is treated as an evil, invincible predator, not just a disease, most people with cancer will indeed be demoralized by learning what disease they have." Sontag's point that people suffer more from conceptualizing about their disease than from the disease itself is, indeed, a well-taken and instructive one.

The upshot of the work on metaphor is that it probably underlies the representation of most of our abstract concepts, and that it structures the ways in which we subsequently perceive, think, and act. Metaphor is the link between the world of *sensus*, anchored in feeling, and the world of *consensus*, anchored in abstraction.

In the legal sphere, the metaphorical capacity allows lawyers, jurists, judges, etc. to understand a value, an attitude, a criminal action, etc. in terms of something more concrete. Laws dealing with abstract concepts such as justice, equality, etc. are grounded in metaphor, and since law systems are based in large part on the same conceptual system that we use in thinking and acting, then metaphorical language is an important source of evidence of what those systems are like.

Whereas legal systems start out in tandem with religious systems as poetic expressions of human needs, feelings, and fears, they are eventually rationalized through constant usage and through continual consensual reworking, becoming disconnected from religion. Highly rationalized cultures differentiate between civil and religious law systems, failing to recognize their common poetic origins. Vico alluded to civil law as a code "dictated by fully developed human reason" (Bergin and Fisch 1984: par. 924).

So, as the discourse in a culture becomes progressively more abstract, so too do its laws. Legal concepts can always be seen, however, to be based on concrete metaphorical gestalten: for example, *justice = a scale* ("the scales of justice," "justice must be balanced," "the jury will have to weigh the evidence"), *justice = blindness* ("justice is blind"); *seeing = believing* ("eyewitness evidence") and similar examples. These surface not only in discourse, but in extrinsic semiosic representations as well: this is why courtrooms in America are often decorated with sculptures of blindfolded figures, of weighing scales, and similar motifs. These metaphorical vehicles betray the concepts that we consider crucial in making and implementing laws.

IV
Concluding Remarks

It is relevant to note here that Vico wrote several works on the nature of law in Latin, which now go under the Italian title *il diritto universale* (universal law) (Verene 1991:18-19). For Vico, the invention of law as poetic expression was "the basis of the human world" (Verene 1991:138); no such thing could ever be found in the animal world. The law begins in the customs forged by poetic logic and is, therefore, rooted in common sense-making. The specific laws that are established at this stage of cultural evolution reflect common-sensical notions and feeling structures. The laws of early cultures tend to be oral agreements on how best to do "what the gods desire." If and when these laws are "written down," they start to assume a different character, commanding "by force like a tyrant" (Verene 1991: 138).

It goes without saying that this analysis of the law is offered here solely as a target for discussion. I follow Vico's suggestion that one should look for the origin of institutions, such as legal systems, in our metaphorical creations. Like myths, stories, works of art, and other products of the *fantasia*, laws start out as poetic gestalten; it is only at a later stage of cultural evolution that they are transformed by metaphor into abstract conceptual systems.

As Arnheim (1969:233) has also aptly observed, it must also never be forgotten that the categories of logic, language, jurisprudence, objective knowledge, and the like have experiential origins: "Human thinking cannot go beyond the patterns suppliable by the human senses." In the universal need to conceptualize what we call spiritual and moral feelings, Vico detected basic human tendencies. This is why all cultures have developed religious, marriage, and burial rites. They are "expressions" of our spiritual nature.

The mental world of abstract conceptualization is a World 3 state of mind, to use the terminology made popular by the philosopher Karl Popper (Popper and Eccles 1977). Popper classifies the world of the mind into three domains. *World 1* is the domain of physical objects and states, including human brains which can affect physical objects and processes by means of neuronal synapses transmitting messages along nerve paths that cause muscles to contract or limbs to move. *World 2* is the whole domain of subjective experiences. This is the level at which the concept of Self emerges, as the mind allows humans to differentiate themselves consciously from the beings, objects, and events of the outside world. The interaction between Worlds 1 and 2 is how we first come to perceive, think, plan, remember, and dream. *World 3* is the domain of knowledge in the objectivized sense. It is, in other words, the totally human- made world of culture. Laws, at this level, become rationalized and encoded in language. They are thus subject to the specific categories of the language used and of the communal sense-making agreements that these categories encode. From a Vichian perspective, World 1 can be seen to correspond to the pre-conscious world of instincts and sense impressions. World 2 is anchored in the deep level where knowing is a by-product of the workings of the *fantasia* and the *ingegno*. And World 3 coincides with the surface level of cognition. The *fantasia* converts World 1 states into World 2 ones, and *metaphor* transforms World 2 states into World 3 ones. The legal systems of rational cultures are products of metaphor converting World 2 laws into World 3 ones. As Hayward (1984:49) has similarly pointed out, "Popper's World 3, includes a very large part of World 1 and of World 2," because it "is formed by interacting webs of metaphor gestalts."

WORKS CITED

Anderson, J. A. *The Architecture of Cognition*. (Cambridge, Massachusetts: Harvard University Press, 1983).

Bergin, T. G. and Fisch, M. eds. *The New Science of Giambattista Vico*. (Ithaca: Cornell University Press, 1984).

Black, M. *Models and Metaphors*. (Ithaca: Cornell University Press, 1962).

Black, V. ed. *Vico and Natural Law: Special Issue of Vera Lex*. (Basel: Natural Law Society, 1985).

Bogen, J. E. *Some Educational Aspects of Hemispheric Specialization*. UCLA Educator, 1975, 12: pp. 24-32.

Bosmajian, H. *Metaphor and Reason in Judicial Opinions*. (Carbondale: Southern Illinois University Press, 1992).

Danesi, M. *Vico, Metaphor, and the Origin of Language*. (Bloomington: Indiana University Press, 1993).

Danet, B., Hoffman, K. B., Kermish, N. W., and Rafn, H. J. An Ethnography of Questioning in the Courtroom. In *Language Use and the Uses of Language*, R. Shuy and A. Shnukal eds., pp. 222-234. (Washington, D.C.: Georgetown University Press, 1980).

Fish, S. *Doing What Comes Naturally: Change, Rhetoric and the Practice of Theory in Literary and Legal Studies*. (Oxford: Oxford University Press, 1989).

Goodrich, P. *Legal Discourse*. (London: Macmillan, 1987).

Hausman, C. R. *Metaphor and Art*. (Cambridge: Cambridge University Press, 1989).

Hayward, J. W. *Perceiving Ordinary Magic*. (Boston: Shambala, 1984).

Hoey, M. The Statute as Discourse and the Lawyer as Linguist. In *The Eleventh LACUS Forum*, R. A. Hall ed., pp. 255-262. (Columbia: Hornbeam, 1984).

Hoffman, R. R. Metaphor in Science. In *Cognition and Figurative Language*, R. P. Honeck and R. R. Hoffman eds., pp. 25-46. (Hillsdale: Lawrence Erlbaum Associates, 1980).

Jackson, B. S. *Semiotics and Legal Theory*. (London: Routledge and Kegan Paul, 1985).

_____. *Law, Fact and Narrative Coherence*. (Liverpool: Deborck Charles, 1988).

Johnson, M. *The Body in the Mind: The Bodily Basis of Meaning, Imagination and Reason*. (Chicago: University of Chicago Press, 1987.

Kevelson, Roberta. *Peirce's Esthetics of Freedom: Possibility, Complexity, and Emergent Value*. (New York: Peter Lang, 1993).

_____. *The Law as a System of Signs*. (New York: Plenum, 1988).

_____. Toward a Global Perspective on Legal Semiotics. In *Semiotics, Law and Social Science*, D. Carzo and B. S. Jackson eds., pp. 81-93. (Rome: Gangemi, 1985).

_____. *Inlaws/Outlaws*. (Lisse: Peter de Ridder, 1977).

Kövecses, Z. *Metaphors of Anger, Pride, and Love: A Lexical Approach to the Structure of Concepts*. (Amsterdam: Benjamins, 1986).

_____. *The Language of Love: The Semantics of Passion in Conversational English*. (London: Associated University Presses, 1988).

_____. *Emotion Concepts*. (New York: Springer, 1990).

Kurzon, D. Thomas, Hypethemes and the Discourse Structure of British Legal Texts. *Text*, 1984, 4: pp. 31-55.

Lakoff, G. *Women, Fire, and Dangerous Things: What Categories Reveal about the Mind*. (Chicago: University of Chicago Press, 1987).

Lakoff, G. and Johnson, L. *Metaphors We Live By*. (Chicago: Chicago University Press, 1980).

Lakoff, G. and Turner, M. *More than Cool Reason: A Field Guide to Poetic Metaphor*. (Chicago: University of Chicago Press, 1989).

Langer, S. *Philosophy in a New Key*. (Cambridge, Massachusetts: Harvard University Press, 1942).

Mead, R. *Courtroom Discourse*. (Birmingham: West Midlands Publishing, 1984).

Nuessel, F. Metaphor and Cognition: A Survey of Recent Publications. *Journal of Literary Semantics*, 1991, 20: pp. 37-52.

O'Barr, W. *Linguistic Evidence: Language, Power and Strategy in the Courtroom*. (New York: Academic, 1982).

Parisi, D. A Three-Stage Model of Language Evolution: From Pantomime to Syntax. In *Glossogenetics*, E. de Grolier ed., pp. 419-433. (Utrecht: Harwood, 1983).

Peirce, C. S. *Collected Papers of Charles Sanders Peirce*, vols. 1-8, Charles Hartshorne and Paul Weiss, A. Burks, eds. (Cambridge, Massachusetts: Harvard University Press, 1931-58).

Perrine, L. Four Forms of Metaphor. *College English*, 1971, 33: pp. 125-138.

Philips, S. U. The Social Organization of Questions and Answers in Courtroom Discourse: A Study of Changes of Plea in Arizona Court. *Text*, 1984, 4: pp. 225-248.

Pollio, H., Barlow, J., Fine, H., and Pollio, M. *The Poetics of Growth: Figurative Language in Psychology, Psychotherapy, and Education*. (Hillsdale: Lawrence Erlbaum Associates, 1977).

Popper, K. and Eccles, J. *The Self and the Brain*. (Berlin: Springer, 1977).

Richards, I. A. *The Philosophy of Rhetoric*. (Oxford: Oxford University Press, 1936).

Scott, W. T. Law, Semiotics, Coding, and Communication. In *Recent Developments in Theory and History*, T. A. Sebeok and J. Umiker-Sebeok eds., pp. 493-513. (Berlin: Mouton, 1991).

Sebeok, T. A. In What Sense is Language a "Primary Modeling System?" In *Proceedings of the 25th Symposium of the Tartu-Moscow School of Semiotics*, H. Broms and R. Kaufmann eds., pp. 67-80. (Helsinki: Arator, 1987).

Solomon, J. *The Signs of Our Time*. (Los Angeles: J. P. Tarcher, 1988).

Sontag, S. *Illness as Metaphor*. (New York: Farrar, Straus & Giroux, 1978).

_____. *AIDS and its Metaphors*. (New York: Farrar, Straus & Giroux, 1989).

Tulving, E. Episodic and Semantic Memory. In *Organization of Memory*, E. Tulving and W. Donaldson eds., pp. 23-36. (New York: Academic, 1972).

Verene, D. P. *Vico's Science of the Imagination*. (Ithaca: Cornell University Press, 1981).

_____. *The New Art of Autobiography: An Essay on the Life of Giambattista Vico Written by Himself*. (Oxford: Clarendon, 1991).

Wheelwright, P. *The Burning Fountain: A Study in the Language of Symbolism*. (Bloomington: Indiana University Press, 1954).

Chapter Three

THE SINGULAR EXPERIENCE of the PEIRCE BIOGRAPHER

Joseph Brent

> Upon this first, and in one sense, the only rule of reason, that in order to learn you must desire to learn and in so desiring not be satisfied with what you already incline to think, there follows one corollary which itself deserves to be inscribed upon every wall of the city of philosophy.
>
> **Do not block the way of inquiry**.
>
> C. S. Peirce to the Harvard philosophers, 1898

Charles Sanders Peirce, the United States' greatest philosopher, died some eighty years ago on 19 April 1914. In 1957, when I began to think about a dissertation in the history of American ideas at the University of California at Los Angeles, he was attractive as a subject because, unlike his celebrated contemporaries William James, Josiah Royce and John Dewey, he was the only major figure in the entire field without major studies concentrating upon his life. There were very few biographical studies about Peirce of any kind, none of which, significantly, was based on the large Harvard collection of Peirce's biographical manuscripts. This odd fact was intriguing in itself. The first of these studies, apart from contemporary sketches in such compendia as the 1906 *Biographical Dictionary of America*, was Morris Cohen's Introduction to *Chance, Love, and Logic* in 1923, the first and limited collection of Peirce's philosophical work, drawn from his best known published sources. Cohen, a student of Josiah Royce who was deeply indebted to Peirce for his late work, called Peirce "the founder of pragmatism" and, unlike James's and Royce's successors for sixty years among the Harvard philosophers, found him a major philosophical figure:

> In the essays gathered together in this volume we have the most developed and coherent available account of the philosophy of Charles S. Peirce, whom James, Royce, Dewey, and leading thinkers in England, France, Germany and Italy have placed in the

> forefront of the great seminal minds of recent times. Besides their inherent value as the expression of a highly original and fruitful mind, unusually well trained and informed in the exact sciences, these essays are also important as giving us the sources of a great deal of contemporary American philosophy.[1]

In 1934, there was Paul Weiss's tantalizing essay in the *Dictionary of American Biography*, based largely on obituaries and interviews. Weiss called Peirce "the most original and versatile of American philosophers and America's greatest logician" and described how Benjamin, Peirce's father, was aiming him at genius:

> From time to time they would play rapid games of double dummy together from ten in the evening until after sunrise, the father sharply criticizing every error ... His father also encouraged him to develop his powers of sensuous discrimination, and later, having put himself under the tutelage of a *sommelier* at his own expense, Charles became a connoisseur of wines.[2]

In 1949, Philip Wiener, inspired by Dewey's famous essay "The Influence of Darwin on Philosophy," published *Evolution and the Founders of Pragmatism*. Three years earlier he had already announced his major findings, which were very damaging to those who attributed the origin of pragmatism to Peirce:

> Not a single reference to Peirce's "Metaphysical Club" supposed to consist of [Chauncey] Wright, James, O. W. Holmes, Jr., John Fiske, Nicholas St. John Green, Joseph B. Warner—the latter four trained in law—F. E. Abbot, and Peirce has been found outside of Peirce's inconsistent accounts [in the *Collected Papers*] in any of their writings or accounts of their lives by their friends, so that Peirce's claim that he first formulated the principle of pragmatism in that group is doubtful. But the group did symbolize the great effect of Darwin's work on American thought in the diverse forms of pragmatism that appear in the works of these men in methodology of science, law, history, and theology.[3]

In 1952, Max Fisch had published an intriguing description of Peirce's career as lecturer at The Johns Hopkins University from 1879-84, based almost entirely on Hopkins sources, which suggested that President Gilman fired Peirce, despite the promise of tenure because

> the limit of eccentricity and emotional instability which Gilman could indefinitely tolerate in a man of genius was marked by [the British mathematician J. J.] Sylvester; that Peirce had overstepped the limit; and that ... Gilman took the first politic occasion to remove Peirce. If Peirce's unorthodox economic, political, and social views found expression during his Hopkins years, they also must have weighed heavily against him.[4]

And lastly in 1954, there appeared Perry Miller's biographical sketch in his anthology *American Thought: Civil War to World War I* in which he offered the typical Harvard view

> Peirce is a complicated and difficult mind. He published no philosophical book in his lifetime, only a series of articles which his ardent admirers often found incomprehensible. He lived a rather shoddy existence, never considered respectable enough to be offered a chair of philosophy, got such income as he could by working for the Geodetic Survey or receiving alms from friends. He was cantankerous and isolated, and only in recent years, when his scattered pieces and manuscripts are at last being printed, has he come into his own. In fact, there already exists something of a Peirce cult, and possibly the danger is no longer that he be neglected, but that too much be made of him.[5]

Miller went on to report that professors of philosophy, presumably idealists and naturalists including those at Harvard, accused Peirce of "vulgarizing the mind into a way of satisfying animal appetites or anxieties."

Except for obituaries, scattered biographical references in the first six volumes of the *Collected Papers of Charles Sanders Peirce*, his letters to Lady Welby about signs and his life as a gentleman farmer,[6] a few memoirs, notably by his students Joseph Jastrow and Christine Ladd-Franklin,[7] some occasional sketches, and glancing mention in histories of American thought and books about Peirce's philosophy,[8] these essays contained the only biographical information available in 1957, (Arthur Burks' volumes XVII and XIII of the *Collected Papers* and Carolyn Eisele's "Charles S. Peirce: Nineteenth Century Man of Science" did not appear until 1958 and 1959, respectively) and none of these earlier ones reflected the Peirce biographical manuscripts which the Harvard philosophers had bought at Royce's insistence from Peirce's widow in 1914. Obviously, there was a great need for a biography of Peirce and these few biographical sketches were so provocative that I decided, in my naive ambition, to apply to the Harvard Department of Philosophy for permission to consult their Peirce papers for a biographical dissertation. On 17 March 1958, Roderick Firth the chairman, informed me that "this Department is willing to allow you to consult the C.S. Peirce collection at Harvard," for a biographical dissertation, subject to its approval of the material I intended to use.[9] As it happened, I was the first and at that time the only researcher to whom the Harvard philosophers had given wide permission for such a study. As a graduate student from the hinterlands, I naturally felt extraordinarily fortunate and queasily uneasy at the same time.

My pursuit of Peirce, which still continues, began toward the end of June 1958, when I arrived in Cambridge. Despite the letter of permission, the Widener Library archivist did not allow me to begin research in the papers until he could verify its authenticity, which did not occur for over two months. As I waited, calling and writing the department every week, I began with very limited success to examine the library's holdings for books from Peirce's library of at least 12,000 volumes, which was also brought to Harvard by Royce, finding and spending several fascinated weeks with his annotated copy of the *Century Dictionary*. I also began asking questions about Peirce of a wide group of persons connected with Harvard, including retired professors and, indeed, anyone likely to have information about Peirce who would entertain my questions.

What I discovered astonished me. Most of those I questioned thought of Peirce as an eccentric and debauched genius who was a rich source of unrelated and unformed ideas, significant, if at all, only for having thought of the bright glimmer of ideas like pragmatism, which James had christened and which James, Royce, Dewey, and others then developed into important major systems of thought. One person mentioned his brilliance in logic as well-known and fundamental and another spoke reverently of Peirce as a great, misunderstood, and mistreated thinker whose genuine importance had been suppressed. Almost all of them told stories about his evil ways. Did I know that he was a drunkard, a drug addict, a homosexual, a libertine who had died of syphilis; that he was an atheist who had married the granddaughter of an esteemed Episcopal bishop, who fled him when he tried to seduce her into sexual perversion; that he then had a long adulterous affair with a French whore, whom he married for her money; that he had several bastard children by several women, one a Negress? These accusations and others were a common currency in the older Harvard intellectual community. Few of those I asked showed enthusiasm for a Peirce biography. All of them were concerned with the consequences for Harvard's reputation by bringing such things to light about one of their own; after all, Peirce was Harvard, Class of 1859, his father was a distinguished Harvard astronomer and mathematician, and his grandfather was the first college librarian, who also wrote the first history of the school. Others were distressed about the effects on the Peirce family's feelings and suggested that they would surely sue me for making these embarrassing revelations. Indeed, as I was to learn years later, this general view of Peirce among the Harvard *cognoscenti* had been summarized in 1892, twenty-two years before Peirce's death, by George H. Palmer a Harvard philosopher, when he wrote to President William R. Harper of the University of Chicago, who was considering hiring Peirce. The characterization remained unchanged in 1958, forty-four years after Peirce's death:

> I am astonished at [William] James' recommendation of Peirce. Of course my impressions may be erroneous, and I have no personal acquaintance with Peirce. I know, too, very well, his eminence as a logician. But from so many sources I have heard of his broken and dissolute character that I should advise you to make the most careful inquiries before engaging him. I am sure that it is suspicions of this sort which have prevented his appointment here, and I suppose the same causes procured his dismissal from the Johns Hopkins.[10]

I did my best to dismiss these unsettling slanders of the man in whose greatness I already firmly believed and joined the Charles S. Peirce Society (founded in 1946 by Frederic H. Young), whose secretary-treasurer Edward Madden announced in its bulletin in February 1958, that "Mr. Joseph L. Brent, Department of History, U.C.L.A., would appreciate receiving any obscure biographical references to Peirce" (there were no responses). At the same time, I had initiated correspondence with Arthur Burks, Jackson Cope, Carolyn Eisele, Max Fisch, Thomas Goudge, Murray Murphey, Paul Weiss, and Philip Wiener, all Peirce scholars (and Harvard outsiders) with a biographical interest in him, whose work treated his ideas as important and original.[11] None claimed a current interest in a Peirce biography, all supported my plan, and some provided me with advice and counsel, especially in their warnings to me that, for reasons they could only speculate about, any project involving the Harvard philosophers and the biographical part of their Peirce collection was a dangerous undertaking. It was from them that I learned that the Harvard philosophers had (at a time unknown to me at this writing) restricted both the study and the use of his extensive biographical manuscripts. *The Development of Peirce's Philosophy*, by Murphey, published in 1961 (and reissued in 1993) was and remains, the only detailed book-length study based chronologically on any genuine knowledge of Peirce's extraordinary life. As Murphey was aware, because he tried so hard to get it, a thorough knowledge of that life would have made his book much better, but, like the other would-be Peirce biographers of the time, Murphey made do with what he could get permission to use. He even went so far as to refuse my offer that he make use of my extensive biographical notes, many of which came from the Harvard collections, because, as he recently wrote me:

> Yes, I do agree with you that Harvard's boat should have been rocked and sunk. The reason I did not try to do so was because I was fairly sure that the boat that was rocked and sunk would be mine. I didn't have the money to take Harvard to court, and I did not see any other way of bringing pressure on them that would work. I think that cumulatively all of us did finally force them to do something, which was of course to bring in Max [Fisch]. Arrogance is certainly the word to describe those people; they were impossible.[12]

In his review of my 1993 biography, *Charles S. Peirce: A Life* (for which permission to quote from their Peirce collection was finally granted by the Harvard philosophers thirty-one years after I completed the Peirce dissertation), Murphey wrote that the biography[13]

> would have been published long before this had not the Harvard Department of Philosophy ... refused him permission to quote from a number of the manuscripts. Here again, as so often in the past, the Harvard Department of Philosophy acted to obstruct research on Peirce, thus continuing the Harvard vendetta against Peirce which lasted from Eliot's ascension to the presidency of Harvard in 1869 until the advent of Putnam, Scheffler, and a new breed of Harvard professors. The history of the Harvard Department's conduct with respect to the Peirce manuscripts is one of the sorriest tales in American academic history.[14]

It is finally time to establish in brief the major reasons that lie behind this harsh and, I believe, well-deserved indictment.

Obviously, the Harvard philosophers had their reasons for the policy of censorship, even though these have never been clearly and openly stated, only vaguely insinuated. At the very least, they believed that there was something dangerous in bringing Peirce's life to light. Their position is expressed in a letter to Murphey of March 1952, in response to his request to see the restricted papers in aid of his account of the evolution of Peirce's philosophy:

> Dear Mr. Murphy [sic]:
>
> I have made inquiries about the confidential Peirce papers in consequence of your letter of March 10 and have learned that they include material to which it is impossible to permit access. I hope that steps can be taken to separate these papers in such a way that some of them could be made available to scholars. We have had to refuse a number of earlier requests similar to yours and this makes it all the more desirable that some such reclassification be brought about. The situation is sufficiently complicated to make it impossible to effect such a rearrangement very soon and I fear, therefore that whatever might be done in this direction would occur too late for the immediate purpose of your thesis.
>
> Sincerely yours,
>
> W. V. Quine
>
> Chairman[15]

This segregation was begun in 1954 and completed in 1956. Whether, as part of this process, specific papers were chosen for destruction remains a question. When, in September 1958, I began working through the manuscript correspondence collection in the attic of Widener Library at Harvard University, what I found was dusty, dirty chaos. There was an incomplete list of holdings by box number. Some attempt had been made at some earlier time to organize the letters by correspondent name in folders stuffed into now disintegrating boxes, but a substantial minority of letters was simply scattered. Some individual files seemed complete, others obviously were missing letters, sometimes a few, sometimes many, often almost all. There was no consistent chronological order. It was sometimes impossible to take letters out of their boxes without tearing them, but I was not allowed to change the existing place or order of any document, or to replace the damaged boxes or folders. The collection of letters written by Peirce was the most confused; there were multiple drafts of many letters, often undated and unaddressed, many pieces of philosophical writing (some of them lengthy), bits and pieces of his inventions and plans for projects, receipts for wine, drugs, coffee, and other purchases, scraps of legal matters, and many other odds and ends. Major parts were obviously missing. One personal file, though, of great interest for and understanding of the development of his life and thought was intact—his application (and various materials connected with it) for a grant from the Carnegie Institution of Washington in 1902-3, when he was sixty-three, to write out his philosophy in thirty-six "memoirs." It contained a number of drafts in which Peirce tried, as well, to explain his inability to finish and publish a major work of philosophy and other personal failures.

Thinking that perhaps the biographical files were considered unimportant, I surveyed the philosophical manuscripts and found them also to be in dangerous condition and in extraordinary confusion. (It was possible, however, to identify those manuscripts used by Hartshorne and Weiss by their green cover sheets.) With that discovery, I concluded that the Harvard philosophers had no interest in preserving Peirce's work, and that they considered it to be of little value. Nathan Houser has described, in a preliminary but accurate essay, the sad history of the Peirce papers from the time of their acquisition from Peirce's widow, in 1914, until the present.[16]

For the first two years because of Royce's enthusiasm and respect for Peirce's work, considerable progress was made in sorting and arranging the amazing confusion of manuscripts, but after Royce's sudden death in 1916, although sporadic efforts were made to honor his intentions, the project was allowed to decline and the papers were seriously maltreated. Apparently, some papers were carried away to be studied by teachers, students, and others. Some were simply pocketed, some of the Peirces' intimate letters were removed to the William James collection, and, perhaps, even destroyed. An unknown number was given away as scrap paper to the war drive. His large annotated library, which Royce had promised Peirce's widow would be protected, was dispersed without any record of disposition, many to other universities, including some in Japan. Only twenty-five of Peirce's books are now part of the Peirce Collection; others that remain at Harvard are kept on open stacks. Ten years after Royce's death, Charles Hartshorne, a recent Harvard Ph. D. in philosophy with a deep interest in idealism, but no background in logic and mathematics, was hired to prepare an edition of Peirce's papers in two volumes. Houser quotes him on what he found in a room on the third floor of the Widener Library:

> [The papers] were in a small number of big piles on a large table. I don't remember whether there was any label on the top of each pile. I think there were about eleven piles. On the shelves there were, I seem to recall, just fifty-two empty boxes, each of which was labelled, showing that the manuscripts had been sorted under fifty-two categories, but my predecessor on the job had evidently taken them out of these boxes and resorted them into a much smaller number of piles... .
>
> There was, I think, nothing else in the room. This was the room for the Peirce papers during the three years I worked on them. I remember having the impression that these fifty boxes were labelled in a reasonable way and that probably there'd been a pretty good classification which my predecessor had destroyed.[17]

In the fall of 1926, Paul Weiss, an impoverished, gifted, and ambitious graduate student who had studied at the City College of New York under Morris Cohen (editor of the of the first collection of Peirce's philosophy called *Chance, Love and Logic* published three years before), casually joined Hartshorne in the project. Luckily, he was competent in logic and mathematics and had a forceful character. He convinced the department to expand the project to six volumes. He discovered in a basket marked "to be discarded" one of Peirce's most important papers in logic. Written about 1880, while Peirce was at Hopkins, it proposed a Boolean algebra with one constant and was "a striking anticipation" of the Harvard philosopher H. M. Sheffer's proposal to the same effect, published in 1913.[18]

Neither Hartshorne nor Weiss had any editing experience and Weiss recalls that at no time did any of the Harvard philosophers instruct or oversee their labors, neophytes that they were, nor did they advise them concerning any points of philosophical importance. According to Weiss, only one change was ever suggested in their editing of the papers, and this occurred when he requested that Lewis go over volume 4, "The Simplest Mathematics," and is represented by a footnote.[19] Weiss also recalls that no members of the department ever made more than a perfunctory visit to their workroom during the periods they worked on the papers, although Hartshorne recalls taking a number of manuscripts at different times to A. N. Whitehead for his comment. (I wonder if Whitehead would have written in just the way he did without knowledge of Peirce's work. In *Process and Reality*, which appeared in 1929 (based on his Gifford Lectures of 1926-7), Whitehead proposed that a philosophical system should be conceived as being generated recursively from a few basic metaphysical categories, which is precisely what Peirce described as his procedure in the manuscript of "A Guess at the Riddle" and in "The Architecture of Theories" published in *The Monist* series of 1891-93. The issue of the extent of Peirce's unrecognized influence is a genuine one.) When Weiss left for his first appointment at Bryn Mawr College in 1931, he took with him all the manuscripts required for the fourth volume of the *Collected Papers*, which contains a selection of Peirce's most important then unpublished work on logic and mathematics. He returned them to Harvard two years later, but the Harvard philosophers had made no record of what he had taken and had not requested their return.[20]

Despite these facts, the Harvard philosophers stated in the introduction to the *Collected Papers* that:

> Nearly all the members of the Department during the last fifteen years, as well as many others who were interested in Peirce, have devoted much time to the very often very intractable material of the manuscripts. But the final and laborious work of selecting, arranging and preparing the papers for the press has been done by Dr. Charles Hartshorne, formerly Instructor in Philosophy at

> Harvard, and by Dr. Paul Weiss, who is at present an Instructor in Philosophy at this university ... [21]

Weiss and Hartshorne both remember that the original intention of the Harvard philosophers was to name themselves, as the members of the department, as the editors of the *Collected Papers*. Weiss recalls that it was only with the greatest difficulty that he convinced R. B. Perry that to do so would be unjust, with the consequence that he and Hartshorne appeared on the title page as editors.

The papers languished for ten years. In 1941, another Harvard graduate student started to organize and number (the McMahan numbers) the collection in sixty-one boxes, including correspondence, for transferral to Widener Library. Three years later, in 1944, just before the transfer under the chairmanship of C.I. Lewis, there occurred a "give away" of Peirce's manuscripts, in which the Harvard philosophers and their friends took whatever struck their fancy. After strong objections, Lewis issued a recall, but we cannot know now, except by chance, what and how much was taken, or what was returned. (It is fairly said of Lewis that his successful career as a logician grew out of his two year study of Peirce's unpublished logic papers in the early twenties and his earlier knowledge of Peirce's published work in the field, to which he was introduced by Royce. In the first edition of his first important work, *A Survey of Symbolic Logic*, published in 1918, Lewis devoted twenty-eight pages to Peirce's pioneering work in the field and called it as important as George Boole's. In later editions and in other works, the account of Peirce's importance is left out.) Houser writes:

> ... some important manuscripts were quietly returned many years later by an eminent Harvard graduate who confirms that the "give-away" did occur and that he kept certain papers because he thought they would be safer in his care. Among the papers returned by this single graduate were such important writings as Peirce's "A Guess at the Riddle," a manuscript on Darwinism and synechism, part of a manuscript on selfishness and political economy, a paper on religion and politics, and notebooks on phaneroscopy.[22]

The papers were transferred from the Widener to Houghton Library in 1960, which already had nineteen boxes of Peirce manuscripts, probably originally sequestered by R. B. Perry in the early 30's, while he was working on his biography of William James. (It seems likely that a number of the Peirces' intimate letters were destroyed by Perry in an effort to sanitize Peirce's relationship with the Jameses. Perry gave Hartshorne, on condition that he destroy them, a small number of Peirce's widow's letters to James's wife, which, among other things, described Peirce's addiction to drugs and alcohol. The letters are now at the Peirce Edition Project in Indianapolis. In a 1934 letter to Gifford Pinchot, Juliette described how Peirce, as a young man, helped William James to master psychological method and added that "Harry James [William James's son Henry Jr.] is most anxious to get from me the early correspondence and lessons between the two men [Peirce and William James] and he offered to buy them ... "[23] The letters have never been found.) A last substantial addition to the Houghton collection was made in 1969, when an old desk filled with important Peirce manuscripts, whose history remains unclear, was found in the underground passageway connecting the Widener and Houghton libraries. The Peirce Collection is now permanently housed in the Houghton. At least a quarter of the philosophical papers, numbering over 80,000 pieces, are still misarranged and the biographical material remains in a state of confusion.

In November 1958, after a month of disordered research, when I inquired about a particular box, the archivist informed me that the Peirce collection had been searched for evidence of certain aspects of Peirce's life and that those portions had been restricted. The box I had asked for was one of four so classified. At that point, like my predecessors who tried to study Peirce's life, I seriously considered giving up the entire venture. I sought advice from McGeorge Bundy, then dean of the Harvard faculty, and asked him to intervene in support of my request to consult the restricted boxes. He agreed to look into the matter and suggested the name of an attorney used by the Harvard Corporation to counsel me, but at the same time he gently and elliptically asked me to consider carefully the personal danger I risked in proceeding against the power of Harvard University. The attorney thought I might prevail in a suit, but added that, after bringing the possibility of a suit to the department's attention, he believed that the Harvard philosophers would see to it that my career was ruined. I conferred several times with Firth, the department chairman, who apologized for the great difficulties his mistake, in giving me permission in the first place, had caused; he offered to write a letter of explanation to my department and to give me

$500 for my troubles. When I refused the offer, he invited me to apply to the department for appointment as the official Peirce biographer (I did not take the offer seriously, for I was a mere graduate student, and I wrote him to that effect). The outcome was that I was allowed to continue to do research, but kept from the restricted boxes. Max Fisch was eventually appointed the official biographer in 1959.

Shortly before my move to Cambridge to begin research in June 1958, Fisch wrote me:

> Any further work I do on Peirce is likely to proceed so slowly that I see no reason why you should not go ahead as if I were not involved in any way or degree ... You have a fair chance to make a major contribution to American intellectual history, in which Peirce seems to me the key figure.[24]

Murphey, a historian, wrote to me soon after I had agreed to the restriction imposed by the Harvard philosophers that:

> I think you are in a very difficult situation ... A good biography cannot be written without access to all data ... Whatever Peirce did was of a highly immoral nature ... Harvard has a real interest in keeping this quiet. I do not believe it is inertia; there is something dangerous there which they want to keep under cover.[25]

My decision in November 1958, to proceed without access to the restricted boxes was based on two assumptions. The first was that, very probably, the Harvard philosophers did not know what was in the biographical materials. Their dismissal of Peirce's importance, and their disgust at his life made it seem to me unlikely that they had made a serious effort to find out what was in the restricted boxes. I also believed that the available material probably had indications of what they were trying to hide. Fisch wrote me later, as he was considering the Harvard philosophers' offer in April of 1959, that he had once surveyed the restricted boxes and "I can assure you that what they add to what a diligent researcher can dig up elsewhere is much less than the restrictive policy assumes."[26] Fisch here illustrates a point that research historians consider obvious: it is unlikely that significant events are recorded by only one source. I soon discovered important biographical information about Peirce in many collections, nine at Harvard itself. Within a week of my decision to continue with my research into Peirce's life, I discovered much revealing but disconnected material about Charles's personal life in the collection of his father Benjamin's letters. These included many family papers commenting on Charles in addition to his father's letters. The collection was restricted at the request of the Harvard philosophers before I had quite finished studying them. I found some 10,000 pages of Peirce manuscript in the National Archives in the Coast Survey papers, his employers for thirty years. The Hopkins archives included some information not used by Fisch in his Hopkins essay. Other university archives contained papers of Peirce's correspondents. So did the Library of Congress, the Massachusetts Historical Society, and other depositories. Many likely sources for Peirce's life and thought still remain unexplored at this writing.

By the end of April 1959, when Fisch conditionally accepted his appointment as Peirce's biographer, I had amassed nearly 2500 notecards on Peirce's life. In our correspondence, I kept Fisch informed of my progress and of my troubles with the Harvard philosophers. Despite this, he expressed a strong interest in a collaboration to save him time and effort. By the end of June, I had completed my study of the Coast Survey material and of several collections at the Library of Congress, the Smithsonian Institution, the National Archives and the Carnegie Institution of Washington, and had accumulated more than 3000 notecards. During a visit with Fisch in the summer of 1959 at his home, we cordially discussed at length how we might work together. We agreed that we would write separate Peirce biographies, expressing our different interests, but would collaborate in and pool our research, some of which I would do as his assistant, which I had, in fact, already done at his expense in Milford, Pennsylvania, Peirce's home for the last thirty years of his life. There, I conducted interviews, examined the local newspapers, official records, and a Peirce letterbook in the possession of a Milford resident. Fisch also offered to advance my cause with the Harvard philosophers, especially in the matter of seeing the restricted papers. I offered to let him make copies of all my notes, including leads, which he immediately did. Those notes, with Fisch's annotations, are part of the Peirce Edition Project's collection.

That autumn, an event occurred which quickly led to the end of our friendship and our collaboration—and for thirty years, to my ambition to write a Peirce biography. Fisch received a telephone call from a retired Peirce scholar and devotee (perhaps cultist in Miller's sense), and member of the Peirce Society who had, on impulse, made a pilgrimage to Milford with a friend to visit the appropriate shrines and talk with the elders about their memories of the Peirces. In doing so, they learned about my earlier presence, misinterpreting it to mean that I was an imposter who claimed to be Harvard's official biographer. Fisch wrote to me:

> My informant became quite exercised about the matter; ... so he made a trip to Harvard, had a visit with his old friend Donald Williams (who is apparently to be chairman [of the philosophy] department this year), heard from Williams about the department's difficulties with you, and urged Williams to write to key people in Milford stating that I am the biographer chosen by Harvard, that you do not represent Harvard in any way, etc. It is my impression that Firth had not yet showed Williams my letter about you, so he was not in a position to set my informant straight ... Well, my informant then went back to Milford, conveyed his authoritative information ... and I'm afraid also the information about your difficulties with Harvard and its view of you. Then he began getting other reports in Milford according to which you were my agent, or assistant, or collaborator ... I provided him what I could over the telephone. He seemed relieved but still puzzled that I should be accepting help from someone of whom the Harvard department thought so ill. ... I shall do what I can by correspondence, but perhaps the cloud of misunderstanding will not lift until after personal conversations at Harvard in February and at Milford sometime later.[27]

Fisch also said that, until this unexpected event, he had intended to send me copies of the notes Jackson Cope had earlier made for him on the restricted papers. He now was reluctant to ask Harvard's permission to do so, which he thought necessary. Though Fisch did his best, the Harvard philosophers would not agree to anything involving me with themselves. Fisch acquiesced in their decision to deny me access to the restricted papers (or to any other Peirce biographer excepting, in some instances, Eisele and, of course, Burks, who had earlier screened the papers for volumes VII and VIII of the *Collected Papers*, without making much use of them). In giving in to their stipulations, Fisch also broke off our agreement and did not afterwards share any of his research results with me, as he had agreed to do.

Fisch's appointment as the official biographer had two major effects, one destructive and the other constructive. On the one hand, he became the Harvard philosophers' gate-keeper in all matters affecting access to and use of their biographical information about Peirce. In practice, this meant that no other would-be Peirce biographer had any chance at it. He often exercised this function with a high degree of caprice, allowing a few to read tantalizing bits, but refusing them permission to use what they had seen. Surprisingly, the secrets were kept, though, occasionally, a Peirce scholar took advantage of these glimpses of the extraordinary figure Peirce was.[28] On the other hand, Fisch plunged with single-minded devotion into the chaos of Peirce manuscripts. By 1970, with the help of his wife Ruth, Don D. Roberts, Richard Robin (author of the annotated catalog and identification numbers for the Harvard Peirce *Collection)*, Eisele, Murphey, and other independent scholars, he had managed to bring sufficient order to the philosophical manuscripts so that they could be used on microfilm, though with difficulty, by scholars anywhere. In 1973, he presented "A Plan for a New Edition of the Writings of Charles S. Peirce" to a group of scholars who agreed to ask Harvard to give them permission to make electroprint copies of, and to use the Peirce papers to publish a multivolume chronological selection of Peirce's work. Harvard agreed to the arrangement. The copies were deposited the next year with the Institute for Studies of Pragmaticism at Texas Tech University in Lubbock, Texas, a place far removed from the refined hotbed of ideas, culture, and inspiration that Cambridge and Harvard University had been for Peirce in his youth and young manhood. This exile was an appropriate consequence of what Murphey calls "the Harvard vendetta against Peirce." In 1975, the entire project was moved to Indianapolis, bringing it a little closer to home. There, founded and directed by Edward C. Moore and funded through his efforts by Indiana University, The National Endowment for the Humanities, and the National Science Foundation, The Peirce Edition Project began. Moore appointed Fisch as general editor with a staff of four. The staff has put most of the materials in order and five volumes of a projected thirty have been published by the Indiana University Press. Over the years, Fisch also collected Peirce materials of various kinds from a large number of sources, and also brought together a large library on 19th century American thought. In 1989, Fisch retired, too ill to write his biography. He left a legacy of a well-conceived, usable and ongoing center for the study of Peirce as a fitting sign of his persistence and devotion.

In the meantime, I had become an outcast among Peirce scholars. Some of them publicly accused me at meetings of the Peirce Society of slander and character assassination (a still lingering reputation), which led to the surreptitious reproduction and distribution of my dissertation here and in Europe. Several presses and scholars showed an interest over the years in publishing a revision, but the Harvard philosophers told them that no permissions would be forthcoming. In 1977, for example, Charles Crittenden, a philosopher then interested in Peirce, and John Clendenning, editor of the Royce papers, urged me to publish it. Crittenden wrote:

> ... It seems to me that it could pretty well be published as it stands. The picture given is not altogether favorable to Peirce, of course, but then that may be as it should be. In any case as the Peirce project proceeds there will be great interest in the life of this fascinating man, and your biography will be a prime source of information ... let me commend you for a fascinating account of a fascinating and difficult figure, and for your (as it seems to me) sound judgments throughout.[29]

I sent the letter to Fisch who discouraged the possibility, writing that, " ... you have a vision of Peirce that is unlikely to reach print ...," and reporting that it was most unlikely that the Harvard philosophers would relent.[30] In thirty years, the dissertation was cited only twice. With sardonic amusement, I realized that I felt a sense of kinship with Peirce in his long-held anger at Harvard's treatment of him.

Then, in 1990, entirely unexpectedly, long after I had moved into other fields of interest and had given up on the biography, Thomas A. Sebeok, a distinguished semiotician, linguist and Peirce scholar (who is not an academic philosopher), found my dissertation and asked me to revise it for publication, including in my text, where I thought it appropriate, the results of Peirce scholarship since 1960. In December 1991, at the request of Indiana University Press, the Harvard philosophers, who could no longer find sufficient reason to deny it, gave me permission to publish selections from their Peirce *Collection*. In January 1993, the Press published my biography and Houser, the new director of the Project, allowed me to study the restricted papers, which I had vainly asked to see thirty-five years before, as well as Fisch files. All Peirce materials at the Project and at Harvard are now accessible to scholars, making it possible, at last, eighty years after his death, to freely study not only Peirce's philosophical manuscripts, but (with the addition of new research into collections likely to have Peirce material but not yet examined) the entire record of his extraordinary and tragic life as well. This opening up of the Harvard and Project sources of Peirce biography—this belated unblocking of the way of inquiry—will mean that we will be able at last to place him more accurately and fully in the fabric of the history of ideas, and to state more rigorously the range of his relevance to the manifold worlds to which he claimed his discovery of *semeiotic* gives privileged entry.

ENDNOTES

Citations to works other than those by Peirce are given in the usual form. Those for Peirce are given in abbreviated form: for the *Collected Papers of Charles Sanders Peirce*, CP 1.1 means volume 1 paragraph 1; for *Writings of Charles S. Peirce: A Chronological Edition*, W1:100 means volume 1, page 100.

1. M. Cohen, 1923:iii.

2. P. Weiss, 1934:398-403.

3. P. Wiener, 1946:181-2, 1949:24-6.

4. M. Fisch, 1952:277-311.

5. P. Miller, 1954:xxxi.

6. I. Lieb, 1953.

7. C. Ladd-Franklin, 1916:715-722; J. Jastrow, 1914:571, 1916:723-726.

8. Lewis, C. I., *A Survey of Symbolic Logic*, 1918, pp. 79-106; Anderson and Fisch, "Charles S. Peirce," *Philosophy in America from the Puritans to James*, 1939; Schneider, *A History of American Philosophy*, 1946, pp. 334-337, 516-523, 546-550; Buchler, Justus, *Charles Peirce's Empiricism*, 1939; Feibleman, James K., *An Introduction to Peirce's Philosophy Interpreted as a System*, 1946; Goudge, Thomas A., *The Thought of C. S. Peirce*, 1950; Gallie, W. B., *Peirce and Pragmatism*, 1952;

Thompson, Manley, *The Pragmatic Philosophy of C. S. Peirce*, 1953. For what was then thought to be available about Peirce, see Fisch's bibliography, 1964, pp. 483-514.

9. Allen, Ruth, secretary to the department, to author, 17 March 1958.

10. W4: lxv. Introduction by N. Houser.

11. Burks had published on Peirce's theories of probability and abduction, his categories, and on his system of signs, and had just finished his work on Vols. VII and VIII of the *Collected Papers*, for which he had access to the Harvard Peirce biographical manuscripts, but he made limited use of them and declined Harvard's offer to write the official biography; Eisele was at the beginning her major work on Peirce, the mathematician and scientist, having published his correspondence with Simon Newcomb, on his gravimetric and astronomical work at the Smithsonian, and other subjects; Fisch had published on O. W. Holmes, Jr. and pragmatism, on Peirce at Johns Hopkins, and on Alexander Bain and the origins of pragmatism; Goudge had published *The Thought of Charles S. Peirce* and on Peirce's theories of induction and abstraction; Madden had published on Peirce's methodology; Murphey was completing *The Development of Peirce's Philosophy;* Weiss was co-editor, with Charles Hartshorne, of Vols I-VI of the *Collected Papers*, and had published on Peirce's architectonic; Wiener, in addition to his *Evolution and the Founders of Pragmatism*, had published Peirce's correspondence with Samuel P. Langley and, with Frederic Young, had edited the first volume of *Studies in the Philosophy of Charles Sanders Peirce*. Of these, only Burks had the chance to study the Harvard biographical manuscripts; Eisele, Murphey, Fisch and Wiener had to use other sources, such as the Smithsonian, the Coast Survey, Johns Hopkins and the personal correspondence of others. For more detail, see Fisch's bibliography, 1964.

12. M. Murphey to the author, 13 May 1994.

13. J. Brent, 1993.

14. M. Murphey, 1993:723-728.

15. W. Quine to M. Murphey, 13 March 1952.

16. N. Houser, 1992:1259-1268.

17. N. Houser, 1992:1261.

18. CP 4.12n. H. M. Sheffer, 1913:14:481-88.

19. CP 4.19n*.

20. The recollections by P. Hartshorne and P. Weiss were made in conversations with the author between 1992 and the present.

21. CP 1.vi.

22. N. Houser, 1992:1262-63.

23. Juliette Peirce to Gifford Pinchot, 10 September 1934. Pinchot *Family Collection*.

24. M. Fisch to the author, 18 April 1958.

25. M. Murphey to the author, 27 February 1959.

26. M. Fisch to the author, 18 February 1959.

27. M. Fisch to the author, 17 September 1959.

28. For example, Auspitz, 1983:51-64. He used manuscript material concerning Peirce's addiction that Fisch had not cleared.

29. Charles Crittenden to the author, 11 January 1977.

30. M. Fisch to the author, 18 May 1977.

WORKS CITED

Auspitz, Josiah Lee. "The Greatest Living American Philosopher," *Commentary*, 1983, 76: pp. 51-64.

Brent, Joseph. *Charles Sanders Peirce: A Life*, (Bloomington: Indiana University Press, 1993).

Buchler, Justus. *Charles Peirce's Empiricism*, (London: Keegan Paul, 1939).

Eisele, Carolyn. "Charles S. Peirce: Nineteenth Century Man of Science," *Scripta Mathematica*, 1959, 24: pp. 305-24.

______. "Charles S. Peirce and the History of Science," *Yearbook of the American Philosophical Society*, 1954, 353: p. 358.

______. "The Charles S. Peirce-Simon Newcomb Correspondence," *Proceedings of the American Philosophical Society*, 1957, 101: pp. 409-433.

______. "The Scientist-Philosopher Charles S. Peirce at the Smithsonian," *Journal of the History of Ideas*, 1957, 18: pp. 537-547.

Feibleman, James K. *An Introduction to Peirce's Philosophy Interpreted as a System*, with a forward by Bertrand Russell, (New York: Harper & Brothers, 1946).

Fisch, Max H. "Alexander Bain and the Genealogy of Pragmatism," *Journal of the History of Ideas*, 1954, 15: pp. 157-59.

______. "Charles Sanders Peirce," Introduction to Part 4, Section 20 in *Philosophy in America: From the Puritans to James*, Edited in collaboration with Paul Russell Anderson, (New York: D. Appleton Century, Reprinted New York: Octagon Books, 1939/1969).

______. "Draft of a Bibliography of Writings about Charles Sanders Peirce," (with Barbara E. Kretzman and Victor F. Lenzen) *Studies in the Philosophy of Charles Sanders Peirce, Second Series*, eds. Edward C. Moore and Richard S. Robin, (Amherst: University of Massachusetts Press, 1964).

______. "Peirce at the Johns Hopkins University," (with Jackson I. Cope) *Studies in the Philosophy Charles Sanders Peirce*, eds. Philip P. Wiener and Frederic H. Young, (Cambridge, Massachusetts: Harvard University Press, 1952).

Gallie, W. B. *Peirce and Pragmatism*, (New York: Penguin Books, 1952).

Goudge, Thomas A. *The Thought of C. S. Peirce*, (Toronto: University of Toronto Press, 1950).

Houser, Nathan. "The Fortunes and Misfortunes of the Peirce Papers," *Signs of Humanity/L'homme et ses signes*, General Editor Gérard Deledalle, Vol 3 *Semiotics in the World/La sémiotiques dans le monde*, Edited by/Edité par Michel Balat and Janice Deledalle, (The Hague: Mouton de Gruyter, 1992, pp. 1259-1268).

______. "Introduction," *Writings of Charles S. Peirce: A Chronological Edition*, Vol. 4, (Bloomington: Inidana University Press, 1986).

Jastrow, Joseph. "The Passing of a Master Mind," *Nation*, 1914, 98: p. 571.

______. "Charles S. Peirce as a Teacher," *Journal of Philosophy*, 1916, 13: pp. 723-26.

Ladd-Franklin, Christine. "Charles S. Peirce at the Johns Hopkins," *Journal of Philosophy*, 1916, 13: pp. 715-722.

Madden, Edward H. "Chance and Counterfacts in Wright and Peirce," *Review of Metaphysics*, 1956, 9: pp. 420-432.

Miller, Perry, editor. *American Thought: Civil War to World War I*, (New York: Holt, Rinehart and Winston, 1954).

Murphey, Murray G. *The Development of Peirce's Philosophy*, (Cambridge, Massachusetts: Harvard University Press, reprinted with a new preface and appendix Bloomington: Hackett Publishing Company, Inc., 1961/1993.)

Peirce, Benjamin, *Family Papers*, (The Houghton Library, Cambridge, Massachusetts).

Peirce, Charles Sanders. *Chance, Love and Logic: Philosophical Essays by the Late Charles Sanders Peirce, The Founder of Pragmatism*, edited with an introduction by Morris R. Cohen, (New York: Barnes & Noble, Inc., 1923).

______. *Collected Papers of Charles Sanders Peirce*, edited by Charles Hartshorne and Paul Weiss, Vols. I-VI, (Cambridge, Massachusetts: Harvard University Press, 1931-35).

______. *Collected Papers of Charles Sanders Peirce*, edited by Arthur Burks, Vols. VII-VII, (Cambridge, Massachusetts: Harvard University Press, 1958).

______. *Letters to Lady Welby*, ed. Irwin C. Lieb, (New Haven: Whitlock's, 1953).

______. *Papers*, The Houghton Library, Harvard University, Cambridge, Massachusetts.

______. *Writings Edition*, Edited by the Peirce Edition Project, Projected in thirty volumes, (Bloomington: Indiana University Press, 1982-).

Peirce, Juliette, *Papers*, Peirce Edition Project, (Indiana-Purdue University, Indianapolis, Indiana).

Pinchot, Gifford, *Family Papers*, (Library of Congress Manuscripts, Washington, D. C.).

Robin, Richard S. *Annotated Catalogue of the Papers of Charles S. Peirce*, (Amherst: The University of Massachusetts Press, 1967).

Schneider, Herbert W. *A History of American Philosophy*, (New York: Columbia University Press, 1946).

Sheffer, H. M. "A set of Five Independent Postulates for Boolean Algebra, with application to logical constants," *Transactions, American Mathematical Society*, 1913, 14: pp. 481-88.

Thompson, Manley. *The Pragmatic Philosophy of C. S. Peirce*, (Chicago: University of Chicago Press, 1953).

Weiss, Paul. "Charles S. Peirce," *Dictionary of American Biography* S. v., 1934.

Wiener, Philip P. *Evolution and the Founders of Pragmatism*, (Cambridge, Massachusetts: Harvard University Press, 1949).

______. "Peirce's Metaphysical Club and the Genesis of Pragmatism," *Journal of the History of Ideas*, 1946, 7: pp. 218-233.

______. "The Peirce-Langley Correspondence and Peirce's Manuscript on Hume and the Laws of Nature," *Proceedings of the American Philosophical Society*, 1947, 91: pp. 201-228.

Wiener, Philip P., and Young, Frederic H., eds. *Studies in the Philosophy of Charles Sanders Peirce*, (Cambridge, Massachusetts: Harvard University Press, 1952).

Chapter Four

THE EMPIRE of SIGNS and the INFORMATION REVOLUTION

W. T. Scott

I
Introduction

This paper considers some aspects of the effects of globalized, converged information technologies on the semiotic frameworks of which postmodern cultures are constituted in particular ways.

The main argument is that the speed and quantity of intercultural communication forces those of us living in such conditions yet further away from embeddedness in a stable, intelligible, and distinctive, seemingly-authentic, cultural framework of action and experience, and deeper into the mutability, diversity and inauthenticity of postmodernity, as identified by Jameson (1984) and many others since.

II
The Philosophical Framework

In recent times, a perennial struggle within academe—and beyond, in other domains where the fundamental academic concerns of interpretation, understanding and knowledge are important issues—has been waged in a radically-polarized manner.

On the one hand, there are those who cleave to an essentially Enlightenment vision, in which the methods of rational inquiry and debate are trusted to roll back ignorance, superstition, error, injustice, oppression, deprivation and all the other remediable miseries that our human family endures, and by which the march of Progress is hampered. Ideally, in the philosophical sense of a hypothetical-desirable, imaginable state of affairs, there exists a real world understood in common as such by all members of the family, each of whom is capable of employing a shared discourse within a common interpretive framework of values, protocols and procedures. On this view, we can make real, better sense together about the several real worlds, physical, social and psychological, that matter to us.

On the other hand, there are all the modern forms of scepticism now massed beneath the banner of postmodernism, or rather, "postmortemism," given the necrophiliac glee with which many of its proponents celebrate the violent deaths of elements in the opposing forces, from specific concepts such as "speech-community" or "author," to the great abstractions of the Enlightenment program, such as Truth, Reference (Semiosis generally), Knowledge, Reason, Legitimation/Justice, and Sovereignty (personal; collective), to cite but a few.

For example, in what remains one of the best introductions to this second perspective on the perennial struggle between stasis and kinesis, the general and the particular, (*After Philosophy*—end or transformation?) an excellent General Introduction contains the following summary of certain scholars' views on the fundamental notion of *reason*.

> To the necessity that characterizes reason in the Kantian view, they oppose the contingency and conventionality of the rules, criteria, and products of what counts as rational speech and action at any given time and place. To its universality they oppose the irreducible plurality of incommensurable language games and forms of life, the irremediably "local" character of all truth, argument, and validity—to the *a priori* the empirical, to certainty fallibility, to invariance historical and cultural variability, to unity heterogeneity, to totality the fragmentary, to self-evident givenness ("presence") universal mediation by differential systems of signs, to the unconditioned a rejection of ultimate foundations in any form. (Baynes, *et al* eds., 1987:3-4)

The general Introduction to this collection of extracts and essays, each individually introduced and contextualized, goes on to highlight several other key tenets of the essentially-negative perspective on our hopes for the making of sense: a rejection of the notion of a sovereign rational subject (person); a critique of the idea that such subjects can come to know an independent world by creating valid, reliable and neutrally-communicable representations of it; a denial that any form of discourse is relatively stable, and sanitary in the sense of neutrally-transparently representing that independent domain of signifieds, thus collapsing logos, logic, the literal, the argumentative into their traditional counterparts in philosophical writings.

To describe the perspective in hand as "essentially-negative" is unjust and inaccurate within the confines of this collection, which contains several extracts from within the vast literature of Critical Theory/Postmodernism that offer partially-positive, or minimally-negative, positions. For example:

> while all [the authors represented] start from the pluralism of language games and forms of life, not all agree that this is an *irreducible* pluralism of *incommensurable* language games. (Baynes, *et al* eds., 1987:7)

Distinguishing "transformation-of-philosophy" thinkers from "end-of-philosophy" thinkers, the Introduction offers several passages that give succour to those who hope above all that interpretive social actions, such as making sense of evidence and dispensing justice, might yet be justifiable on grounds other than the arbitrary exercise of semiotic power, however sanitized or cosmeticized. Habermas, for example, is said to claim:

> --that there are, as a matter of fact, cross-cultural universals of cognition, speech and action, which can be captured in fallible, but nevertheless general reconstructions of species-wide competences. There is no need to tie universality to necessity and certainty; forswearing these marks of the *a priori* in no way precludes searching for empirical and hypothetical, yet universal, theories of basic human competences. (Baynes, *et al*, 1987: 8)

On the following page, Taylor is summarised thus on his belief that philosophy must continue as "the tradition of self-critical-reason":

> Reflection on the indispensable conditions of intentionality reveals that we are first and foremost embodied agents in a world. Our propositional knowledge of the world is grounded in our dealings with it; and there can be no question of totally objectifying the prior grasp gained by agents within it ... Philosophy as a self-clarification of the conditons of intentionality leads to a better understanding of what we are as knowing agents; it thereby provides insight into the anthropological questions associated with our moral concerns. (Baynes, *et al* eds, 1987: 9)

However, the end-of-philosophy, more radical and negative views, stand against these comforting reassurances that some stable foundation might be available to save us from the ever-shifting oceans of relativism and revisability, adrift on which we can only cling to such flotsam as chance provides, for example the myths and fictions that we mistake for genuine understanding, or even Truth when meta-myths such as Scholarship or Science shape our beliefs.

These negative views of our possibilities and capabilities have dominated the humanities and social sciences in recent times, for various reasons too numerous and complex to explore here. Note, among them and only in passing, the triumphalism displayed not long ago by the varieties of positivism, which endorsed science or at least scientism, marginalized discussion of the bases of knowledge, and disparaged other objects, and ways, of understanding.

Note, also, the apocalyptic millenarian mood of our troubled epoch. Modernity is beset by many social evils which may plausibly be traced to the values and practices indicted and recoiled from by the proponents of postmodernism/Critical Theory.

Before turning to the main concerns of this essay, one important point convincingly made in a recent book to which we will return below needs to be highlighted. It is the paradoxical insight that Modernity, the fruit of the Enlightenment, and Postmodernity are *not* mutually-contradictory, but contiguous stages in an evolution for the particular cluster of concerns that we think of as The Enlightenment. To take but one strand, locating in the individual our human power to reason our way forward from ignorance, superstition and other forms of benightedness, can lead very naturally to the overvaluing of the idiosyncratic individual pursuing a private agenda. The best-known formulations of this are the Romantic genius, freely-expressing that uniqueness in radically-distinctive creative texts intelligible only to an elite; the untramelled capitalist baron; the innumerable micro and macro choices that theoreticaly constitute free markets; and many other manifestations of the individual held to defy or disable the collective and the social.

The circle is complete. We return to (allegedly) pre- Enlightenment conditions, in glorification of whatever is bizarre, deviant, mysterious, irrational, and much else on or over the edge, including the criminal. Evil is not only more interesting, as Pound put it, but more glamorous, particularly when perpetuated by the charismatic individuals whose role in secular, administered cultures—that is, in Modernity—so preoccupied

Weber and, of course, Neitzche. The tortured artist and the artist of torture, creative genius and destructive psychopath, become notoriously difficult to distinguish—certainly in moral terms—in a discursive framework that constantly emphasises the centrifugal, oppositional aspects of our cultures and our conduct.

If the continuity just asserted between high Enlightenment themes and those of the most foundationless, relativizing postmodernist is allowed, then we might be tempted to arrive at the altogether duller view that the possibility for groundedness by-passed on the way is just what Habermas and others propose, the normative social order.

Within this, and only within this is the individual free to generate out of innate, abstract competences the specific capabilities and knowledge that not only guarantee individuality of person-hood, social being and non-trivial originality in action, especially talk, but also help to reproduce and develop non-randomly the normative social order itself. To be human, therefore to understand human actions and cultural products (or any other object of interest) as scholars, we must track endlessly around *all* of the quartiles below.

POSITIVE/NORMATIVE

UNIVERSAL/STABLE PARTICULAR/TRANSIENT

NEGATIVE/DEVIANT

III
Cultures and Communication

The apparently-pedestrian and disappointingly compromise-laden conclusion to the above was, perhaps, predictable given the way in which the assertedly-false opposition between Enlightenment and Postmodern perspectives was handled. However, when we consider more closely some particular aspects of our modern cultures, above all the much discussed information-revolution that increasingly enables the signal traffic we enjoy/endure, some important if familiar issues may be addressed in an illuminating, even enlightening, way within the framework now in place.

It is at once a cliche and a caricature to assert that whatever we mean by a culture is virtually co-extensive with the communicative resources and practices of the people who consider themselves members (totally and exclusively, or partially) of a group whose behaviour embodies the culture. We immediately think of language as a resource salient in enabling a collectivity to share meaning, including notions of itself *as* a collectivity, by means of texts both secular (such as one-off conversations, enduring proverbs, sayings, songs, stories, etc etc.) and sacred (nowadays, Constitutions, Declarations of Rights, legal scripture, contracts of all sorts, as well as the various religious or other value-bearing texts).

The use of singular terms in the preceding paragraph ("a" language; "a" culture) prompts a return to the four-part diagram above. Even within the most stable and unpenetrated society, where cultural transmission over time and space is undisturbed and near perfect, (a theoretical construct is clearly now in place) there will be small differences and discontinuities within the flow of everyday action and reaction. (Hence the "near-" on "perfect.") Any "thick" description of specific encounters and exchanges in real situations will confirm that even a relatively-sealed social system is never monolithic and perfectly-replicating over time and internal space. Were that state of culture to exist, perfect redundancy would prevail, members would act and react like automata, and their behavior would have no significance to them or other participants within the system, all from first principles of communication theory (Scott 1990).

Theoretical and nightmarish though this vision is, it is useful in helping us to calibrate the ways in which real cultures not only sustain themselves and develop, but relate to others, an inevitability in modern conditions where contact and contamination by means of intercultural traffic is now so intense, as we will discuss below.

In the sealed, stable society, where high levels of replication hence predictability prevail, what is cultural hence artificial (in various ways, not only because it is overwhelmingly semiotic) fades from visibility. Social conventions and personal habits, and the specific instances of behavior they generate, are experienced as natural rather than cultural, observed but not observed in the other sense of "noticed". Truly spontaneous actions of all sorts may seem as natural as breathing or as invisible as the fluid on the eyeball, to insiders.

Such undisturbed, innocent societies are the philosopher's stone of anthropology while, for the rest of us, powerful myths such as that of Eden, or of childhood itself, are analogous. These are, to make no bolder claim, necessary imaginings, against which we can measure the forms and degrees of disenchantment that members of virtually all cultures now experience. We know different (if not better) with regard to our personal and collective being-in-the-world as a result of inter cultural transmission, and, of course, our powerful, semiotically-well-nourished, imaginings. The normal, hence invisible and unproblematic is "made strange" by contact and contrast with otherness, so that even in our most cherished and natural-seeming actions we are, in various senses, alienated.

To paraphrase Eliot and the Christian myth of the Fall, after such knowledge, what innocence and spontaneity, what sort of freedom, condemned as we are to wander the real and the electronic highways of a world in which we can never be just ourselves, spontaneously-authentic, but must self consciously signify and interpret not only the external, but the semiotically-constructed internal, other? Tourism begins a home.

We may recall the phrase quoted from Taylor earlier here describing philosophy as the "self clarification of the conditions of intentionality." Lash and Urry (see below) in their study (Lash and Urry 1993) show convincingly that "reflexivity"—critical self awareness as we decode-encode remorselessly—is a necessary condition and burden in the information saturated cultures.

On the positive side, of course, we may stress the rich, indeed infinite possibilities of invention and creativity thus forced-upon our niche-less species of displaced persons, each endowed with cognitive and semiotic resoures more than adequate for the task of fabulating and fabricating some sort of interpretive framework, however transient and permeable.

Cross-cultural contact, if not communication and cultural transmission, (although the proliferation and rapid development of trade jargons, pidgins, and various types of hybrids is powerful evidence that these are both desired and achieved) has been, from all the evidence, widespread across the planet from the earliest times. Consider explorers, conquerors, settlers, emigrants, colonists, travellers, and tourists of all sorts, missionaries, traders, salesmen, marketeers, anthropologists ... *people* moving across the globe carrying with them their cultural baggage and depositing their litter.

In more recent times, the physical movement of people, raw materials, and goods has grown enormously, but so also has the movement of "information," in every sense of that troublesome word.

There is a frantic scramble going on in the 1990's to create vast conglomerates converging all the forms and uses of information technology: telephone companies gobbling up computer companies gobbling up news and entertainment businesses to create global systems of a size and power never before seen. Geography, history, culture, politics, jurisdictional boundaries, matter little to such global conglomerates. Notoriously, these are owned and run in the developed world, where dwell the winners, so far, in the processes of modernization.

A substantial component of the traffic that flows through our global information systems involves trade, hence financial transactions of some sort and in some representational form. Money, a means of representing value and crucial to the development of efficient capitalist markets, is, of course, a type of information dependent upon a semiotic system. Cash and other embodiments of worth have long since been supplemented by other, vastly more efficient, means not only of representing value here and now, but of storing it up, and moving it around over space and time. Exchange value has long since been detached from real objects and commodities, thereafter from actual currency or negotiable abstractions such as bonds and shares. The monetary system is now perhaps the semiotic process par excellence. Signifiers flow everywhere that the swelling global bitstream reaches, regardless of the boundaries, frontiers and other barriers that exist or are vainly-erected to stem it and/or the other, more solid, correlatives that may follow, such as commodities, tourists, factories, ideologies ... or soap operas.

The information flows, like tourist traffic, are mainly one-way, from us to them, through our systems, propagandizing, directly or indirectly, our images and ideas. What is perceived as the misrepresentation and annihilation of indigenous cultures—in short, as "electronic colonialism" —is a major complaint, and not only in the so-called Third World or less developed countries whose concerns were eloquently expressed in the MacBride Report of 1980. In Europe, the French and the speakers of other minority languages, continue to struggle against the erosion of their cultural integrity, in the maintenance of which a language and its related cultural forms—literature, jokes, movies, etc.—is arguably fundamental. (During 1993, the French were prepared to imperill the GATT negotiations, which had lasted seven years, involved some 150 countries, and were widely-considered vital to global economic recovery, just to protect their audio-visual culture from inundation by "*les* Anglo-Saxons.")

IV
The Information Revolution

Before considering further some implications of "the information revolution" for, in particular, notions of authenticity and legitimacy in cultural life, it is important to consider these and other general aspects of the controversy concerning information technology and its impact on our semiotic world (Dordick and Wang, 1993; Traber (ed.) 1986; Woodward (ed.) 1980).

Once again, we encounter a clear bifurcation. There are, on the one hand, numerous enthusiasts for all the miracles that the information revolution has wrought, and is about to deliver in a nannosecond or so. A vast literature, enthusiastic to the point of evangelism, already exists. Recent hyperbole about and on The Internet is simply the latest verse in a continuing paen of worship.

A long standing belief is that Information Technology will liberate us all in various ways: from *isolation* (modern telephones and computer networks, computer cottages); from *ignorance* and other limitations on our intellectual powers (computer-aided learning, automatic literature searching); from *political tyranny* which thrives on controlling information (see below); and from *drudgery and inefficiency* (a commuter-free world where repetitious, brainless and even skilled tasks will be done by "robots"—a linguistic import from Russian, where it means, ironically, "worker").

There are two broad camps among the sceptics hostile to all this optimism and euphoria.

The first group has already been mentioned, those who fear a homogenized, Americanized world brought about by electronic colonialism and other cultural transmissions: fast food is but one example. However, a book published in 1993, *The McDonald-isation of Society* is not particularly a study of that type of product. It is concerned with the underlying technical and managerial *systems of control* whereby a standardized, completely *specified*, product from a fixed range of options rolls off assembly lines in the food industry's best emulation yet of "Fordism" in manufacturing. A specified, implicitly high, quality at minimum cost is achieved, allegedly to maximum advantage of consumer and producer alike.

However, we should not pass over too easily the reality underlying the rhetoric of total quality management, accountability, client-satisfaction, and so on, none of which is objectionable *per se*. The underlying issue is that of *power*, the power to control processes, to annihilate the diverse and unpredictable product. *Uniformity* is the basic value embodied in McDonaldization, and recoiled-from by the first group of sceptics, who inevitably face jibes about being Luddite, nostalgiac romantics, etc. In their turn, they do not deny that globalization is possible or wholly undesirable in certain respects, although they fear that we could all end up living in a shared world (top-left in the diagram) that is an impoverished and centrally-controlled Orwellian one. As the title of the MacBride Report (Many Voices, One World) suggests, multiculturalism is their ideal, with nation speaking unto nation in a free but balanced flow of information through our global systems.

In the second camp of sceptics are those who reject this possibility of a single world culture, in some cases gloomily, for this theoretical yet superficially benign construct represents the extreme antithesis to the relativism and even solipsism which they contend prevails at all levels of human experience. The Babel metaphor is the most apt for this perspective, located bottom-right in the diagram. Other, less nihilistic, opponents of the wonders of global wiring seize upon misunderstanding and discontinuity, partly as a means of subverting the homogenization/control referred to above. They promote an ideology of difference, stressing the mutability of texts, the permanent de-ference of final, unequivocal, settled meanings which we never reach, swimming along forever on this or that current of discourse. Whenever we feel convinced, or that we have at least understood, we have merely been overpowered. We have submitted, probably to a local version of one or other of the master narratives put out by the powerful, such as scholarship or religion, and promoted as guaranteeing a particular quality of meaning of which probability and truth are two instances. To make the point explicit (once more), were truths to exist, they would be irresistibly the same everywhere for everyone able and willing to "see" them, regardless of whatever semiotic formation they were presented within. They would be uniform, universal, time and culture-independent: top-left in the diagram.

Many sceptics implicitly deny that any such quality of meaning is possible. Even if it is allowed as a theoretical possibility, it is considered undesirable, because it is usually employed in the service of the powerful against the powerless, by the owners of capital in all forms (including, crucially, in our times, information/knowledge) against the impoverished, and dispossessed, the silent, the unknowing, and the invisible.

In academic and social practice, all of the sceptics take their stand bottom-right in the diagram, promoting subversion, resistance, and denial, a cleaving to the local and the different and a shunning of whatever crosses borders while allegedly remaining the same.

These debates about meaning and culture merely re-enact classic oppositions that underly *all* debates, about any topic, not just those arising in the themes of this paper, and as adumbrated in the opening section. We can put the opposition in stark terms as follows.

On the one hand, we humans can proceed on the hope and assumption that we are capable of achieving better qualities of understanding than we now possess by using our powers of reason and imagination. A concomitant, perhaps necessary further assmption is that we can share these insights, revelations, new beliefs, even truths, with others by using neutral, already shared specialised semiotic resources such as scholarly language, or mathematics. By these means of meaning, we can reasonably hope to recreate unaltered in their minds the convictions we have formed in ours. Commonality, communality, equivalence, progress, reason, and lots of other keywords of modernism inhabit this master narrative.

On the other hand, we can deny the neutrality and superiority of any code, specialized or not; deny the possibility of context-free meaning; deny the possibility of decoding, for there is only recoding, or limitless interpretation with no hope of "the fixation of belief," to use Peirce's phrase. Difference is the key term here, and difference takes many different forms.

It is easy to discredit extreme versions of both positions. If sameness is overemphasised, it removes the need for acts of communication because we already share so much that is the same, out there in our replicating one-world and in here in our personal experiences. (This nightmarish prospect has already been discussed.)

If difference is overemphasised, then our argument self- destructs, by intelligibly and persuasively denying or condemning intelligibility and persuasion.

They can, of course, be reconciled. We can argue that a distinction, and a specific relationship, exists between our resources for meaning—our *codes*—and the uses to which they are put in our *messages*. Most importantly, these do not exist at the same logical and ontological level. Such resources are generative, that is, their complex rules and units guarantee an infinity of diverse, well-formed output. Because the output is rule-generated (structured) it is potentially intelligible, and because the output is so diverse, it is interesting, or at least informative in a special sense. The potentiating resources are abstract and common, in principle, the concrete output infinitely diverse, and in need of perhaps equally diverse interpretation, sometimes massively so and demanding great skill, imagination, and perseverance.

These resources—English, mathematics, TV grammar, basic legal-political concepts—are increasingly internationalized. This is quite compatible with acknowledging that we all acquire our experience in the use and abuse of such resources within our local context(s). This international spread of semiotic resources enables, and is part of, radical changes in the economy of signs and communication now known as globalization. Space (geographic; cultural) and time, are substantially overcome by rapid mass transport (permanent or temporary) of products and peoples. The different kinds of spaces between us are defeated most spectacularly by electronics, especially satellite-carried, computer-driven systems providing near instantaneous words, and images from the heart of the action, as it happens before our very eyes.

Our notion of "news" has been greatly affected by these developments in instantaneous dissemination, as have our consumption habits with regard to the quantities we consume, (or are offered all day every day); the media we use for this sort of information (rarely newspapers); and the manner in which we relate to the information. The intensely-personal, indeed intimate, concrete-image dominated medium of television, creates a form of direct viewer involvement with participants and "reporters on the spot" which has profound implications for journalistic values, such as those of detachment, impersonal reporting, considered selectivity, and respect for privacy, to name but four. At the time of writing, the trial of the American athlete and film star O.J. Simpson is providing many vivid examples of difficulties for one semiotic domain, the law, created by another, that of the media, difficulties directly caused by the power of electronic mass communication.

Concern for privacy, or, at least, non-interference in events that external scrutiny tends to disable, has its obverse in the exhibitionism evident in much popular television. Typical examples are chat shows with celebrities talking about themselves, to artificially-engineered opportunities for members of the general public to have fun being made fun-of, most recently in the self-inflicted form of home videos submitted for transmission to huge audiences, at least in the U.S.A. and the U.K.

In their valuable study, *Economies of Signs and Space*, Lash and Urry deal in depth with various profound consequences of the global reach of converged media technologies, some of which have been sketched in this section. They write, for example, of the way in which the acceleration-multiplication of traffic across cultural boundaries that were once relatively-sealed results in an "emptying-out" of once *imbedded* and once *meaning-ful* elements of self sufficient cultures. The real, or the electronic, tourist gazes upon what is simply there to be seen, or, increasingly, has been put there to be seen, and by thus drawing attention to whatever "typical curiosity" is concerned, disables the spontaneity and innocence of the cultural practice concerned for members of the culture. Ex-members of cultures, such as expatriates or their descendants, returning in person or otherwise to their roots, are particularly demanding with regard to what is to be seen, eaten, etc. and what not, in other words, what is properly emblematic and authentic (= traditional) or not. They are frequently disappointed or startled by the differences between expectation and reality, which are especially stark in our times. There is therefore pressure on insiders to perform what rapidly becomes an empty travesty of whatever the visitor (more and more vital in many cultures as a source of income) expects. Even in the renascently nationalistic nations of Central Europe, the resultant distaste for, and abandonment of, traditional forms is evident.

Evidently, the self-consciousness of reflexivity discussed by Lash and Urry can easily lead to self-disgust for the social double-agent, or at least embarrassment.

Because electronic systems destroy not only space and time but also categories, the older processes of influence, assimilation and naturalisation collapse beneath a flow of foreign semiotic material (or materials whose principal value is semiotic—cultural "icons," for example—rather than their use or exchange value). Eroded and imploded within, diluted, polluted, or even enriched from without, the wired-in, postmodern cultures display many symptoms of disequilibrium, or dynamic change, if that interpretation is preferred.

From the semiotic point of view, the mongrelization that follows upon the super-abundance, promiscuity and pervasiveness of information—of phenomena overwhelmingly or substantially put together and put out as requiring interpretation, as being about something else—guarantees confusion, bafflement, and that characteristic malaise of our cultures, an all-pervasive sense of phoniness. This is over and above the basic fact of our constantly rediscovered dependence on the represented rather than the real, which already condemns us to a life-world not only artificial and contentious, because everything could be otherwise, but all-too colonizable through the ramified and mediated public domain. When our inner and public social lives are indeed colonized—over-run—not only by someone else's agenda-items, but by travesties, substitutes, and caricatures and other reductive imaginings/imagings, especially when performed in the knowingly-ironic manner so familiar from spoof Westerns, self-satirizing chat shows, in-joke architecture, and the like, when seriousness is only possible as tentative speculation or masked by flippancy, the times are not propitious for those who hanker after substance, for cultural matter of at least potentially-transcendent worth. The sheer speed with which cultural matter circulates merely compounds these forms of malaise by adding instant disposability to tawdriness and phoniness.

As one example, what are we to make of the fact that the cafe once used by the novelist Virginia Woolf and her fellow-members of the elite Bloomsbury group, is, though still located in the same fine and atmospheric hotel building, now (mid-1994) trading as Virginia Woolf's Burger Bar? We know what the words mean, but fathoming the "real significance" in our times returns us to the considerations of foundationless relativism with which this essay has been concerned, with the emphasis now as much on value-relativism as on meaning-relativism.

Another, explicitly intercultural, example is drawn from the Baltic Republics in 1990, when Mikhail Gorbachev (having just resorted to the use of tanks) went there in person hoping to persuade the people of these Republics to stay within the Union. In much of the media coverage, he was shown being greeted by crowds holding placards not in any of the indigenous languages, but in English. They were pointed as well as aimed not at Gorbachev, or at fellow citizens. They would not, perhaps, have understood the specific messages, but they would have understood the real significance. Their purpose and significance was to reach the West via the electronic media, focussed at that time on the disintegrating Soviet Empire and its principal actor. Many of us in the Western world will recall other key images from that period in recent history: Yeltsin on the tank outside the Parliament Building, Sheverednaze's white hair as he strode through the crowd to join him.

These examples allow us to end on a positive note, for the lie has surely been given at last to one of the gloomy predictions advanced by opponents of the evolving global information economy. The proliferation of media technologies, in particular since their integration by the use of computing techniques, has not created and will not create the Orwellian police state. Infinite and comprehensive surveillance is just as impossible as effective censorship (against pornography or whatever other "abuse" of the networks we may wish to prevent). Within cultures—if that is nowadays a meaningful statement—heterogeneity rather than featureless homogeneity controlled from central points is widespread, with the emotional debate in the USA about multiculturalism (versus both monoculturalism and disntegrationism, at either extreme) as a contemporary illustration of the continua along which we all career in our attempts to make and take sense in an information-saturated, semiotic cornucopia.

WORKS CITED

Baynes, K. *et. al.* eds. *After Philosophy: End or Transformation?* (Cambridge/London: MIT Press, 1987).

Dordick, H. and Wang, G. *The Information Society - A Retrospective View*, (Newbury Park/London/New Delhi: Sage, 1993).

Downing, J. *et. al.* eds. *Questioning the Media - A Critical Introduction*, (Newbury Park/London/New Delhi: Sage, 1990).

Financial Times International Telecommunications, Survey Supplement, 17 October 1994.

Jameson, F. "Postmodernism, or the cultural logic of late 1984 capitalism," *New Left Review* 146:53-92.

Lash, S. and Urry, J. *Economies of Signs and Space*, (London: Routledge, 1994).

MacBride, S. *Many Voices, One World:The Report of the International Commission for the Study of Communiction Problems*, (Paris/New York/London: UNESCO, 1980).

Ritzer, G. *The McDonaldisation of Society: An Investigation into the Changing Character of Contemporary Social Life*, (Newbury Park, Calif.: Pine Forge Press, 1993).

Scott, W. T. *The Possibility of Communication*, (Berlin: Mouton de Gruyter, 1990).

Traber, C., ed. *The Myth of the Information Revolution*, (Berkeley: Sage, 1986).

Woodward, K., ed. *The Myths of Information: Technology and Postindustrial Culture*, (London: Routledge and Kegan Paul, 1980).

Chapter Five

NJAL'S HOUSE: LAW and JUSTICE in MEDIEVAL ICELANDIC SAGAS

William Pencak

The five great Icelandic sagas—*Njal*'s, *Grettir*'s, *Egil*'s, *Eyrbyggja*, and *Laxdaela*—dealing with the social problems of the island republic are about many things. People struggle to survive in a harsh environment; they quarrel over inheritances; they fall in love but sometimes marry for wealth; they are torn between loyalty to their uniquely free society, which endured from 870 until 1262, and the desire for fame, heroism, and treasure, only obtainable if they travel to Norway and fight for its king. But at the center of all the sagas is the relationship of law to the republic's survival. Iceland possessed legal rules handed down orally by its Law Speakers. It contained four (later five) quarter courts, and the Althing, a combined supreme legislature and court where freemen and the chiefs to whom they owed allegiance annually tried to settle the titanic feuds engendered by scarce resources and explosive Viking tempers.

This essay discusses the themes of my forthcoming book, *The Conflict of Law and Justice in the Icelandic Sagas*. The five lengthy sagas were written either just before or shortly after Iceland was forced to submit to the Norwegian monarchy its population had once fled. Capitulation was necessary to obtain required supplies of grain and timber—the island had neither of its own—and end the ferocious wars of a handful of chiefs who had taken over the republic. The sagas present profound, complex, yet ultimately indecisive meditations on the legal and moral issues raised by Iceland's republican existence. Was the Althing an adequate forum that regulated the conduct of free men until it declined, or was a republican, representative government marred by violence and injustice from the start? Were monarchy and the Christian church better solutions for keeping order than the Althing, or were they the last-resort, pathetic aftermath of a republic that had squandered its precious freedom?

The sagas are great literature—only the Greek tragedies, in my estimation, deserve comparable praise—because they raise the fundamental issues of the human condition through the medium of

Iceland. From the perspective of law, the sagas invite a panoply of interpretations crying out for and anticipating a semiotic perspective. They deal with questions such as should an innocent yet contentious man be outlawed for the sake of civic peace; should the form and technical points of law be preserved even if injustice is done to individuals; should people take the law into their own hands to undo unjust verdicts; should compromise solutions which placate powerful interests override the claims of aggrieved people to absolute justice? The sagas ultimately pose the question whether a republic of free people is viable, or must it ultimately succumb to aristocracy which begets feuding, monarchy which begets tyranny, or Christianity which begets passivity? The sagas give us no answers, but provide a canvas as broad and colorful as life itself to allow us to reach our own conclusions.

Instead of illustrating the sagas' approach to law and justice with examples from my book, I will turn to the little-known *Saga of Droplaug's Sons*. It was probably written in the early thirteenth century by someone from the Fljotsdale region in eastern Iceland where the action takes place. As with most sagas, it opens with an episode from the heroic age of Iceland's founding (c. 870-930) before the Althing was established. Here problems which later cause bloodshed and political strife were resolved consensually. Saga-writers held up this idealized past as a model for a corrupted republic that would eventually destroy itself. In this case, the decent treatment of women is shown as a principal bulwark of the social order. Ketil the Rowdy settles down in Iceland, as did his Viking forbears, and proves himself anything but that: he buys the freedom of Arneid, daughter of the King of the Hebrides who had been enslaved by Vethorm. He is rewarded for this good deed when she finds a chest of silver and he offers to return her to her people. Ketil and Arneid symbolize the first wave of immigrants to Iceland who found there peace, prosperity, and freedom lacking overseas. Arneid chooses to remain, marries Ketil, and their homestead is named after her, not him, a tribute to the role of great women in Iceland's founding and preservation.

The rest of the saga centers on the rivalry of Helgi, Droplaug's son (Helgi D.), and Helgi, Asbjarn's son (Helgi A.). Helgi D. is brave, quick to anger, and has no problem either taking vengeance or manipulating the law when someone violates his rights or those of his friends and kin, which both Icelandic law and honor compel him to support. Helgi A., on the contrary, is reluctant to take up suits and slow to anger, yet his legal and moral obligations as a chief require him to back unsavory characters. We watch law and society unravel in Iceland through the dual tragedy of these two very different Helgis. It is not so much a question of right vs. wrong, but of insoluble dilemmas which pit different codes of law and morality against each other. These are represented by contrasting personality types, both of which—properly held in check by a healthy legal system and social order—were necessary for Iceland's republican survival.

The honor of women is the first test of Icelandic justice. Droplaug is a widow raising her two sons Helgi and Grim. Word gets back to them that Thorfin and Thorgrim Dungbeetle have accused her of committing adultery while her husband lived. She broods, her son Helgi asks her what is the problem, and she responds: "But you won't avenge this insult, or any other I have to suffer." Depending on how these words are declaimed, she is either complaining that the boys permit her to be abused and are cowards, or else she is ordering them not to take vengeance on her behalf. Ambiguity, innuendo, and rumor propel more than one murder in the sagas, adding to the semiotic density which prevents definitively locating who starts a feud or where justice resides. In this case, the fact that Helgi is only thirteen and Grim only twelve makes the situation even more complicated: is a heartless mother sending off children to fight or is a wise matron protecting her young?

The upshot is that Helgi kills Dungbeetle. Helgi A. reluctantly takes up the lawsuit for financial compensation for the man's death. Helgi D., dissatisfied that it must be paid, learns the law and uses it to institute prosecutions of various sorts against Helgi A.'s supporters. Already Thing or court justice is in trouble. Compromises and payments do not slake Helgi D.'s thirst for true justice—or is it vengeance? In any case, he perverts the court from its purpose of settling disputes among the obstreperous Vikings who settled Iceland into the means of instigating new quarrels. He acts legally, but not admirably or justly, to avenge a situation in which he was paradoxically denied true justice, for his defense of his mother's reputation is from one perspective admirable and just.

The next test of Icelandic justice is over power. Helgi A.'s grandfather Hrafnkel wants the young man's chieftainship. Helgi D. comes up with a scheme whereby the old man persuades An the Clown, who is always sycophantic to Helgi A., to give him even more gifts, in this case, fine horses, in return for being put on a jury at the next Thing.

Helgi A. arranges this, but has An appear wearing a hood as he does not want people to know he has appointed a disreputable character who has obviously been bribing him. Helgi D. comes to court, pulls off the hood, and demands Hrafnkel replace so irresponsible a chief. The Helgis are about to fight it out when a peacemaker persuades Helgi A. to allow Hrafnkel to hold the chieftainship for as long as his grandson had. Then the two will share it equally.

It is impossible to locate justice in this episode. Is Helgi A. being disrespectful to his grandfather, or is the old man being greedy? Are Helgi D. and Hrafnkel doing justice in intriguing with An the Clown to expose Helgi A. as susceptible to bribery and favoritism? Or is Helgi A. simply trying to do a favor for a loyal supporter and much-maligned man? But there are two points to this incident. First, the Thing, where juries and prominent men arranged compromises which prevented such insoluble predicaments from leading to bloodshed and social chaos, still worked. Second, the chiefs who came to dominate Iceland, and who could not achieve peace except in the short run, ruled through corruption and nepotism.

The third dispute of the Helgis concerns the scarce economic resources which plagued an island bereft of timber and good farmland. A henchman of Helgi D.'s sues a supporter of Helgi A.'s over some stolen sheep. Helgi D. presses the lawsuit, demands self-judgment, and insists that the sheep be replaced by far more valuable cows. A wrong is avenged, but overly so, by a lopsided payment which feeds the very anger court settlements were supposed to reduce. Helgi D. this time works technically within the law but against its spirit and purpose. People defend "the law" or set themselves outside its limits in the name of "justice" as suits their convenience.

Episode four broaches the question whether one ought to lie in court to escape punishment for a deed which, although illegal, satisfies moral law. A young woman married an old kinsman of Helgi D.'s for his money and was seeing a more desirable supporter of Helgi A.'s on the side. After warning the lover twice to stay away, Helgi D. kills him. When Helgi A. cannot find the body he claims Helgi D. had it buried at sea, which was in fact the case. But Helgi D. and his accomplices swear that this is untrue, and Helgi A. pays one hundred ounces of silver to end the case. Was a justly exacerbated Helgi D. acting with restraint after having warned an adulterer to stay away? Or was Helgi A. acting nobly in making a financial sacrifice to clear up a morally ambiguous situation? Or both?

There is further ambiguity about the incident which leads to Helgi D.'s death, and about what it means for Iceland and its law. Droplaug is remarried to Hallstein. There is no love lost between him and his stepson. Helgi D. had a long conversation with the slave who murdered Hallstein, although he instantly killed the slave and there was no proof of his complicity, only the suspicions which are at the heart of so many sagas.

The first effect of the murder is Droplaug leaves the country and moves to the Faroe Islands. Whereas her ancestress Arneid found refuge from injustice in republican Iceland, Droplaug's emigration implies Icelanders must look overseas not only for justice but for simple peace. Norway's takeover in the 1260s is heralded by this earlier saga in which Droplaug's removal marks the end of Iceland as a stable, law-abiding haven.

Helgi A. prosecutes the murder. Helgi D. does not stand a chance. Even his best friend tells him people are tired of his arrogance, and he has almost no supporters. Justice at the Thing is coming to depend on the size of your following rather than the validity of your case. Helgi A. makes him pay an enormous fine and outlaws him for three years. But it may be the pushy, obnoxious Helgi D. who stands for justice in slaying his step-father's murderer, and the overtly admirable representative of the social consensus, Helgi A., who in fact perverts true justice. Whether or not it is right to outlaw someone like Helgi D. without a sound case, the saga tells us the decision was inevitable: outlawry existed not to do absolute justice—which was impossible—but to rid Iceland of troublemakers. Society united behind its legal system of compromises to keep the peace.

But Helgi D. will not compromise. He remains in Iceland, moves north, and continues to attend courts. He meets his doom when he helps a kinswoman divorce a supporter of Helgi A.'s; she throws his possessions and clothes outside into a cesspool. The man complains to Helgi A. that he permits Helgi D.'s outrages against his supporters to go unavenged. Such weakness threatened a chief's authority as his men would then seek protection from another chief. Is Helgi D. the perpetual trouble-maker, or the hero who knowingly risks death by helping out a kinswoman in distress? That we are not informed of the circumstances of the marriage in question adds to the dilemma, for it puts us in what was probably the position of the two Helgis. They were obliged to support their people regardless of their clients' personalities or their knowledge of the situation.

Helgi D. is overwhelmed by a large party of men, but only after Ozur, whom the saga tells us sprinkled water on him when he was born, betrays him, for Helgi D. turns his back on this man whom he trusts. Now we are told in the last line of the saga that Helgi D. was killed the year after Christianity was first preached in Iceland, about 998. So it seems at first that Ozur did not "baptize" him, and the saga's editor speculates the sprinkling of infants may have been an old pagan custom. But since the sagas are works of creative writing and moral edification rather than true history, and baptism is used anachronistically later in the saga, so we may guess that the author deliberately introduced a "baptism" for two reasons. First, to show that Christianity did not bring a higher level of morality or social stability to Iceland. Second, Ozur, the surrogate Christian, turns on the child he blessed. That Christianity betrayed a heroic Iceland is one possible interpretation of many of these tales hidden symbolically as the sagas were written in Christian Iceland.

Alternatively, however, we may consider Helgi D. the murderer and troublemaker, the representative of a pagan Iceland Ozur did well to eliminate and Christianity did well to replace. The text's judgment is further complicated by a reference to Thangbrand in the final line. His mission from Norway brought turmoil rather than harmony; other proselytizers had to replace him. Helgi was thus killed at precisely the moment (998-1000) when Iceland was in chaos as pagans fought with Christians. It thus suggests a parallel message to the reason Iceland officially adopted Christianity: not for religious reasons, or because most pagans thought it superior, but simply to end a lawless situation which threatened the republic's existence. Similarly, Helgi D. dies because Ozur must choose between staying out of the fight and permitting Helgi D. to kill his chief, Helgi A., or remaining true to his legal obligation and supporting the latter. An insoluble conflict of laws, principles, and, symbolically, visions of Iceland's future, face us. It is almost as though it did not matter who survived, or which religion triumphed, as long as the warfare came to an end.

The irony is, as the rest of the saga shows, it did not end. The Christian settlement appears as an unsatisfactory makeshift. Helgi D. may therefore stand for pagan Iceland, Helgi A. for Christian. The former is headstrong, warlike, heroic, and unwilling to compromise either his anger or his principles. The latter is cautious, calculating, yet corrupt, willing to subordinate justice to order and to make deals with people like Hrafnkel to keep power in the hands of elite families. This was the ultimate fate of Christian Iceland: as the Althing proved useless in settling disputes—as between the Helgis—the level of violence escalated.

Helgi's brother Grim is badly wounded in the battle, but he survives and is secretly nursed by his aunt Grua, who becomes a surrogate mother. This means that the spirit of old Iceland survives underground in the new Christian, elitist order—literally, for Grim hides out in a cave. Once more, as in Droplaug's case, a woman acting courageously signifies preservation of justice and tradition, whereas the superfluous abuse of an old woman by one of Helgi D.'s men just before the battle—he threw a snowball at her—heralds disaster. Conversely, women such as Droplaug and Grua can be seen nursing feuds and keeping alive vengeance sensible men were trying to put to rest.

In any case, fear overwhelms Iceland once the Althing is rendered useless and Helgi D. is killed. Claustrophobia sets into a saga where Helgi D. once ranged free and wide, ignoring threats to his safety and the limits of law. Both Grim and Helgi A. have to live in hideouts in terror of each other's vengeance. In fact, it is when Helgi A. throws caution to the winds, opens his house to a number of guests as in the hospitable days of yore, that Grim is able to sneak in and stab him in his sleep. Helgi D.'s heroic death in battle, which the saga describes in detail and most excitingly, gives way to the stealth and ambush of Helgi A.'s demise. There is one poem in this saga, and poems in sagas always signal important lessons. After gloating over the death of Helgi A., and praising the great death-struggle of his brother Helgi D., Grim sings of the new paranoia that has overcome a lawless society: "I had to be up at dawn for four days in fear, after I won the fight."

But the feud is not over. Grim still must hide out from the vengeance of Helgi A.'s kin. He is finally undone by a good deed. He protects the sister of a young man who is harboring him from a berserk who would seize her. But after killing the berserk, the man's mistress, pretending to be a doctor, spreads poison on a wound Grim received and kills him. The saga thus concludes with a powerful reminder that women played a key role in provoking and nurturing feuds, that they could serve as either facilitators of peace or instigators of vendettas. Perhaps by concluding in this way the saga's author was attempting to justify the reduction, in late republican Iceland, of women to the more subordinate status they held in most of Europe. (In the sagas they hold chieftainships, divorce men, and exercise great influence.) Or perhaps he was ending with a final, courageous woman not afraid to avenge her man. At any rate, Grim dies taking Holy Communion—an anachronism, but one which suggests Christianity may be the death of Iceland, that it did not bring the peace it promised. For the saga ends with no satisfactory resolution, but with further vengeance for Helgi A. and then with mention of Thangbrand's provocative mission. As was true by the time *The Saga of Droplaug's Sons* was written, Iceland was a collapsing society at war, ready to embrace the Norwegian absolute rule it once had spurned.

The Saga of Droplaug's Sons thus illustrates the point my book will make about the longer, more famous sagas. A semiotic reading which provides a spectrum of interpretive possibilities—looking at both the contexts in which the sagas were written and the context of a particular episode within a saga—is the only way to do justice to these complex works. I will briefly describe now how the major sagas may be interpreted semiotically.

Njal's Saga most explicitly makes the law its theme, for Njal is identified as Iceland's greatest legal sage. He is born in 930, the year the Althing was founded. The burning of his house, himself, and most of his family and followers is the saga's central incident. Most of the first half of the saga describes the efforts of Njal and Gunnar—the bravest, most virtuous of Icelanders, the republic's spirit as Njal is its law—to contain an escalating feud spurred on by their wives. Njal may be a hero, vainly trying to keep the peace; yet he may also be the cause of his own demise, as his efforts coincide with furthering the personal advantages of his family and followers. Similarly, Gunnar refuses to accept his outlawry, bursting out in the only paean to Iceland's natural beauty in any saga, that he cannot leave his home. He thereby brings on his death. Njal, similarly, will not leave his house when it is attacked, trusting that his adversaries will fight fairly and let his people come outside. Symbolically, he is refusing to desert the law, just as Gunnar cannot sever his identification with Iceland itself. But the lawman, the house of law, and the hero are all destroyed.

In their wake arise alternatively savage vengeance and Christian forbearance. Kari avenges Njal by slaughtering the followers of Flosi, leader of the burners. The two are ultimately reconciled, and undertake pilgrimages to Rome where they obtain forgiveness. Christian forbearance has replaced the Althing's system of paying off victims' families, outlawry, and compromise. But Iceland is now not only subservient to Rome, but to Norway: Flosi dies on a voyage to Norway to buy timber for his house, symbolically reenacting Iceland's submission to the Norwegian monarchy. And shortly before the saga ends, Icelanders are dispersed to other countries, where they continue to fight. The pagan Valkyries' cries are heard shattering the Christian peace, and blood miraculously spoils Easter services in Iceland. Njal may have been overly nepotistic and conciliatory, but he at least struggled valiantly to preserve the society of free, heroic people embodied by his friend Gunnar. An Iceland without a Njal simply joined the rest of Europe as a fief of king and church.

Njal's Saga tests the possibility of republican justice from the perspective of a great legal sage. *Grettir's Saga* views Iceland's institutions from an outlaw's vantage point. Grettir is perhaps the most obnoxious child in literature, preferring to murder his father's animals rather than taking care of them, refusing to help the crew on a voyage to Iceland, and injuring people at the sporting events where Icelanders sublimated their aggressions. Yet he only gets in serious trouble when he tries to do good deeds: he must kill the inhabitants of a Norwegian house in self-defense where he has sought refuge because he looks like a troll after a fierce storm. The influential father of two of the slain men has Grettir outlawed in Iceland, thereby barring Grettir's own access to justice for the murder of one of his brothers.

For the next nineteen years Grettir lives by his wits: women, outlaws, and the poor befriend him. Respectable people whether Christian or pagan use his great strength for their own purposes and then cast him out. He is finally undone through a pagan curse, and in death attains the justice denied him in life: all pagan rituals are banned from Iceland and his nemesis Thorbjorn Angle, although technically within the law when he murdered Grettir, is himself outlawed for the sorcery he employed to do so.

A final ironic comment on the disparity between real and institutionalized justice occurs in the saga's epilogue. Grettir's brother Thorstein pursues Thorbjorn all the way to Constantinople and kills him. But while Thorstein is awaiting death he is saved through the machinations of a noblewoman who falls madly in love with him, uses her connections and wealth to divorce her husband, and then marries him. They live together before repenting by taking holy orders in Rome.

Grettir's Saga presents the disjunction of law and justice: Grettir is a noble outlaw in the tradition of Robin Hood. His death shames Iceland into finally doing justice, but the saga's message warns us not to identify real justice with any political system or religion. That Grettir's just avenger is spared not because his rescuer is moved by his case, but by sexual lust, and through the perversion of the Byzantine legal and moral order concludes this most cynical of sagas.

Egil's Saga is the tale of a great poet. Like many important writers of modern times, he is no effete intellectual, but a warrior and adventurer in the mold of Ernest Hemingway or Lord Byron. The Althing makes a late appearance in *Egil's Saga*. Most of his adventures occur in Norway and England, where he must use his poetry to praise tyrannical kings who have stolen his property or threatened his life. When Egil, in his late forties, finally settles in Iceland, his poetry deepens. The great verses in which he laments his drowned sons—he nearly committed suicide but his art cheered him up—and praises his friend Arinbjorn who saved him from the wrath of unjust kings are genuine, unlike the work he and other court poets who appear briefly fashion for their royal masters.

Similarly, Egil settles down in Iceland as a farmer and patriarch: his transformation symbolizes the establishment of peace, justice, and a far better poetry or culture in a republic of free men than under the Norwegian kings. When Egil appears in his magnificent battle regalia in Iceland, it is to win a suit at the Althing, to establish peace and do justice, rather than to serve a tyrant's cause or win personal glory. The final lines of *Egil's Saga*, the only one of the five in which the action was completed before Christianity came to Iceland, link the achievements of Icelandic republicanism with paganism while joining monarchy and tyranny to Christianity. The best of Egil's grandsons participates in the battle in which King Olaf, who brought Christianity to Iceland and Norway, is killed. Perhaps *Egil's Saga* slyly hints that the creative forces of art, freedom, and paganism can overcome the Christian monarchy to which Iceland was forced to submit.

The *Laxdaela Saga* really ought to be called *Gudrun's Saga*, for its protagonist is termed the most exceptional woman in Iceland's history. Sympathetic treatment of women, such as the plight of an old Irish nurse left behind when she could easily have been sent to Iceland to end her days with the child she raised, suggests that of all the anonymous sagas,

Laxdaela was the most likely to have been written by a woman. This is not a far-fetched notion. Icelandic women, far less numerous than men in a frontier society, held chieftainships, owned property, and could marry or divorce as they chose during the early republic when the action of the great sagas takes place. One may speculate that some of the sagas scapegoat women as the hidden hand in major feuds—Njal's and Gunnar's troubles are largely blamed on their wives—because Icelandic women were being reduced to a status more typical of medieval Europe once Norway took control.

Laxdaela Saga's women completely outshine the men. In a very long prologue, Unn the Deep-Minded is a fierce foe of monarchical tyranny and the matriarch who first settles the region of Iceland's Lax River. However, once Iceland settles down, there is no more room for a woman of Gudrun's intelligence and fiery temperament than there is for a Grettir or Gunnar. Gudrun at age fifteen is forced into marriage with a wealthy old man; she next impulsively marries a weakling. Gudrun loves only Kjartan, the most outstanding young man in Iceland, but he returns belatedly from a trip to Norway. In the meanwhile, informed either in good faith or not (the saga is ambiguous) by Kjartan's bosom friend Bolli that Kjartan will not return, she marries Bolli as a second choice. But Kjartan does return, Gudrun and he feud, and she engineers a plan in which Bolli kills him. This escalates into a vicious feud in which Bolli also dies; the warring campus are led by Gudrun and Kjartan's mother Thorgerd. Only in late middle age does Gudrun find peace in her life after her thirst for vengeance against Bolli's killers is slaked. She then marries Thorkel, a man worthy of her who dies when his reach exceeds his grasp: he is shipwrecked returning to Iceland with an enormous shipload of timber to build a church larger than the King of Norway's. Gudrun then becomes Iceland's first nun and abbess, a sign that Icelandic Christianity may have been a vehicle through which its outstanding women, frustrated under republican institutions, could shine, whereas it doomed its heroic men through the symbol of Thorkel's death. Here, *Laxdaela Saga* reverses the perspective of the other four sagas, but that is as it should be in a woman's saga. The Althing too is significantly absent: Gudrun only uses it to arrange peace once she has carried on a vendetta against Bolli's killers for sixteen years and is finally satisfied. Ultimately, *Laxdaela Saga* leaves open the question of whether Gudrun is a heroine or a monster.

It is fitting to save *Eyrbyggja Saga*—the saga of the people of the Eyr region—for last. It lacks a protagonist comparable to the others. Instead, virtually every conceivable problem that causes feuds in the Icelandic republic is presented, from runaway slaves to arguments over beached whales, from quarrels over land to adultery, from ambitious chiefs to the tensions between Christians and pagans. The Althing is powerless to stop a succession of feuds which lead to the destruction of the virtuous pagan priest Arnkel at the hands of the shifty Christian Snorri. Fathers turn against sons, Arnkel's successor finds himself in a battle against his own grandson. Thorolf Mostur-Beard, a wise pioneer of Iceland who could compromise his feuds, is succeeded by Thorolf Twist-Foot, a savage, cruel man who has to be buried twice and his body burned to put a stop to his senseless rages and murders committed by his ghost. The saga ends with the exhaustion of both sides and new quarrels brewing. The only heroes are the community of free men who vainly try to stop the aristocratic vendettas which in fact led to the destruction of the republic shortly before *Eyrbyggja* Saga was written.

The sagas I have discussed invite semiotic interpretation on three levels. First, the leading characters signify the potential for greatness of sages (Njal), heroes (Gunnar, Grettir), women (Gudrun), poets (Egil), and a community of free people (*Eyrbyggja Saga*) in the context of a consensual republic. We may ponder the social costs and advantages of maintaining such people in a free (Icelandic) context rather than a Norwegian (monarchicial) one, compare their behavior in both situations, and judge the relative merit of the two sorts of states from different perspectives.

Second, Iceland was a consensual and anarchic republic—in the sense of a community enforcing laws without coercive state power. Only assent to the Althing's decisions, which had to convey legitimacy, that is appear just, held Iceland together. Cases which were technically decided according to the rules but failed to satisfy an underlying sense of justice frequently led to further strife. Various formal and informal codes of law came into conflict—Christian vs. pagan, compromise vs. eye-for-an-eye justice, aristocratic vs. republican. (Two tales I have not discussed—the *Bandamanna Saga* and the short story of "Ale-Hood" show how clever commoners, using trickery, could achieve real justice by corrupting power-hungry, greedy chiefs who had already corrupted the Althing and thus justice itself.) In the background is the conflict between Icelandic republican and Norwegian monarchical institutions, a projection into the past by saga-writers of the merits and necessity of Iceland's submission to the monarchy in 1262. All the competing legal codes had virtues and defects; the reader is again left to ponder and judge.

Finally, no body of literature I know of centers so consistently around judicial decisions, their consequences, and the nature of law. Iceland was the only republic to survive for a long period between the decline of Rome and the rise of Switzerland, and was well aware and proud of its unique status. Other assemblies of free men in Europe were either brought into line with the monarchies of the times, or else became vehicles through which feudal lords contested their power with kings. But in Iceland, only during the republic's decline did the freeholders lose their voice to a handful of great families, and with disastrous consequences. For about three centuries, a century longer than the United States, the world's oldest republic among the world's major nations excepting Switzerland, Iceland endured as an alternative model of law and government to the European norm. While it lost its independence in 1262, which it did not regain until 1944, the sagas' examination of the pluses and minuses of republican rule stand as a monument to Icelandic civilization, much as the Greek tragedies and works of Thucydides, Herodotus, and Plato remain meditations on the glories and limitations of Athenian democracy. The sagas' warning—that economic scarcity leads to class divisions and aristocratic domination, which in turn leads to factionalism only resolvable through arbitrary power—was the lesson of both the Greek philosophers and the historical fate of the Roman republic. It is a lesson we ought not to forget.

WORKS CITED

In addition to my own *The Conflict of Law and Justice in the Icelandic Sagas*, forthcoming from Rodopi Publishers of Amsterdam and Atlanta, 1995, the reader is referred to the following:

Andersson, Theodore M. *The Icelandic Family Sagas: An Analytical Reading* (Cambridge: Harvard University Press, 1967).

Byock, Jesse L. *Medieval Iceland: Society, Sagas, and Power* (Berkeley: University of California Press, 1988).

Clover, Carol J. "Regardless of Sex: Men, Women, and Power in Northern Europe," *Speculum* 68 (1993), pp. 363-388.

Fox, Denton and Hermann Palsson, translators, *Grettir's Saga* (Toronto: University of Toronto Press, 1974).

Haworth, Eleanor and Jean Young, translators, *The Saga of Droplaug's Sons* and *The Fljotsdale Saga*, Everyman Book (London: J. M. Dent & Sons, 1990).

Magnusson, Magnus, Hermann Palsson, and Paul Edwards, introductions to the Penguin Books translations of all the above sagas (except *Grettir's Saga*). Miller, William Ian, *Bloodtaking and Peacemaking: Feud, Law, and Society in Saga Iceland* (Chicago: University of Chicago Press, 1990).

Schach, Paul, *Icelandic Sagas* (Boston: Twayne Publishers, 1984).

PART III

Chapter Six

THE WAY of CREATING NEW SIGNS in LAW: the TREATY of MAASTRICHT —a SIGNAL for a NEW STATE?

Ingo J. Hueck

I
Introduction

As to my topic, I would like to mention a few things before I start: I have been dealing with the Treaty of Maastricht for quite some time, actually since the discussion about its aims started. Especially during my time at Mainz University I had a number of interesting and controversial discussions with Professor Rupp, a well-known expert in constitutional law who was opposed to the treaty. In the name of a citizen he brought a lawsuit against it before the German Constitutional Court.

I myself have always pleaded for the continuation of the European integration, particularly with respect to the preservation and expansion of a peaceful and socially just order for eastern Europe. The Treaty of Maastricht is an important and necessary step to which, however, conventional legal methods and categories are no longer applicable. Neither did a new European state come into existence with the Treaty of Maastricht, nor was the foundation laid for the "United States of Europe" as Chancellor Dr. Helmut Kohl meant. The European Union (EU) is the legal basis of the European Community (EC) and at the same time a supra-national institution aiming at a more efficient political co-operation of the member states, and at a more efficient social, economic and cultural integration in Europe. The German Constitutional Court has therefore named it "*Staatenverbund*" (association of states): it does not *subordinate* different states to a new form of a state as a federation does, but *associates* different states without forming a new state. This differentiation in (state) law is based on a specific theoretical method or presupposition of (state) law: no state without a political community!

In the following I would like to remind you of the development of the treaty until its becoming valid. Then I will present the different methods and conceptions of how the treaty is regarded in relation with the national constitutions of the member states. That part of my paper will be concluded by a short summary of the decision of the German Constitutional Court about the question of whether the treaty is in keeping with the German Constitution. And finally I would like to show you the way of creating this new sign in (state) law and the consequences for the development of the EU.

II
The Treaty of Maastricht

After months of uncertainty about its fate and trouble with its ratification the Maastricht Treaty has gone into effect on 1 November 1993. The twelve Member States of the European Communities[1] established among themselves by the Treaty, according to its article A, the European Union. The Treaty was concluded on 7 February 1992 in Maastricht. The name of this town in the Netherlands should become the symbol of European unification and progress for the adherents of the Treaty and of European centralization and loss of sovereignty of the Member States for its opponents.

One striking feature about the manner in which the Treaty was negotiated was the secrecy which accompanied the inter- governmental negotiations. Fundamental requirements of democracy like transparency, information, and public discussion were ignored.[2] The price some of the governments had to pay was the delay of the ratification procedure in their countries. This delay was the consequence of a now intensive public discussion about the Maastricht Treaty and the future way of european unification and it was the consequence of constitutional problems which the Treaty caused in some States.

The Maastricht Treaty itself determines in Article R that ratifications by all parties of the Treaty are necessary according to their constitutional provisions. Three States held a referendum on the Maastricht Treaty: Denmark, Ireland, and France. In Denmark a majority of 50.7 per cent voted on 2 June 1992 against the transfer of sovereign powers to the European Union. The European goverments had to realize that a lot of citizens of the European states did not completely agree with the contents of the Treaty! The "no" in Denmark was the incent for critical public discussion on the Treaty. However, the referendum in Ireland of 18 June 1992 brought a clear majority in favour of the Treaty. The discussion on the Maastricht Treaty in France, linked with several internal political problems, seemed to divide the whole nation. In the French referendum the Treaty finally gained a narrow majority of 51 per cent of the votes.[3] As the ratification by Denmark was irrevocable the parties of the Treaty entered into negotiations version on a special status for Denmark.[4] The modified version of the Treaty was approved by 56.8 per cent of the citizens in the second Danish referendum on 18 May 1993.[5] The United Kingdom had waited for the second Danish referendum before discussing the Treaty in Parliament. The Treaty was misused by the political parties in the UK as a weapon in the fight for power. On 20 May 1993 the Parliament decided in favor of the Treaty[6] which was ratified by the United Kingdom on 2 August 1993.[7] At this time only one state had not ratified: Germany!

The Constitution of the Federal Republic of Germany—maybe the *Grundgesetz*—was amended in order to enable Germany to ratify the Treaty.[8] But this fact did not entail the delay in the procedure of ratification. Amendments of the Constitution had also been necessary in France and Spain. The French *Conseil Contitutionnel*, the Constitutional Council competent for the control of French legislation, held in a decision of April 1992 that transfer of sovereign powers enforced by the Maastricht Treaty would touch the national sovereignty of France. Essential conditions were altered, which would determine the execution of national sovereign power.[9] The French Constitution was amended on 23 June 1992 in order to render the ratification of the Treaty possible.[10]

In Spain the Constitutional Court (*Tribunal Constitucional*) decided that also the Spanish Constitution had to be amended to allow the ratification of the Maastricht Treaty. The Court saw the reason in the provision of the Treaty which entitles every Union citizen to stand as a candidate at municipal elections in the Member State in which he resides.[11]

Finally it was the German Constitutional Court—the *Bundesverfassungsgericht*—which removed the last hurdles for the Maastricht Treaty. In a decision of 12 October 1993, the Court confirmed that the Treaty was compatible with the *Grundgesetz*. As the Treaty would not establish a European Federal State, the provisions of the *Grundgesetz* on the transfer of sovereign powers would allow the necessary shifting of competences to the Union.[12] Germany could ratify the Treaty and the Treaty entered into force on 1 November 1993.

III
The Maastricht Treaty and the European Community

The Provisions of the Maastricht Treaty

By the Maastricht Treaty the contracting Parties established among themselves a European Union (EU).[13] The EU is built on three pillars. The three existing Communities contiune to exist, but the three Treaties are amended. Some distance away from the three Communities are standing two distinct pillars, one on Common Foreign and Security Policy and the other a combination of home affairs and judicial cooperation.[14] The two latter pillars are not adjusted to the Community approach. They are almost entirely intergovernmental in nature. Concerning those two pillars, the Maastricht Treaty is a Treaty under the regime of public international law.[15] The amendments of the already existing Community Treaties are based on art. 236 of the European Economic Treaty, art. 204 of the Euratom Treaty, and art. 96 of the Coal and Steal Treaty. The whole contruction is not a masterpiece. The user-unfriendliness has been augmented and transparency can hardly be discovered. The Maastricht Treaty is one of the most complicated treaties of the last forty years. Even during the negotiations before the German Constitutional Court there were many misunderstandings and obscurities concerning the meaning of some conditions, particularly because the German translation differed in some points from the English version.

The Monetary Union

The crucial points of the Maastricht Treaty can be found in the first pillar, especially in the admended EEC Treaty. The "E" for Economy is dropped and the name changed to "Treaty on European Community". The scope of application of the EC Treaty is extended explicitly to purely non-economic matters, for example the Community shall contribute to the flowering of the cultures of the Member States[16] or contribute towards a high level of health protection.[17] However, the most important step realized by the Maastricht Treaty has economic character. Also part of the EC Treaty are the provisions on the Economic and Monetary Union. The Monetary Union[18] touches the sovereignty of the Member States even harder than the Economic Union.

The Economic Union

The Member States keep their sovereign power in economic policy. They will not be enpowered to print money but they will keep the final decision how to spend it. However, Member States regard their economic policies as a matter of common interest and shall coordinate them in the Council according to the framework given by the EC Treaty.[19] The key of this framework is art. 102a EC Treaty determining that the Member States and the Community shall act in accordance with the principle of the open market economy with free competion, favoring an efficient allocation of resources. Goal is the closer coordination of economic policies and the convergence of the economic performances of the Member States.[20] To this end, the Council, on the basis of reports submitted by the Commission, monitors economic developments in the Member States and the Community.[21]

Member States shall avoid excessive government deficits.[22] The Commission is empowered to control budgetary discipline. The art. 104c EC Treaty contains incisive measures of enforcement. Following a recommendation of the Commission, the Council can decide with qualified majority whether an excessive deficit exists in a Member State. After having given recommendations, which the Member State did not put into practice, the Council can decide on measures for deficit reduction and can fix a time-limit for the Member State to apply these measures. The Council acts by a majority of two-thirds of the votes. With this majority the Council may even require the Member State to make a non-interest-bearing deposit of an appropriate size or may impose fines if the Member State does not comply with the decisions taken by the Council. The Economic Union is based on the final responsibility of the Member States.[23] But the freedom of decision on economic policy is limited by the Community framework.[24]

Cooperation of the Member States

The second and third pillar of the Maastricht Treaty contain more or less classical means of cooperation. Source of the idea to strengthen the cooperation on certain matters was the perspective that more and more problems cannot be resolved on the national but only on the European level. But concerning the Common Foreign and Security Policy (CFSP) and the Cooperation in the fields of Justice and Home Affairs (CJHA), the EU is not entitled to take decisions binding for the Member States.[25] The Jurisdiction of the European Court of Justice completely includes the first pillar, but it is not extended to the second pillar (CFSP). It can be extended to matters of the third pillar (CJHA) by a special agreement.[26]

On the other hand it cannot be denied that a system of cooperation on the European level may influence decision- making in the Member States. For example Article J.1 al. 4 of the Maastricht Treaty imposes an obligation on the Member States to support the Union's external and security policy actively and unreservedly and to refrain from any action which is contrary to the interests of the Union. On the long term, the framing of a common defense policy is intended.[27] The Western European Union is seen as integral part of the Union and shall develop into the defence arm of the Union. But this development shall made compatible with the policy of the NATO. The design of this framework has just begun.

In regard to the policy of Cooperation in the fields of Justice and Home Affairs the Maastricht Treaty defines in art. K.1 matters of common interest, on which the Member States shall cooperate. In matters like combating terrorism, drug addiction or fraud on an international scale, cooperation on the international level is irrenouncable. Another central matter ist the aslyum and immigration policy.[28] Parts of the matter are integrated in the EC Treaty. The new art. 100c EC Treaty empowers the Council to determine the third countries whose nationals must be in possession of a visa when crossing the external borders of the Member States. This provision is embodied in the EC Treaty, not in the parts of the Maastricht Treaty on cooperation!

European Union and Democracy

The Maastricht Treaty strengthens democracy in the EC, but it did not abolish the fundamental defect. The Council is the legislator, not the European Parliament! And the Council is composed by one representative of the government of each Member State, meaning that the composition varies depending on the subject matter to be discussed. From the perspective of democratic legitimacy, this is a defect but it is still a feature of the Community system.[29] However, Maastricht improves the participation of the European Parliament in legislation. The decision-making for a lot of matters will be performed according to the new co-decision procedure instead of the already existing cooperation procedure.[30] In the cooperation procedure[31] the Council can take a decision even against the will of the Parliament. In the co-decision procedure[32] under certain circumstances the Parliament can prevent the forthcoming of a legal act. This procedure applies for example in decision-making on free movement of persons and services, mutual recognition of diploma or the implementation of the Common Market. If the Parliament says "no" the Council cannot decide against it, the legal act falls.[33] This kind of destructive procedure does not allow legislation by Parliament. But it allows, in the cases in which it is applicable, an effective parliamentary control. If a legal act fails in this procedure, the competence of ruling falls back to the Member States. Nevertheless, Commission and Council may try to reform the legal act and start the legislative procedure again.

Under the aspect of democracy the Maastricht Treaty brought further news: the mentioning of political parties on a European level,[34] the right of the European Parliament to set up a temporary Commitee of Inquiry,[35] or for example the right of any citizen of the Union to adress a petition to the European Parliament.[36]

An improvement for parliamentary control brings Article 158 al. 2 EC Treaty.[37] The governments of the Member States nominate the members of the Commission. But the Commission as a body will be subject to an approvement by the European Parliament. This contruction strengthens the formal and above all the factual influence of the Parliament in the process of choosing members of the Commission.[38]

Linked to democracy is the respect of human rights. The Maastricht Treaty incorporates the fundamental rights as guaranteed by the European Convention for the Protection of Human Rights and Fundamental Freedoms of 1950 and as they result from the constitutional traditions of the Member States.[39] Thereby, the jurisprudence of the European Court of Justice, creating fundamental rights for the Community, is acknowledged.[40] This is the reason that the discussion has started again if the European Community may adhere to the European Convention of Human Rights and Fundamental Freedoms, an idea favored by the European Parliament!

IV
The Treaty of Maastricht: A Signal for a New State? A Discussion About the Proper Theory for the EU

The Maastricht Treaty shifts the Community towards the federal nation-state, but it does not constitute a new, federal state.[41] This is also the result of the German Constitutional Court—the *Bundesverfassungsgericht*.[42] However, the Treaty creates and defines some certain elements pointing into the direction of a federation.

The integrational process in Europe in general and the evaluation of the Maastricht Treaty especially are seen in three different ways:[43]

(1) The followers of the *national perspective* state that the European communities are not to be compared to other international organizations. Even the EEC possessed special competences which were obliging for the member states, and had therefore the character of a federation, or was at least similar to a federation.

(2) From the *international perspective* the European treaties are regarded as traditional international organizations. This perspective is based on a treaty in international law between the United Nations and the European communities from 1982. It contains a definition of international organizations negotiated with the EEC[44] in which the EEC declares to be an international organization with special competences.

(3) The *European perspective* avoids a traditional view and defines the integrational process in Europe and the European organizations as unions of states *sui generis*, of a special quality.

V
The Decision of the German Constitutional Court

Already in its first decision concerning the European integrational process in 1967, the German Constitutional Court had decided that "the community itself is not a state, nor is it a federal state," but a "community of a special quality."[45] This vague phrase became more precise in the Court's decision on the Maastricht Treaty where it was named "*Staatenverbund*" (association of states), thus rendering it impossible to view the European integration from a traditional perspective. EC and EU are no longer to be regarded as supra-national organizations, yet they are neither federal states nor confederacies, in spite of their having some elements of a state. In addition to that, it is not only deficits concerning state law, but, much more so, social deficits which render the quality of being a state dubious.

Citizenship of the Union

With Article 8 EC Treaty a citizenship of the Union is established. But this citizenship does not replace national citizenships. It is a label for a collection of rights which in part have already existed in Community law.[46] Freedom of movement and residence, right to address petitions are elements of the Union citizenship as well as the right to vote and to stand as a candidate in municipal and European elections in whatever state a citizen resides.[47]

Federalism of the Member States

The Union is obliged to respect the national identities of the member states including for example the federal character of the Federal Republic of Germany.[48] In fact, the Federal Republic faces a double federal structure. The EC in its present shape already acts as legislator for a lot of matters and as administrator in a few matters. As the administration in the Federal Republic is to a large extent carried out by the federal states and not by the federation, the position of the federal states has lately been improved by an amendment of the Constitution.[49] However, for the Community the federation is the direct partner.[50] The Community has to consider in the relation to the Member States art. 5 EC Treaty stipulating federal loyalty, but more in the sense of loyal cooperation! The position of the German federal states versus the Community is defined by the German federation not by the federal states themselves.

So there are two levels in the European system: Community and federation. Within Germany there are three levels: federation, federal states and municipalities. The attempt to make those two systems compatible results in a complicated structure of mutual information and participation in decision-making.

The EU does not only respect federal structures of Member States like Germany, Beligum or Spain. Structural elements of federalism were implemented to the Union itself. A Committee consisting of representives of regional and local bodies, the Committee of the European regions, was established. It is to be consulted by the Commission or the Council if the EC Treaty so provides and shall enable these institutions to take into consideration the different interests of the regions.[51]

Principle of Subsidiarity
With Article 3b EC Treaty, the highly discussed principle of subsidiarity was introduced into the legal framework of the Community. It determines that the Community only takes action if and in so far as the objectives of the proposed action cannot be sufficiently achieved by the member states and can therefore be better achieved by the Community. Object of discussion are the meaning and the effects of this principle and the question if the European Court of Justice can control its application.[52]

The juridical contents of art. 3b EC Treaty are limited. The notions leave large margins of interpretation to the political institutions.[53] The Council tried to give guidelines for the application of the principle of subsidiarity.[54] The principle concerns the "if" and "how" of an action. In an interinstitutional agreement the European Parliament, the Commission, and the Council have described the procedure of application of the principle of subsidiarity.[55] The Commission is obliged to justify every proposal for an action taking into consideration the subsidiarity. The Parliament has to justify every amendment of a proposal of the Commission. All three institutions monitor, on a regular basis, if the planned actions are compatible with the principle of subsidiarity. The Commission enacts an annual report on this question.[56]

VI
The Consequences for the Development of the EU: the EU as a Political Unity

The EU does not have the competence to create competences of its own.[57] It is only entitled to decide on its own right to take action on a certain subject.[58] Still, the Member states are the final source of legitimacy.[59] The Maastricht Treaty may have the effect of an incentive to closer cooperation and more harmonization. But the Treaty does not create a European federal or any other European state. The only and limited autonomous law systems of the Community and the member states are closely connected with one another. However, the mutual influence does not constitute the coherent law system of a federal state.[60]

The principle of limited authorization prevents the EU from being an European federation.[61] The Maastricht Treaty shows definitely that the EC, not the Union as a whole, cannot be explained only by the patterns of public international law. At least now, the Community is at a point of no return.[62] There is no way back to traditional national policy-making in Europe. The *Bundesverfassungsgericht* held that the further transfer of sovereign powers to the Community can be allowed as along as the EU is not a federal state.[63] The EU must not become a union in the sense of international law. It must not become a federal state or a confederacy. This is the reason why the name "*Staatenverbund*" (association of states) was coined.[64] It expresses that on the one hand the idea of a common European policy has been originated, but on the other hand that supreme power and the character of a state with respect to the member states have been limited.[65] A "*Staatenverbund*" is a supra- national community of national states concerning law and joint actions, which, with the Maastricht Treaty, has given itself a sound and lasting basis for a common policy. Yet the EU and the EC have only limited supreme powers and a limited democratic legitimation, and above all a limited political homogenity. Thus an imaginable European state would first of all lack a European people, because:

> Democracy is to be the conscious political formation of a unity from the bottom to the top, all representation must always be juristically depending on the will of the community. The people as the many parts is to bring itself consciously into the form of a people as a whole. There must be a certain degree of homogenity in order to make the formation of a unity possible.[66]

The German Constitutional Court has followed Heller's view, and understands the Maastricht Treaty as a positive further step towards the European integration, yet not in the sense of the formation of a new state but more as a cultural and social integration. Therefore the decision has another consequence unforeseen by its followers:

> By saying that Europe must not become a state the Court has formulated the borderline for further developments in Europe. Anything goes as long as no European state results from it.

ENDNOTES

1. Belgium, Denmark, Federal Republic of Germany, Greece, Spain, France, Ireland, Italy, Luxemburg, the Netherlands, Portugal, United Kingdom.

2. Deirde Curtin, The Constitutional Structure of the Union: A Europe of Bits and Pieces, 30 *Common Market Law Review* 18 (1993).

3. *Europäische Zeitschrift für Wirtschaftsrecht* 623 (1992).

4. A discription of the special status for Denmark gives Gunnar Schuster, *Der Sonderstatus Dänemarks im Vertrag über die Europäische Union, Europäische Zeitschrift für Wirtschaftsrecht* 177 (1993).

5. *Frankfurter Allgemeine Zeitung*, 21 May 1993 (no. 116), p. 1/4.

6. Winfried Münster, *Keine Sonderbündelei in Europa, Süddeutsche Zeitung*, 22/23 May 1993 (no. 116), p. 4; see also *Frankfurter Allgemeine Zeitung*, 21 May 1993 (no. 116), p. 4.

7. Eckart Klein/Andreas Haratsch, *Neuere Entwicklungen des Rechts der Europäischen Gemeinschaften -1. Teil-, Die öffentliche Verwaltung* 785, 787 (1993).

8. *Bundesgesetzblatt* 1992, part one, 24 December 1992 (no. 58), p. 2086.

9. Conseil contitutionnel, Decision no. 92-308 (9 April 1992), *Revue Du Droit Public* 608-616 (1992).

10. Matthias Herdegen, *Die Belastbarkeit des Verfassungsgefüges auf dem Weg zur Europäischen Union, Europäische Grundrechte Zeitschrift* 589 (1992).

11. *Tribunal Constitucional*, declaration 108/1992 (1 July 1992), *Europäische Grundrechte Zeitschrift* 285 (1993).

12. *Bundesverfassungsgericht*(BVerfG), decision of 12 October 1993, *Europäische Grundrechte Zeitschrift* 429 (1993); comments and reviews for example by Karl Matthias Meesen, Maastricht nach Karlsruhe, *Neue Juristische Wochenschrift* 549 (1994); Christian Tomuschat, *Die Europäische Union unter der Aufsicht des Bundesverfassungsgerichts, Europäische Grundrechte Zeitschrift* 489 (1994).

13. Art. A of the Maastricht Treaty.

14. Martin Seidel, *Zur Verfassung der Europäischen Gemeinschaft nach Maastricht, Europarecht* 125 (1992).

15. Franz Ludwig Graf Stauffenberg/Christine Langenfeld, *Maastricht - ein Fortschritt für Europa, Zeitschrift für Rechtspolitik* 252 (1992) [Graf Stauffenberg is a member of the European Parliament].

16. Art. 128 EC Treaty; see Georg Ress, *Die neue Kulturkompetenz der EG, Die öffentliche Verwaltung* 944 (1992).

17. Art. 129 EC Treaty; see Robert Lane, New Community Competences Under the Maastricht Treaty, 30 *Common Market Law Review* 939 (1993).

18. Malcom Crawford, One Money for Europe?, The Economics and Politics of Maastricht (1st ed. 1993); Barry Eichengreen, Should the Maastricht Treaty be saved?, *Princeton Studies in International Finance* No. 74 December 1992.

19. Art. 103 al. 3 EC Treaty

20. Seidel (*supra* note 14), at 136.

21. Art. 103 al.3 EC Treaty.

22. Art. 104c al. 1 EC Treaty.

23. Seidel (*supra* note 14), at 136.

24. Karl Albrecht Schachtschneider, *Süddeutsche Zeitung*, November 25, 1992 (no. 272), p. 15, 1st column.

25. Thomas Oppermann/Claus Dieter CLassen, *Die EG vor der Europäischen Union, Neue Juristische Wochenschrift* 5, 10 (1993).

26. Art. K.3 al. 2 lit. c; for some details see Andreas Middeke/Peter Szczekalla, *Änderungen im europäischen Rechtsschutzsystem, Juristenzeitung* 291 and passim (1993).

27. Art. J.4. of the Maastricht Treaty.

28. Kay Hailbronner, *Perspektiven einer europäischen Asylrechtsharmonisierung nach der Maastrichter Gipfelkonferenz*, in: Kay Hailbronner (editor), *Asyl- und Einwanderungsrecht im europäischen Vergleich*, (1st ed. 1992); Albrecht Weber, *Die Harmonisierung der europäischen Einwanderungs- und Asylpolitik, Zeitschrift für Rechtspolitik* 170 (1993).

29. Georg Ress, *Über die Notwendigkeit der parlamentarischen Legitimierung der Rechtsetzung der Europäischen Gemeinschaften*, in: Georg Ress/Wilfried Fiedler (editors), *Gedächtnisschrift für Wilhelm karl Geck*, 1989, p. 625-684; Peter Michael Huber, *Die Rolle des Demokratieprinzips im europäischen Integrationsprozeß, Staatswissenschaften und Staatspraxis* 349 (1992).

30. Oppermann/Classen (*supra* note 25), at 7.

31. Art. 189c EC Treaty.

32. Art. 189b EC Treaty.

33. Reffering Philip Raworth, Too Little, too Late? *Maastricht and the Goal of a European Federation, Archiv des Völkerrechts* 34 (1994).

34. Art. 138a EC Treaty.

35. Art. 138c EC Treaty.

36. Art. 138d EC Treaty; see also art. 138e (Ombudsman).

37. Oppermann/Classen (*supra* note 25), at 7.

38. Georg Ress, *Die Europäische Union und die neue juristische Qualität der Beziehungen zu den Europäischen Gemeinschaften, Juristische Schulung* 989 (1992).

39. Art. F al. 2 of the Maastricht Treaty.

40. Hans-Werner Rengeling, *Grundrechtsschutz in der Europäischen Gemeinschaft* 13 (1st ed. 1993); Gert Nicolaysen, *Europarecht* I 56, 60 (1991).

41. Raworth (*supra* note 33), at 26.

42. BVerfG (*supra* note 12).

43. Summary by Michael Schweitzer/Waldemar Hummer, *Europarecht* 210 (4th ed. 1993).

44. Schweitzer/Hummer (*supra* note 43), at 211: Art.1 Annex IX of the Sea Law Convention of the United Nationen, 10 December 1982.

45. BVerfG, vol. no. 22, p. 296.

46. Stefan Hobe, *Die Unionsbürgerschaft nach dem Vertrag von Maastricht, Der Staat* 245 (1993); Oppermann/Classen (supra note 25), at 7; Ress (supra note 38), at 987; Hans Georg Fischer, *Die Unionsbürgerschaft, Europäische Zeitschrift für Wirtschaftsrecht* 566 (1992).

46. Art. 8a, 8b EC Treaty. See Manfred Degen, *Die Unionsbürgerschaft nach dem Vertrag über die Europäische Union unter besonderer Berücksichtigung des Wahlrechts, Die öffentliche Verwaltung* 749 (1993).

48. Art. F al. 1 of the Maastricht Treaty. See on the participation of the German constituent states in the European Community Manfred Zuleeg, *Die Stellung der Länder und Regionen im europäischen Integrationsprozeß, Deutsches Verwaltungsblatt* 1329 (1992) [Prof. Zuleeg is judge at the ECJ]; Michael Schweitzer, *Beteiligung der Bundesländer an der europäischen Gesetzgebung, Bayerische Verwaltungsblätter* 609

(1992); Detlef Merten, *Föderalistische Mitgliedstaaten in einer Europäischen Union*, in: *Staatsrecht und Staatswissenschaften in Zeiten des Wandels, Festschrift für Ludwig Adamovich*, 446 (1st ed. 1992).

49. The new art. 23 of the *Grundgesetz*.

50. Walter Rudolf, Federal States, in: *Encyclopedia of Public International Law*, vol. 10, 165, 174 (1st ed. 1987).

51. Art. 198a-c EC Treaty.

52. From the many comments see: Deborah Z. Cass, The word that saves Maastricht?: The principle of subsidiarity and the devision of powers within the Eureopean Community, 29 *Common Market Law Review* 1107 (1992); A. Toth, The principle of subsidiarity in the Maastricht Treaty, 29 *Common Market Law Review* 1079 (1992); Wolfgang Kahl, *Möglichkeiten und Grenzen des Subsidiaritätsprinzips nach Art. 3b EG-Vertrag, 118 Archiv des öffentlichen Rechts* 414 (1993); Helmut Lecheler, *Das Subsidiaritätsprinzipsim Europäischen Gemeinschaftsrecht, Festschrift für Werner Thieme 431 (1993); Clemens Stewing, Subsidiarität und Föderalismus in der Europäischen Union* (1st ed. 1993); Gerhard Konow, *Zum Subsidiaritätsprinzip des Vertrages von Maastricht, Die öffentliche Verwaltung* 405 (1993); Peter M. Schmidhuber, Das *Subsidiaritätsprinzip im Vertrag von Maastricht, Deutsches Verwaltungsblatt* 417 (1993) [Mr. Schmidhuber is a member of the European Commission].

53. Stauffenberg/Langenfeld (*supra* note 15), at 255.

54. European Council in Edinburgh on December 11 and 12, 1992, conclusions of the presidency, published in: *Bulletin der Bundesregierung*, no. 140, 1277 at 1278 (28 December 1992).

55. Agreement of 25 October 1993, text for example in: *Europäische Grundrechte Zeitschrift* 603 (1993).

56. *Id.*, at 604, considerations 22, 23, 24 and 27.

57. BVerfG (supra note 12), at 441; Carl Otto Lenz, *Vertrag von Maastricht - Ende demokratischer Staatlichkeit?, Neue Juristische Wochenschrift* 1962, 1963 (1993) [Mr. Lenz is General Attorney at the European Court of Justice]; Ulrich Everling, *Überlegungen zur Struktur der Europäischen Union und zum neuen Europa-Artikel des Grundgesetzes, Deutsches Verwaltungsblatt* 936, 942 (1993) [Mr. Everling is a former judge at the European Court of Justice].

58. Herdegen (*supra* note 10), at 590.

59. Seidel (*supra* note 14), at 132; different opinion by Joachim Wolf, *Die Revision des Grundgesetzes durch Maastricht, Juristenzeitung* 594, 596 (1993).

60. Werner von Simson/Jürgen Schwarze, *Europäische Integration und Grundgesetz*, 42 (1st ed. 1992); Oppermann/Classen (*supra* note 25), at 11; Stauffenberg/Langenfeld (*supra* note 15), at 253; different opinion by Hans *Heinrich Rupp, Maastricht - eine neue Verfassung?, Zeitschrift für Rechtspolitik* 211, 213 (1993); Dietrich Murswiek, *Maastricht und der Pouvoir Constituant, Der Staat* 161 (1993); Rupert Scholz, *Grundgesetz und Europäische Einigung, Neue Juristische Wochenschrift* 2593, 2594 (1992).

61. BVerfG (*supra* note 12), at 440-445.

62. Ress (*supra* note 38), at 986, 991; see also Seidel (*supra* note 14), at 138.

63. *Supra* note 61.

64. Paul Kirchhof, *Der deutsche Staat im Prozeß der europäischen Integration, in: Josef Isensee/Paul Kirchhof, Handbuch des Staatsrechts* VII, p. 885, 886 (1st ed. 1992);

65. Kirchhof (*supra* note 64); see also Meesen (*supra* note 12), at 553, 554; Manfred Zuleeg, *Die Eruopäische Gemeinschaft als Rechtsgemeinschaft, Neue Juristische Wochenschrift* 545 (1994).

66. *Politische Demokratie und soziale Homogenität* (1928), in: Hermann Heller, *Gesammelte Schriften* II, p. 421- 433 (1st ed. 1971).

Chapter Seven

WHY CAN'T HE?: the KENTE CASE and LEGAL DISCOURSE

Norma Procopiow

This paper has its origins in a Legal Writing course I gave for pre-law students. In an effort to relate the complexities of legal writing to what is actually going on in today's courtrooms, I assigned a position paper on a case that recently drew considerable notice because of its controversial overtones. A DC Superior Court judge had dismissed a defense lawyer from a case because he refused to remove his African kente stole when appearing in court. The project revealed how the material facts of a case become transformed by processes of struggle and negotiation laden with interpretive codes extending well beyond the legal domain. Specifically, it demonstrated how current political socialization has impacted on legal circumstances, challenging standards and precedents while at the same time generating conflicting discourses in a semiotic field that encompasses the courts, the press, even the entertainment media.

On the most rudimentary level, this case dealt with advocacy. Where, for example, does the semantic of advocacy conflict with the requirement of the non-prejudicial? The court structure, in its formulated ideal, should rest between the right of advocacy and the necessity for impartiality. But this case really dealt with how the external power structure impacts on legal questions which, in turn, originate systems of solidarity that constitute all of our communication exchanges.

Since traditional protocols are being confronted by unprecedented circumstances in civil and criminal cases, our constitutional provisions re-signify through syntagmatic modalities. How, for example, do we signify "free speech" and what are the linguistic strategies whereby legal and socio-cultural versions of the First Amendment clash? The case we examined—which the press provocatively dubbed the "Kente" case—raised these questions, demonstrating the tensions that political correctness imposes on synchronic legal ideology and the presuppositions embedded in diachronic legal doctrine. Indeed, the press paid little attention to the actual criminal case in question; nor was the ulitmate verdict on the defendant (who was appointed a new attorney) ever publicized. What *was* publicized was the debate on whether the lawyer's First Amendment rights had been infringed upon. The argument remains moot; "free speech" is an arbitrary signifier whose meaning is constituted by the differences in legal and political concepts and commitments. The courtroom's hallowed realm—where appropriate or inappropriate attire is defined strictly according to whether it impedes the proper adminimstration of justice—became absorbed into the entertainment industry and carnivalized. Disinterest in justice for the defendant in this case was replaced by banter at the talk-show level. Does or doesn't a lawyer have the right to dress as s/he pleases? And doesn't the ubiquitous three-piece suit convey as political a message as a kente cloth?

Here, briefly, is what happened. In May of 1992 DC Superior Court Judge Robert Scott told John Harvey, who was representing a defendant on charges of assault with intent to murder, that he would not be permitted to wear his African-style kente cloth in front of a jury, claiming that the stole might unfairly prejudice a jury in favor of him and his client, both of whom are black. (It should be noted that, given the trial's location in a District of Columbia court, the jurors were predominantly black.) Harvey refused to comply and the judge removed him from the case. Harvey then filed a petition in the DC Court of Appeals, asking that Judge Scott either lift his ban or recuse himself because he (Judge Scott) was not being impartial and was denying the defendant *his* choice of legal representative. This accusation was double edged: either the judge had abrogated the Sixth Amendment by depriving the defendant of the right to a swift and speedy trial, or the attorney, by refusing to remove the cloth, was himself abrogating the Sixth Amendment, equally depriving his client of a swift and speedy trial.

The power of the court to impose standards of personal appearance or attire is determined by three general considerations: 1) the requirement that the standard be related to the administration of justice; 2) the necessity that the standard be specifically articulated; and 3) the effect of such standards on two constitutional provisions—due process and the guarantee of religious freedom. This standard of personal appearance or attire refers to a court-imposed "dress code," in other words, any standard of good grooming having as its object the maintenance of dignity and decorum in the courtroom. However, this standard does *not* include detachable articles which, though they may be fixed to the garments or person of the wearer, are not donned for the purpose of covering the body. Here, one could instance tools, handcuffs, signs or placards. Clearly, the kente cloth fits into the "detachable articles" category, leaving its relevance to statutes open to question.

An investigation into recent reported cases on such standards yields few analogies. Suffice to say that although courts theoretically have the power to impose standards of personal appearance upon both attorneys and criminal defendants, these standards are more likely to be imposed upon attorneys. In the words of Justice Cardozo, attorneys have been historically regulated with "minute particularity, even in matters so personal as the growth of their beards or the cut of their dress." The appearance standard for criminal defendants more expressly relates to evidentiary purposes, such as exhibiting apparel to facilitate identification at lineups or at trial.

With regard to the Kente case, constitutional issues and the authority of the judge became an interpretive conundrum scooped up by the media, which pandered to their audiences and capriciously interpreted the law. Indeed, on an extra-legal level, the exchange of opinions co-opted a discourse of its own, generating a variety of documents. The primary genre was print coverage. (I am eschewing tv news, since it incorporates extra-linguistic signifiers, such as framing and timing, too extensive to include here.) Three journals presented the story: the *New York Times*, *The Washington Post*, and the *Washington Times*. Constructions of meaning for the three news footages subtly differed in their accounts, as evidenced in each headline caption. For the *NY Times* the text was: "Judge Objects to Lawyer's African-Style Cloth"; for the *Washington Post*: "Showdown Over Kente Cloth: DC Judge Takes Resolute Lawyer Off Case"; and for the *Washington Times* there were two stories and headings: "Courting Contempt: The Great Kente Debate" and "Failing to Dress for Success, Lawyer Dismissed From Case." The editorial stance of the *NY Times* needs no explanation; for those perhaps less familiar with the two archrivals of DC journalism, the *Washington Times*, owned and controlled by Reverend Moon, tends to bring reactionary contrast to the liberal *Washington Post*.

The textual plane for these stories clearly construes fact-finding as interpretation. For the *NY Times* the caption constructs hierarchical markers: "judge"—emphasizes Judge Scott, who is an authority;

"objects"—here the verb provides the mode of expression that he as an authority selects; and "African-style Cloth"—identifies the cause of his reproval. It is interesting that the qualifier here is "African-*style* cloth," a linguistic marker suggesting: now it isn't really African, is it?, directing a certain censoriousness toward the lawyer. For the *Washington Post*, the delivery of the facts highlights the lawyer rather than the judge (that is, here is an interpretant of symbolic freedom of speech resisting authority and promoting advocacy): and with regard to commitment, the lawyer—is "resolute." Moreover, "Showdown" suggests an ideological feud not addressed in the *NY Times* but characteristic of the *Post*. An entirely different meaning informs the *Washington Times* headings, which privilege word play over factuality: that is, the double pun on "courting contempt," the ironic reference to a "great ... debate," the play on semantic rhyme in "failing to dress for success," (yoking *dress* and *success*) and the tactic of jargonizing "kente wearer" into legal semiosis: "kente wearer *tries* (emphasis mine) patience of judge."

The semiosis in the *Washington Times* captions strongly contrasts with that of the other two journals. News footage is generally regarded more factual than language from drama or other fictive texts. Appeals to "truth" or "reality," intrinsically relative to classification on the mimetic plane, are closer in the other two papers; the strategy of aligning figurative markers in the *Washington Times* with reader expectations of the fictive rather than the factual gives the headlines themselves meaning possibilities whereby distortion of genre, with presuppositions regarding expected modes of discourse, reduces its dignity or importance as a news item.

The discourses in the three papers become even more divisive in their varied "narratives." The *NY Times* addressed the problem of proper administration of justice and whether wearing a kente cloth would disrupt or detract from the proceedings of the court. The *Post*, in a subsequent lead editorial, called for the removal of the judge, arguing that his claim that the jurors might be influenced by attire, or that "they might somehow lose their judgment and objectivity" is flagrantly insulting to the jurors. And the *Times* emphasized that judges "have wide discretion to set and enforce courtroom decorum as they see fit..." and that "whatever the lawyer's intent, the verdict on courtroom dress almost always comes from the bench." Clearly, the *Washington Times* makes a direct appeal to authority here. The strategy of juxtaposing word-play headlines with a "factual" reference to court rule enactments places partiality with the judge.

By these readings, the law, seemingly, is allowed to appear only within narratives; different "fact situations" generate from the same set of events. Thus, the case manifests the question of First Amendment guarantee of religious freedom as it applies to a kente cloth, which here functions as a sign of that freedom. But the significance of kente cloth is, in present society, assigned different categories as well. For example, is the cloth a cultural or a religious sign and how do we distinguish between the two? If we apply dictionary definition, we merely add another set of messages. Religion, according to Webster, is a "specific fundamental set of beliefs and practices generally agreed upon by a large number of persons or sects." Culture, on the other hand, is the "sum total ways of living built up by a group of human beings and transmitted from one generation to another." The obvious distinction between the two definitions is that culture carries a connotation of the legacy of time. Yet, how do we separate out "beliefs and practices" in religion from the "sum total ways of living" in culture? Attorney Harvey told the judge that as an officer of the Faith United Church of Christ, he was required to wear the cloth, both in private surroundings and at work, as an expression of religious faith and ethnic solidarity. However, scholars at the Textile Division of the Smithsonian Institution were consulted regarding the meaning and origins of kente cloth. Their response? Kente was an ancient symbol of royalty in Ghana, West Africa. Wearing the cloth became popular during the civil rights movement as a symbol of pride and has remained so to date. They added, however, that applications of kente cloth have expanded to such a degree as to trivialize it and render it little more than a fashion statement. Their assessment, therefore, implied cultural significance.

Various systems of semiotics would propose meaning-making patterns depending on their specific epistemology. For example, social semiotics would anchor this profusion of messages by summarizing the political/cultural domains in operation. Thus, the Smithsonian response is that of a dominant group in our system of social relations; its signifiers express currently stable, relatively controlled meanings. How, then, does the African-American National Bar Association's response function in the discourse? Rather than issuing a defense of the kente cloth for cultural or religious purposes, the Association made this observation: the cloth could “cut both ways,” either eliciting sympathy for the black defendant, or offending the jurors, who might associate it with former Mayor Marion Barry, who wore a similar cloth at his trial for drug use, corruption, and misuse of DC funds. Interestingly, their reading of the issue was as a group whose title had hegemonized them; speaking from a position of power, they, too, qualified as a dominant group. And they chose to pragmatize the situation: the kente cloth has lost its original purpose.

So much for enlisting social semiotics’ distinction between dominant groups and anti-groups. Indeed, in which of these slots would we place the African-American National Bar Association? If we try structural semiotics instead, the Greimasian semiotic square generates such principal contraries as “liberty” and “authority.”

SEMIOTIC SQUARE

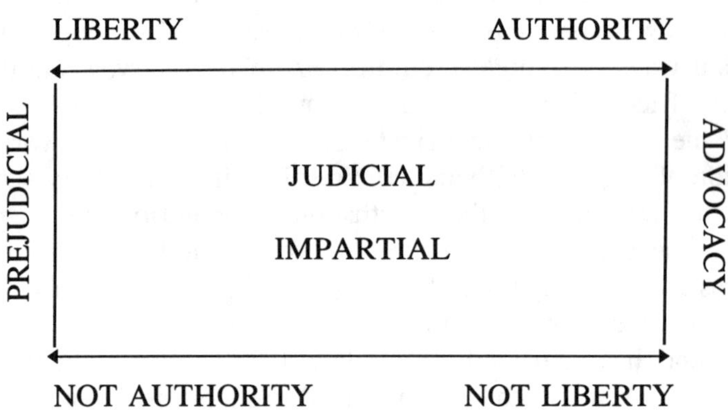

Here freedom of speech is interpreted or poised in conflict between liberty and authority at the point in our square where the lines intersect. Former Supreme Court Justice Warren Burger provides an example of pertinent discourse here. Subsequent to the *Washington Post*’s editorial in defense of attorney Harvey, Burger submitted his rejoinder to the *Post*. The signifiers in his discourse are equally interesting. He states that “Recently a *Post* editorial excoriated a very experienced D.C. Superior Court judge, Robert Scott, for refusing to allow a lawyer to try a jury case wearing a kente cloth sash.” Since time immemorial, he argues, certain dress codes have been part of every society—including even some primitive societies. "What a bizarre business it would be for a Knight of Columbus to appear with his elegant, military-style garb and flowered hat, and perhaps the sword. If a kente cloth is permissible, why not the same rule for Knights of Columbus?" At the risk of second guessing a Chief Supreme Court Justice's motives, we can argue that Burger's editorial fits squarely on the right side of the square. The judge's name, for example, is given, but the lawyer's is not. Also, Burger states that dress codes have been part of every society, adding with innuendo, that they have been part of even some "primitive" societies! Finally, his comparison of the kente cloth with the Knights of Columbus' garb, hat and sword mocks the actual practice by confusing a purely ceremonial situation with clearly confrontational symbolic usage.

But the dress code debate does not end there. The secularizing and commercializing of the First Amendment appears in collective, undifferentiated discourses throughout our popular culture. For example, during the same period the Kente case was being publicized, an episode on the tv series "L.A. Law" featured a dramatized version of the potential consequences of this legal phenomenon. In this episode, a father was brought to trial for allegedly sexually abusing his small daughter. His attorney, who happened to be a nun, appeared in court wearing her habit. The judge instructed her not to appear in court again in clerical garb, claiming that her vestments— perhaps a sign that she was a spokesman for God?—might prejudice the jury in the father's favor. This unlikely and histrionic application of a legal problem converted the First Amendment into a tool for sheer entertainment, exemplifying how tropes for the impartial vs the prejudicial have transformed the law into a code which shapes our society's value judgments.

My final example of First Amendment "pop" relates to a film that appeared several years ago, entitled "My Cousin Vinny." In this variation on the dress code theme, Vinny, your leather jacket, spurred boots, and gold chain breed attorney from a sixth-rate law school in Brooklyn, is confronted by a judge in a courtroom in a southern small-town where the term liberal signifies the enemy and subversion. The judge, whose Harvard Law School diploma is prominently displayed above his desk, warns Vinny that if he appears in court again in similar attire he would be cited for contempt. The next day Vinny saunters into the courtroom wearing the same chains, leather and spurs. The livid judge calls him to the bench and bellows: "didn't I tell you to never ever appear in my court in such disgusting attire?" Vinny, with seeming ingenuousness, replies: "You weren't fuckin' serious, were you, your honor?"

The message in "My Cousin Vinny" is also embedded in the ideological constructs presently discussed. Vinny's casual demeanor, contrasted with the judge's rigidity, signifies that species of American hero we have sentimentalized in our culture for centuries. Against great odds, and townspeoples' efforts to suppress evidence, Vinny, today's Everyman, solves the case, heaping ridicule and ignominy on the sartorial judge.

How, then, do we interpret these varied genres and agents of communication? We have three modes of discourse: legal, journalistic, and fictional. The semiosis moves forward and backward, from the legal sphere to the entertainment sphere and from entertainment back to the legal. In each category the symbolic confrontation of First Amendment rights emphasizes today's essential question: what are the limits to our ability to speak out against the establishment? In entertainment, the producers used the semiotics of costume, an exaggeration to dramatize a political issue. In journalism, the editors found a story which titillates the public's appetite regarding political correctness. And in the courtroom the lawyer *also* used a semiotics of costume to express his independent status as an Afro-American, defying court rules set by precedent and ritual etiquette. Kente as a sign took part in the contest over the arbitrary nature of a right. Just as a signifier does not take its meaning from its connection between itself and its signified, so too a right does not owe its existence to its connection to an individual. Put another way, the concept of kente does not simply re-present previously existing things in the world; rather, it represents the system of differences between legal and "mainstream" moral concepts. As an agent of intertextuality, it is a conspicuous signal and one of the summarizing signs of our currently constitututed political world.

WORKS CITED

Brownstein, Andrew. "Showdown Over Kente Cloth." *The Washington Post.* 12 (June 1992), pp. A1, A16.

Burger, Warren. "The Kente Case." *The Washington Post.* 17 (June 1992) A24.

"Control of Court Over Attorneys Generally." *US Supreme Court Court Digest: Lawyers Edition*, Vol. 3. Section 13 (D), p. 198.

Dubin, Lawrence A. "Pressing the Button for Free Speech." *The National Law Journal*. 4 (November 1991) p. 13.

Margolick, David. "Judge Objects to Lawyer's African-Style Cloth." *The New York Times*. 5 (June 1992), p. B 8.

Metzier, Kristan. "Failing to Dress for Success." *Washington Times*. 12 (June 1992), p. G2.

Piccoli, Sean. "Courting Contempt." *Washington Times*. June 17, 1992: p. F12.

Trenkner, Thomas R., J.D. "Annotation: Power of Court to Impose Standard of Personal Appearance or Attire." *ALR Digest*. 73 ALR 3d 353.

Chapter Eight

FIRST, DO NO HARM: MIXED SIGNALS in our THINKING about LIFE and DEATH

Robert C.L. Moffat[1]

I
Some Meanings of Harm

I invite the reader to think with me about several questions of life and death by examining seven symbols that seem central to that cluster of issues that has come to be popularly known as the right to die.[2] Though the list of symbols could probably be much longer, my present list will suffice to draw our attention to some fundamental issues. Examination of the common assumptions behind basic terms used in thinking about life and death will reveal how answers to serious questions are not given seriously, simply because we typically assume rather cavalierly that the meanings of the terms are obvious.

Take as an example, my first question: what does the phrase "do no harm" mean? If we ask the average doctor that question, we are likely to hear something to the effect that the Hippocratic Oath requires the doctor to do all within her power to extend life. Technically, the oath does not include the phrase "First, do no harm." However, the oath does include the phrase "I will keep [the sick] from harm and injustice." The oath also includes prohibitions on deadly nostrums and abortifacients.[3] Not surprisingly, then, the phrase is typically applied to purely physical well-being, especially by those opposed to any "right" to die.[4]

It may be instructive to consider a contrasting opinion. An excellent example is provided by the recent best seller *How We Die*,[5] by Sherwin Nuland a physician at Yale. Nuland's book has turned out to be surprisingly popular for a serious work describing in considerable detail the processes of death from the most frequent causes. Nuland tells us that doctors have forgotten their pastoral function to minister to the dying, not simply to stave off death at any cost. An ever increasing life expectancy,[6] he says, has led us to deny the certain advent of our own individual mortality so that we approach death unprepared. Today eighty percent of Americans die in hospitals[7] too often tangled in webs of wires and tubes in intensive care units.[8] "Those tucked-away sanctums," suggests Nuland, "symbolize the purest form of our society's denial of the naturalness and even the necessity of death."[9]

Regrettably, Nuland's view contrasts with that of the typical doctor who would be more likely to think of "harm" in terms of failing to preserve physical life.[10] That view of harm as terminating purely physical existence is indeed one possible definition of the "harm" symbol. But there are other possible definitions as well. For example, is it reasonable to think of harm as *extending* painful life? Under some circumstances surely we would consider it sound to judge that prolonging pain was the harm and that terminating the painful physical existence was not harm. We might make a similar judgment when the question is whether meaningless existence should be extended. If Nancy Beth Cruzan has been trapped in a permanent vegetative state for many years without hope of recovery, then it may be reasonable to view extension of that "life" as harm.[11]

These examples of the possible different meanings of harm illustrate the central role of symbols in our thinking. Harm is often used unthinkingly to mean termination of purely physical existence. But once we point to alternative examples of possible harms, the conventional meaning of the symbol loses some of its power. This deconstruction[12] of the signal "harm" is a necessary aspect of the dynamic evolution of the meaning of signs.[13] Roberta Kevelson has shown us that real change is manifested in the evolving signs by which we communicate.[14] Hence, efforts to reform the prevailing code must begin with attention to the signs we employ.[15] One example could be taken from Herbert Marcuse who liked to point out how the phrase "standard of living" is used unthinkingly as a measure merely of economic welfare, while upon reflection the phrase could encompass much more meaningful and various assessments of human condition.[16] But discussion of the dynamic process of language must include not only the role symbols play[17] but also the power of unexamined signs to govern thought and action. I am especially appreciative on this latter point of the work of my colleague Walter Probert as conveyed in his remarkable book *Law, Language and Communication*.[18] In semiotic fashion he urged on us the importance of words consciousness as a means of liberation from the power which words are given to produce inevitable conclusions.[19] Thus, "harm" left unexamined threatens the tyranny of extending painful, meaningless life in the guise of providing us with better medical service. In order to avoid such traps, we must make ourselves aware of the way in which fundamental terms in this discourse are given unexamined symbolic value.[20] Encouraging further development of the moral "code" by enhancing that awareness is the purpose of this essay. To do so I shall consider whether there are worthwhile alternative meanings available for such basic terms in the discussion as life, death, good, playing God, pain, and humane.

However, before we can proceed to examine the other six signals, we must guard against excessive abstraction in our discussion. Therefore, I digress briefly by relating a case study to provide us with a situational context in which to think about how these signals can become mixed in real life application. The case study centers around the end of the life of a woman named Estelle Browning.[21] Mrs. Browning was an elderly woman who lived in St. Petersburg, Florida. She visited some friends in the hospital and saw that they were on life support systems and after seeing these people in this pathetic state, she came home and said, "I never want to be that way."[22] She was so determined about this that she went to see a lawyer and had the lawyer draw up an advance directive, popularly known as a Living Will. However, Mrs. Browning felt that the standard legal boilerplate of the statutory Living Will[23] was insufficient to provide her with the degree of protection she sought. Instead, she instructed her lawyer to add specific tailor-made provisions that neither nutrition nor hydration be provided by gastric tube or intravenously.[24] These additional explicit provisions she had added to the document were, at that time especially, highly unusual as compared with the standard statutory living will. After having this customized document prepared for her, her comment was, "Oh Lord I hope this never happens to me. Thank God, I've got this taken care of; I can go in peace when my time comes."[25]

How did Mrs. Browning's planning work out? Almost precisely one year after she had executed her advance directive with those very specific provisions, she suffered a massive hemorrhage in the left parietal region of the brain—a stroke that destroyed her cognitive control.[26] As a result, she was unable to swallow and so the doctors did a gastrostomy. This consisted of inserting a feeding tube, known colloquially by the gastrointestinal people as a peg, directly into her stomach. The following day she was transferred to a nursing home where her body spent the following two years. I will not prolong this digression by recounting the many adventures her poor body endured during its stay in the nursing home.[27] Later on, her second cousin filed a Petition in Court requesting adherence to her Living Will.[28] Eventually, her case was heard by the Florida Supreme Court which held, after her poor body had mercifully expired, that her Living Will should have been adhered to and that the feeding tube should have been disconnected so that she could die in peace.[29] Now, as it happens, that means her body would have been permitted to starve until it was physically dead. The *Browning* decision written by Justice Rosemary Barkett, recently appointed to the Eleventh Circuit Court of Appeals, typifies leading cases on this topic which hold that while passive measures may be employed to bring life to a close, active measures may not.[30] In other words, you have the right to refuse medical treatment. Not only may you refuse attachment to a ventilator or a machine that will pump your blood for you, but you also have the right to refuse food and water.[31]

II
Some Meanings of Life

Reflecting on Mrs. Browning's wishes, we may now ask was she harmed by the meaningless extension of her life? Can those responsible for prolonging her life claim that they were saving her from harm? There can be little question that her wishes were not fulfilled. Of course, those who oppose her desire for self-determination will claim that she wished to harm herself. We might then raise the question: how do you define the life you purport to prolong? Do you mean quantity of life? That would be the standard answer: pure physical quantity of life.[32] Interestingly enough, this view usually claims to base itself on belief in the sanctity of life, but the life it seeks to sanctify is mere biological function over time. Hence, if a body has human form, and if its heart continues to beat, then that alone is sufficient to qualify as human life.[33] Such a conception of human life, we must take note, excludes social interaction, human potential, and human thought from consideration as factors that define human life.

Could a definition of life properly include such matters? A conception of the signal "life" contrasting to quantity of life is quality of life.[34] A view of life in terms of quality necessarily includes capacity for human thought, although quality implies a variety of meanings, both psychological and social. We might conceive of a definition of quality of life in a social sense as the capacity for meaningful interaction.[35]

Another qualitative definition, less frequently thought of, would focus on essential autonomy. "Life" then would be, as Mrs. Browning wished, living with the knowledge that the wishes of your will are going to be honored.[36] Mrs. Browning's wishes were very important to her; nevertheless they were not honored. It is hard to imagine how anyone could deny that Mrs. Browning would think that her quality of life had been seriously destroyed by the failure to respect her wishes. Certainly, we would consider it morally objectionable if, after the state classified her as dead, her body were treated in ways wildly inconsistent with her wishes. Autonomy seems to make serious claims as a central component of our conception of quality of life.

It is important to note that defining life in purely quantitative terms is inconsistent with a focus on autonomy. But if we desire to respect the wishes of the patient, our moral theory must emphasize autonomy. In that respect, it is interesting to take note of the current attempt to shift the focus from autonomy to pain management. That is the focal point of the recent *U.S. News and World Report* cover story. They purport to be very worried that the publicity given to Dr. Kevorkian's campaign has shifted attention to assisted suicide, thereby eclipsing efforts to provide good pain management.[37] What is noteworthy about this concern is its assumption that the two are mutually exclusive alternatives. If we appreciate the significance of autonomy, it becomes clear that both are equally important. In fact, there seems to be a symbiotic relation between the two. For example, the article mentions the rapidly increasing rate of suicide among the elderly.[38] An important reason for this trend is that people are concerned about losing control and not having their wishes respected, so they go ahead and take preemptive action. I am certain that this concern over losing autonomy has driven some patients to Dr. Kevorkian[39] in precisely those cases where some mainstream moral philosophers criticize his interventions as coming "too early."[40]

The point of autonomy is that, if we make a serious promise to provide reasonable pain control coupled with a promise that when you say you have had enough we will honor your wish, I believe that people will choose to continue, generally speaking, as long as they have any meaningful life, even when the scraps of it look pretty meager to the medical professionals who are looking after them.[41] They will hang around longer than caregivers might expect, as long as the pain is not intolerable and as long as they can be assured that they are not going to lose control. What is clear is that the lynchpin of such decisions is autonomy. Since Mrs. Browning made her wishes very clear, is it not absolutely unforgivable to refuse to honor her efforts to exercise her autonomy? Some critics seek to excuse the failure to honor autonomy by worrying about more difficult questions. I do not deny that such difficult questions exist, both as a matter of theory and also as a matter of being able to decide in advance. But that admission does not alter the fact that a rational person would regard Mrs. Browning's situation as undesirable. That fact makes it clear that anyone can make a Living Will that delineates the things that she definitely does not want to happen. Beyond that, if we have a system in place in which we are assured that our autonomy will be respected, we do not have to worry about solving difficult questions in advance. It is highly likely that we could not decide in the abstract whether we would choose to live like Elizabeth Bouvier, the woman in California who asked that the machines be turned off because she could not stand any more life as a quadriplegic.[42] She claimed that she was so desperate to end her painful existence that she wished to starve to death. Whether we would choose to starve to death if we were caught in her hell is something we cannot know until we have tried it out.[43] But there is no need to decide in advance how we would respond to that challenge. In any dilemma where we remain able to express our wishes, we can decide based on the circumstances at the time, so long as we have a system in place that guarantees respect for our autonomy. Such a system seems the only way to respond to the many elderly couples who are engaging in double suicides or murder suicides. Their fear that they are going to lose control is met by a definition of life that gives primacy to autonomy. If their wishes were respected, I believe that most would choose to continue much longer than they presently do. They are acting preemptively because they fear losing control.

Since autonomy is so central a consideration in thinking about quality of life, it is worth noting that it is also central to the semiotic approach in general.[44] Semiotics stresses that humans are neither static nor isolated.[45] Rather, they are purposive and communicative. This is a notion also developed extensively by Lon Fuller,[46] who was strongly influenced by symbolic interactionism which traces its roots to George Herbert Mead, a fellow pragmatist of Peirce. Although human society is affected in important ways by the environment, the unique human quality is dynamism: the ability to remake the self through experience and reflection. From this postulate we could infer that the social ability to alter the self, the capacity to experience moral growth and to develop further the moral code, is the most human of qualities.[47] Autonomy, therefore, is central to the semiotic method. Semiotics begins from the understanding that humans have a socialpsychological need to exercise control over the choices that allow us to create a self distinct from the rest of humanity. However, once that ability to choose is lost, purpose becomes meaningless, and the specter of mere survival looms. Deprived of our autonomy, we become insignificant products of the environment, relegated to a pathetic actuality. Without choice, we function in a vacuum in which we lose the ability to project ourselves into the environment. Therefore, choice and participation in the process of becoming are crucial elements of the self. In short, to have a self is to possess autonomy. The quantitative view of the symbol "life" is superficial; the self is passive, acted upon by external forces. Only a qualitative view that centers on autonomy includes a genuine, acting self.

III
Some Meanings of Death

But if we ask what is life, then, by the same token, we must ask what is death? As we noted earlier, Sherwin Nuland indicates that the general perception tends to be that it is evil rather than good.[48] That perception is furthered and exacerbated by a widespread mythology of death.[49] Think of the central role that gruesome dead bodies so often play in horror films, in science fiction, in psychodramas and so on. Death is something to be avoided at all costs, not to be thought about, not to be faced, certainly not to be considered a natural part of life. This social attitude is what makes the popularity of Nuland's book so interesting, since that is what his book is about: how we die. Yet, according to the best seller lists, a lot of people are reading it. That development is so interesting, because it involves a shift from our contemporary avoidance of death to the traditional acceptance of death as an inseparable part of life.

Our contemporary irrational fear of death seems due to the escalation of Twentieth Century technology coupled with the isolation from death produced by that technology and the inability of modern "scientific" medicine to accept death.[50] By disguising the decisions which surround death, this society no longer regards death as part of the life process. A century ago virtually any grown person would have had personal experience in laying out a dead body. Today only a very small minority of persons have had that experience. Consequently, the bulk of the population operates under the handicap of the mythology of death. That ignorance makes them potential victims. It sets them up to be exploited by a medical community which takes the easy course: shunting off dying patients into the intensive care unit and isolating them.[51] Visits are typically limited to half an hour at a time and are highly restrictive. The idea of meaningful interaction with your family and friends in a setting not unlike solitary confinement is ludicrous.

That reality contrasts starkly with the widespread image of the classic deathbed scene. Many may have seen the famous portrait of Queen Isabella's signing of her last will, the classic *Masterpiece Theater* view of the deathbed. The Queen is surrounded by family and counselors and physicians while the scribe writes out her last will. That scene contrasts in a macabre way with the setting of the intensive care unit. It is an incredible condemnation of our society that eighty percent of our people are dying in hospitals. That should not happen except under unusual circumstances such as accidental deaths. People should die at home. People should die at home in their own beds.

Upon examination, of course, there are several alternative definitions of death. First, there are physical definitions. The traditional one is cessation of heart and lungs.[52] That has been supplanted by cessation of brain function, the current popular one applied in all jurisdictions.[53] That definition, however, is not quite as simple as it sounds. One might think that there was no meaningful brain function left in Mrs. Browning's body. Were she brain dead, however, her wishes would have been respected. Instead, the doctors diagnosed her condition as a persistent vegetative state which means that reptilian brain function continued, even though she had absolutely no capacity for meaningful interaction.[54] Mrs. Browning's predicament suggests that a possible further working definition of death might be the cessation of meaningful existence. This definition is more imprecise, of course, in that it requires the exercise of some qualitative judgment, but that same drawback is also its merit. Ceasing meaningful existence is a conception of death that is based on pursuing quality of life. As a qualitative definition, it requires of us a more refined understanding of good and evil than the quantitative physical approach.

IV
Some Meanings of Good

This same contest between quantitative and qualitative conceptions is reflected in attempting to understand the meaning of the symbol "good." Is the continuation of life under any circumstances good? Some think so. For example, Conservative Rabbi David Novak in his book *Suicide and Morality*[55] reports approvingly the position of Thomas Aquinas:

> The feeling [of committing suicide] contradicts life which is a real good. Suicide is unnatural because it does not intend a real good. Death is a privation of the real good life. The moral consideration of this situation in the light of the natural inclination to preserve life is to subordinate the suicidal feeling to human nature. Suicidal feelings are not empirically denied but they are denied human value inasmuch as they deprive man of his proper end which is a real good. This consideration will lead to the conclusion that there is no moral justification for suicide.[56]

Clearly, Mrs. Browning, wishing to exercise her autonomy, would disagree. For her, the denial of suicide is clearly not a good. Accepting Novak's conception requires the triumph of the quantitative view over the qualitative view of life.

V
Some Meanings of Playing God

That same contrast applies in viewing the next question: what is playing God? Functionally, it is often merely a variation of the question what is good, even if one had not just been exposed to Aquinas' view. A nice example of typical thinking is provided by a recent occurrence in Florida. The parents of a terminally ill nine-year-old boy became embroiled in a controversy with their school board.[57] The lad has a degenerative nerve disease. The parents resolved that while he was still alive he should live as normal a life as possible and continue to attend the special education classes at his elementary school. In keeping with this plan, they requested school authorities, should the boy's heart stop beating while he happened to be at school, that they not call 911 or resuscitate him. They wished that the boy be allowed to die in peace.[58] This caused all kinds of consternation and the school superintendent made this statement, "In my estimation a reasonable person is going to try to keep a child from dying. Boy, I don't like playing God."[59] Perhaps, the most fascinating aspect of all this is that the superintendent had absolutely no awareness of the irony of his statement. His unspoken assumption was that the natural thing to do was to resuscitate and that *not* resuscitating is playing God. What a terrific question to beg![60]

Not all who think about this subject beg that question. Dr. Donald Murphy at George Washington, one of the medical leaders on standards for resuscitation and improving advance directives, has addressed the question seriously. In his article *Life Sustaining Therapy: A Model for Appropriate Use*,[61] he develops a model designed to suggest those circumstances under which we should presume against resuscitation. There is no need here to explore the complexities of his model, but he demonstrates rather clearly that from both a medical and from an economic standpoint, out of hospital cardiopulmonary resuscitation (CPR) is an inappropriate decision for chronically ill older people.[62] In such cases, the presumption, in the absence of an advance directive to the contrary, should be no CPR.[63] Why? Because the chance of survival to discharge is one percent,[64] which means that the vast majority of patients so situated will expire after some days or a few weeks in the intensive care unit which is both very expensive and very hard on their families.

At the same time, Dr. Murphy would honor advance directives even in very marginal cases.[65] By taking this position, his effort is simply to sort out what presumptions ought to be made. What he is concerned about is the fact that emergency medical technicians are going out and restarting hearts. By the time the patient gets to a doctor, under the current regime, it is too late to undo a mistake. Obviously, some of this concern would be alleviated if we honored individual wishes, including active measures to terminate the remnants of physical life for patients who request such assistance. The existence of such provisions would allow mistakes to be undone by doctors. At present, doctors are justifiably paranoid about having a terminal patient whom they fear they may have to put on a ventilator because there is no advance directive, making it much more complicated to get life support systems turned off.

Although Dr. Murphy's model carefully avoids the need for active measures, the basis of his calculation is still measured in terms of quality of life. Of course, defining life in terms of quality, as something other than an accumulation of years, makes those who oppose active measures nervous, because if we can measure quality, then we implicitly acknowledge that lives may vary in value. Is all life equally worthy of preservation? The quantitative answer is affirmative, but unhelpful in making difficult choices. For example, if we must decide whether to allocate scarce resources to care for a ninety-year-old cancer patient who is unaware of her surroundings and suffering excruciating bone pain or to use them to look after a nine-year-old child with broken limbs, the quantitative model is of no use. Both patients make an equal claim. From a qualitative standpoint, the condition of the ninety-year-old cancer patient makes it evident that her life has reduced value both to herself and to society. Her capacity for meaningful interaction has been almost completely destroyed, and her potential to contribute to society is at an end. If medical resources are finite, it is impossible to provide the same level of life sustaining treatment to all patients in all circumstances. More-over, equal treatment is unlikely equally to enhance the lives of patients in differing situations. It is unrealistic to devote equal resources to preserving the life of the ninety-year-old cancer patient and the life of the nine-year-old accident victim. What criteria can be employed to assist in making such determinations? Thorough qualitative analysis would be complex. But age, health, and prognosis of the patient would be obvious considerations. In most cases, the nine-year-old's potential to contribute to and interact with society throughout the course of a lifetime will be much greater than that of the ninety-year-old. From a qualitative perspective, medical treatment is an investment with future returns. When the suffering of the ninety-year-old is alleviated by medical intervention, that result too is a positive return on the investment, since not only is her pain abated but other members of society are reassured that they will be similarly cared for in their hours of pain. To make assessments of quality is an essential component of exercising choice. But to exercise choice is, as Goethe understood, to play God.

Similarly, is acceptance of the passive euthanasia allowed in Mrs. Browning's case somehow a matter less of playing God than if active euthanasia were permitted?[66] Is that distinction as real as it is often treated as being? The lead story in a recent *U.S. News and World Report* quite boldly proclaims that "[n]ow all 50 states have enacted laws to allow the signing of Living Wills. As a result, passive euthanasia, the act of withholding or withdrawing life sustaining technology like a feeding tube or respirator, is now common practice."[67] I think that statement is both naive and overly optimistic. Very serious efforts will be required to get significant cooperation from nursing homes before such policies become routine and are consistently carried out. But even if we were to accept the "common practice" pronouncement as true, how seriously should we take the active/passive distinction? Should we rest content that Mrs. Browning has the right to have the feeding tube removed and may now starve herself to death? Our reason for contentment would be that we need not play God as long as her death is "passive." On the other hand, active euthanasia (which *U.S. News and World Report* claims is the issue now being debated)[68] *would*, in that view, involve playing God. If we hasten her already certain physical death, should that action make us feel that we are playing God in some significant sense that allowing Mrs. Browning to starve slowly to death does not? As the original resuscitation question shows, exercising choice *is* playing God, and choosing to be passive is still choosing.

VI
Some Meanings of Pain

How should we exercise choice? Focusing on the meanings of pain might be helpful in our deliberations. Is active intervention to carry out Mrs. Browning's wishes more or less painful for her? Normally we think of pain as physical torture. The same *U.S. News and World Report* article trumpets that nearly one-hundred percent of cancer pain is now controllable.[69] Apparently, the writers were presuming that those who had watched loved ones die of cancer would not be reading their lies. Most certainly, the authors did not bother to talk to experts in pain management which is a brand new specialty, the first boards for which were held in October 1993. The claim that we will manage your pain well is much more complicated than it's generally made out to be.[70] These are important reasons why pain management will become more difficult under Hillary's plan, because much pain is too complex for general practitioners to manage competently.[71] Morphine is thought to be the panacea, but it does almost nothing for bone pain or gastrointestinal agony. As a matter of fact, even estimates that ninety percent of cancer pain is controllable may be exaggerated.[72] And we must remember that these assessments fail to account for physical discomfort short of actual pain.[73]

Moreover, our vision is very limited if we confine our attentions to physical pain. Surely, we recognize the pain of psychological torture, which may take many forms, including the loss of a loved one. That notion of pain may seem surprising to some, but therapists working in the field consider such a loss an emotional trauma. From a chemical standpoint, the body is suddenly deprived of the endorphins generated by the intimate physical contact now missing.[74] As a matter of social psychology, that same loss is understood in terms of symbolic interaction as the pain arising from the sudden, tremendous void created in the person's normal patterns of interaction. Yet another form of pain consists in witnessing the physical or mental deterioration of a loved one. I think, for example, of the suffering of my cousins, as they endured the extended vegetative state of my favorite aunt a few years ago. She had suffered a stroke much like Mrs. Browning's, and her body was kept "alive" in a nursing home for well over a year. The suffering of a body in such a vegetative state is really something about which we know almost nothing. But certain it is that the family suffered greatly seeing her in that deplorable condition.

Nor can we forget that a further form of pain may be knowing that the great cost of the meaningless extension of your painful life is bankrupting your family. I am certain that every person knows of at least one situation where family finances have been destroyed by a final illness. One of my friends told me recently that he sends his mother a few hundred dollars every month because all the income she has is her social security check (about half the maximum, so not very much). I expressed surprise, because I knew they had had a successful business. The answer was that his father had had a stroke and the family savings were nearly exhausted for home care during the last few years of his life, because such care is extremely expensive.

Relating the pain of cost back to the exercise of autonomy, there is a recent interesting study which shows that patients with Living Wills have an average of one-third the medical costs for their final illness as patients without a Living Will.[75] However, the savings of cost and pain are much less than they could be, because the authors note only a slight rise in the percentage of people with Living Wills, despite the passage of Senator Moynahan's bill.[76] That law was passed after the Supreme Court's decision in *Cruzan v. Director of the Missouri Department of Health*.[77] Although the law has not had great impact yet, it may eventually lead greater numbers of people to make out Living Wills. The bill requires that hospitals and nursing homes plop a Living Will down in front of you when you are admitted. However, I suspect that the reason for such minor impact so far is that hospitals and nursing homes are often not using patient admissions as an opportunity to engage in counseling and discussion of Living Will issues, to provide patients with the possibility of doing some good advance planning.

Yet another form of pain for conscientious citizens is the knowledge that expensive, but unnecessary care is draining public coffers. Some may find it hard to believe that anyone would worry about cost when insurance companies or governments are footing the bill, but I have known personally such individuals, and knowledge of the unnecessary expense was painful to them. In evaluating the ethical readiness of the legal profession, we should take note of how rarely these costs are mentioned in court opinions in right to die cases. In *Cruzan*, for example, Justice Rehnquist flatly recites, "[A] State may properly decline to make judgments about the 'quality' of life that a particular individual may enjoy, and simply assert an *unqualified* interest in the preservation of human life to be weighed against the constitutionally protected interests of the individual."[78] Yet contrary to the language in *Cruzan*, the interest of a state in preserving life must be qualified by its interest in preserving the effectiveness of its health care system. Indeed, the care of the terminally ill has placed an enormous strain on health care providers and insurers.[79] Traditionally, these costs have been considered irrelevant, while all possible measures were taken to keep patients alive.[80] In reality, such disregard for costs relied upon the capacity for government or insurance to mask expenditures. Today however, with both government outlays and insurance rates skyrocketing, the financial well-being of families, health providers, and society as a whole depends upon controlling such costs.[81] The use of Living Wills and active measures must, therefore, be considered within the range of possible alternatives in light of the health care crisis. Simply put, resources are finite and "[t]he aggressive care of patients with poor prognoses [is] an inappropriate use of resources."[82] Vast outlays are required to sustain patients who have no meaningful chance of recovery. Yet these patients, under current law, are not permitted to waive their right to extend worthless physical life. While they may choose to forego life sustaining treatment by making out Living Wills, extensive resources must still be devoted to controlling their pain and monitoring their condition while they slowly starve their poor bodies to death.

Yet another possible definition of pain is doubting that your wishes will be carried out. A rather poignant example is provided in a recent letter to *Dear Abby*.[83]

Yesterday my father died. My immediate reaction was relief that his prolonged illness had at last ended. This poor soul had suffered a few small strokes, had Parkinson's Disease and Arthritis and last fall we had to admit him to a nursing home when I could no longer continue to care for him.

He had a tube to his stomach, catheter from his bladder and in his last 8 months had been back and forth to the hospital for blood transfusions, oxygen, urinary infections, etcetera, etcetera. The last month he no longer recognized me and was in my opinion 95% dead. We wouldn't allow an animal to suffer this way. The racehorse Secretariat was in pain so they put him out of his misery. Why should a sick old man of 88 endure so much. Could it be that the nursing home collected some $2,400 a month for his care?

He had a Living Will, but this only provided that if his heart stopped that there would be no heroic measures to revive him. Why won't the medical profession let nature take its course? Why do they insist on prolonging a life that really is not living any more?

I was told I had no choice on the feeding tube except to decide if it went up his nose or directly into his stomach. We can't starve a patient, the nursing home spokesman said. It was terrible to see what Dad suffered and I visited him every day.

It was terrible to see the other patients in this nursing home crying out for help when there was nothing that could be done. Thank God it's finally over for my Father, but it was the longest 8 months that he ever lived. When he was able to communicate, he was distressed for me to see him in this condition. Medicare can only go so far so his savings were about depleted.

I can't feel much sadness that he's gone only that he had to suffer so much before his heart finally stopped beating. We can only hope that something in the future will change before any of us have to go through the same misery. I'd do anything to prevent my family from seeing me linger that way.

[Signed] Grieving Daughter.[84]

This letter illustrates quite well the great psychological torture that can be forced upon one in refusing to carry out one's wishes. The pain of denying autonomy should not surprise us, for that is the pain of being a slave. Yet we routinely choose to enslave the dying and force them to endure their torture. Is it not atrocious that we should force Mrs. Browning to starve to death? Patients in vegetative states may not suffer in ways that we can presently fathom. But we do not know what kind of dreams they may have, particularly as the process of starvation proceeds. If we really care about relieving pain, we would employ active measures to allow individuals such as Mrs. Browning to die in a peaceful, dignified, and painless way.

VII
Some Meanings of Humane

By the same token, would we classify our treatment of Mrs. Browning as humane? Is it really humane to extend meaningless life or is it more humane to terminate pain? Is providing treatment or enhancing torture the better way in which to express our common humanity?[85] These propositions have come to be accepted as uncontroversial by the mainstream moral philosophers writing in this area.[86] Yet the pithy conclusions of a James Rachels[87] are ignored by the people who exercise the power, the foot dragging members of the medical and legal professions, whose ethical training is conceded to be terribly deficient by knowledgeable observers.[88] Although their recalcitrance affects society, the problem is nonetheless internal to the legal and medical professions. That is where we need action and re-education, unless we are willing to wait a generation until current ethical thinking trickles down to the nether regions.

Despite the lack of ethical cooperation by the legal and medical professions, is it so difficult to determine what we mean by humane? Suppose that while we were out riding, your horse stumbled and broke its leg in a chug hole. I would then sadly but routinely hand you the revolver. As the owner of the horse, tradition dictates that killing the horse is your honor and responsibility. But suppose that you said this horse was so special to me that I am going to treat it like a human. I love this horse so much that I am going to starve it to death. We know that the probabilities are very good that you would face jail time for animal cruelty on the grounds that you had acted inhumanely to the horse. Is it not time that we begin also to treat humans humanely?[89]

ENDNOTES

1. Copyright 1994 Robert Moffat. I must express my great gratitude for the extensive and very helpful research assistance of Charles Boning. I wish also to thank Roberta Kevelson and the participants in the Seventh Annual Roundtable on Law and Semiotics for their comments and questions when I first presented this paper at the Roundtable. I am also grateful for the helpful questions and discussion of Hans Oberdiek and the participants in a Philosophy Colloquium at Swarthmore College where I presented a related paper "Going Softly: Roles of Law in the Right to Die" on April 17, 1994. Finally, this essay is dedicated to the memory of my late wife Janette Leslie Moffat who is responsible for the moral clarity with which I view these issues. Reprints of this essay are being distributed as an activity of the Janette Leslie Moffat Fund for Law, Medicine, and Bioethics of the University of Florida Law Center Association.

2. J. Boyle & G. Grisez, *Life and Death with Liberty and Justice: A Contribution to the Euthanasia Debate* (Univ of Notre Dame Press, 1979); Derek Humphry, *Final Exit: The Practicalities of Self-deliverance and Assisted Suicide for the Dying* (The Hemlock Society, 1991); Barbra J. Logue, *Last Rights: Death Control and the Elderly in America* (Lexington Books, NY, 1993); Timothy E. Quill, M.D., *Death and Dignity: Making Choices and Taking Charge* (W.W. Norton & Company, NY, 1993); Tom Regan, editor, *Matters of Life and Death: New Introductory Essays in Moral Philosophy* (NY: Random House, 3rd ed., 1991); David Novak, *Suicide and Morality* (NY: Scholars Studies Press, 1975); Sherwin Nuland, *How We Die* (NY: Knopf, 1993); Robert N. Wennberg, *Terminal Choices: Euthanasia, Suicide, and the Right to Die* (William B. Eerdmans Publishing Company, Grand Rapids M.I., 1989).

3. The actual language of the Hippocratic oath is: "I will neither give a deadly drug to anybody if asked for it, nor will I make a suggestion to this effect. Similarly, I will not give to a woman an abortive remedy." See Thomas Mappes & Jane Zembaty, *Biomedical Ethics* 53 (NY: McGraw-Hill, 3d ed 1991) (setting forth the oath in full). It is, however, common to confuse the "First, do no harm" phrase with the Hippocratic oath. See, eg, Quill *supra* note 2, at 43. See also Ludwig Edelstein, *The Hippocratic Oath: Text, Translation and Interpretation, in* Ancient Medicine 6 (Baltimore: Johns Hopkins Press, 1987).

4. M.F. Sullivan, "Oath violations are commonplace," *Gainesville Sun*, July 1, 1994, p. 13A (Letter to the Editor): "[T]he pro-life ethic espoused by the oath ... [is violated by] doctor's complicity in euthanasia, assisted suicide and abortion ...."

5. Sherwin Nuland, *How We Die* (NY: Knopf, 1993).

6. *Id.* at 84-85. Nuland states that while average life expectancy has increased dramatically, the human species has a maximum, genetically determined life span of just over a century. Even if all disease were eliminated, he contends, the "ravages of senescence" would still lead to mortality within narrow and largely predetermined time limits.

7. *Ibid.* at 255.

8. *Id.* at 254: The beeping and squealing monitors, the hissings of respirators and pistoned mattresses, the flashing multicolored electronic signals -- the whole technological panoply is background for the tactics by which we are deprived of the tranquility we have every right to hope for, and separated from those few who would not let us die alone. By such means, biotechnology created to provide hope serves actually to take it away.

9. *Ibid.* at 254.

10. Henk Jochemsen, Ph.D., *Life-Prolonging and Life Terminating Treatment of Severely Handicapped Newborn Babies: A Discussion of the Report of the Royal Dutch Society of Medicine on "Life-Terminating Actions with Incompetent Patients: Part I: Severely Handicapped Newborns,"* 8 Issues L & Med 167, 176 (characterizing human physical and spiritual existence as a unity, and concluding that "[m]edicine should always be practiced in an attitude of assistance to the life of the patient, not the death of the patient."); but see *Bouvia v. Superior Court*, 225 Cal. Rptr. 297, 305 (1986): "It is incongruous, if not monstrous, for medical practitioners to assert their right to preserve a life that someone else must live, or more accurately, endure ...."

11. Paul Kurtz, Ph.D., The Case For Euthanasia: A Humanistic Perspective, 8 Issues L. & Med. 309, 315 (1992) (describing an alternative view of "harm"):

> Another moral principle that should be taken into consideration is nonmalfeasance. We ought not to harm those persons whom we love or those people whose care we are entrusted with. This means that we ought to be concerned with what will benefit the person. It is not always to the benefit of the active patient to be kept alive at all costs. You may be doing good to the active patient to help him die and thus not harm him by prolonging his agony. In other words, if you keep someone alive against his will who might otherwise die with some dignity, you may be hurting him and inflicting cruel and unusual harm on him. That is immoral.

12. Robin Paul Malloy, "Introduction to the Symposium: Law and Economics and the Semiotic Process," 42 *Syracuse L. Rev.* 1, 2 (1991): "The reading of signs therefore requires a deconstruction and reconstruction of the stimuli confronting the reader or unknowing semiotician."

13. *Ibid* at 3: "Signs, in a semiotic sense, are always in motion. Signs are always changing and are part of a process of creative evolution.... [S]igns ... are dynamic, changing, and contextual." Although some writers in this field make distinctions between terms such as "signal" and "sign" or "symbol," I use them interchangeably in this essay.

14. Roberta Kevelson, *The Law as a System of Signs* 35 (1988): An open society, in which an open legal system usually predominates, rests not on the assumption that the world is fully created once and for all, but rather on the belief in the possibility of real change in the world, that is, on the conviction that the universe *becomes* and not that it is, that something really new may be created, and that this real novelty is not manifest in the actual order of things but is present in the evolving concepts of signs which stand for a reinterpretation of values and meanings of relationships between things.

15. Roberta Kevelson, "Semiotics and Methods of Legal Inquiry: Interpretation and Discovery in Law From the Perspective of Peirce's Speculative Rhetoric," 61 *Ind. L. Rev*. 355, 355 (1986): "[I]n Peirce's view no code is ever complete, and thus all judgments may be regarded as provisional only, capable of reinterpretation and reformation."

16. Herbert Marcuse, *An Essay on Liberation* 24 (Boston: Beacon Press, 1969).

17. Kevelson, supra note 15, at 355: Peirce's semiotic methodology ... seeks to account for the development of meaning in verbal signs in all acts of inquiry, such that a sign is shown to interpret its previous sign, or referent in discourse, and to bring a cumulation of meaning forward in a dynamic and open-ended process.

18. Walter Probert, *Law, Language and Communication* (Springfield, IL: Chas. C. Thomas, 1972).

19. Probert, "Words Consciousness: Law and the Control of Language," 23 *Case-Western Reserve L. Rev*. 374 (1972). See also Probert, *supra* note 18, at 16:

> I have said that application, invocation, and interpretation of laws (and we should add facts) are not automatic. But it can seem to be. There is the rub. To say that decision is not just a matter of logic or that it is a value process, or that it involves policy questions, or underlying moral issues, are some of the ways of pointing out that in a psycholinguistic sense, in the ways that words can be used, there is choice. But to the person who is not aware of the psycholinguistic possibilities or who in a given situation is convinced, conditioned, threatened, or maybe insensitive if not intolerant to ambiguity, there is no choice. *That-is-the-way-it-is* and the other way does not make sense, is not reasonable, or is even absurd.

20. Probert, supra note 18, at 144. "The master form of the word as it appears in print or in sound tends to cover or conceal, to act as camouflage, for the deeper complexities within the dynamics of what we like to call the concept represented by the mere sound or letter." *Ibid*.

21. In re: *Guardianship of Estelle M. Browning*, 568 So. 2d 4 (Fla. 1990).

22. *Ibid*. at 9.

23. Fla. Stat. Sec. 765.04 (1987).

24. *Browning*, 568 So.2d at 8.

25. *Ibid*. at 8-9.

26. *Ibid*. at 8.

27. *Ibid*. at 8: "During the course of her stay in the nursing home, Mrs. Browning was plagued with physical difficulties, including complications with her feeding tube, which became dislodged. The gastrostomy tube was replaced by a nasogastric tube on May 19, 1988." Further difficulties she experienced are catalogued in the court's footnote:

> The ailments included numerous episodes of vomiting; numerous bed sores, some of which evidenced profuse drainage; bruises and blisters on extremities; swelling of the hands, feet, and ankles; ingrown toenails; sporadic vaginal bleeding; and rectal discharge. The complications included leakage from the tube; drainage from the incision around the tube; plugging of the catheter bulb, which required frequent replacement and insertion; and leakage from the catheter.

Ibid. at 8 n.3.

28. *Ibid*. at 8.

29. *Ibid*. at 17.

30. *Cruzan v. Director, Missouri Dept. of Health*, 110 S.Ct. 2841, 2846-51 (1990)(examining the right to refuse treatment). "As [the] cases demonstrate, the common-law doctrine of informed consent is viewed as generally encompassing the right of a competent individual to refuse medical treatment." *Ibid*. at 2851. See also In re *Estate of Longeway* 133 Ill.2d 33, 139 Ill.Dec. 780, 549 N.E.2d 292 (1989); *McConnell v. Beverly Enterprises---Connecticut, Inc.*, 209 Conn. 692, 553 A.2d 596 (1989); In re *Quinlan*, 70 N.J. 10, 355 A2d 647 (1976).

31. *Bouvia v. Superior Court*, 179 Cal.App.3d 1127, 1143-45, 225 Cal.Rptr. 297, 305-06 (1986) (allowing for the withdrawal of nutrition from a quadraplegic patient). See also *Cruzan*, 110 S.Ct. at 2852: "[F]or the purposes of this case, we assume that the United States Constitution would grant a competent person a constitutionally protected right to refuse lifesaving hydration and nutrition."

32. Timothy E. Quill, M.D., *supra* note 2, at 49 (1993)(assessing what he refers to as the "medicalization of death"): "In medical training and practice, the prolongation of life is given a much higher value than the lessening of human suffering, even in the care of the dying."

33. This notion is rigorously perpetuated by certain disability activists, the Christian Defense Coalition, and reactionary elements in the Roman Catholic Church.

34. Barbra J. Logue, Last Rights 9-19 (NY: Lexington Books, 1993) discussing the reduced quality of life enjoyed by many elderly patients. "[P]eople [are] living longer, living longer with, and in spite of, very disabling chronic conditions, which the health care system can 'manage,' but not 'cure.'" *Ibid.* at 13. See also Marvin Kohl, Ph.D., *Altruistic Humanism and Voluntary Beneficent Euthanasia*, 8 Issues L. & Med. 331, 333 (number 3, 1992)(assessing how qualitative factors might impact treatment decisions):

> [A] life that is not totally full is not necessarily empty, and further that one can be happy with a life that is far from ideal, and that being abnormal, disadvantaged, or disabled does not necessarily mean that one cannot lead a relatively rich, busy, and contented life. Similarly, we understand that a life that is, on balance, unhappy is not necessarily an empty one. It may still possess opportunity for great moments of satisfaction. Exiting from an unhappy life is, therefore, one thing; exiting from an irreversibly meaningless or agonizing existence is another.

35. Marvin Kohl, Ph.D. *Altruistic Humanism and Voluntary Beneficent Euthanasia*, 8 Issues L. & Med. 331, 337-38 (1992); Barbra J. Logue, *supra* note 34, at 4, 126-27 (Lexington Books, N.Y., 1993): "Although modern techniques of pain management can substantially alleviate physical pain ... [they create] a deathlike state in which the person has no conscious experience, no significant communication with others, no joy, no movement toward personal goals--in short, no life."

36. Logue, *supra* note 34, at 140: "For families who supply direct care for elders ... fears about their ... future well-being that inevitably arise--are good examples of the human costs associated with long-term care provision."

37. Joseph P. Shapiro with David Bowermaster, *The Case of Dr. Kevorkian Obscures Critical Issues and Dangers*, U.S. News & World Report (April 25, 1994).

38. *Ibid.*

39. Julia Pugliese, Note, "Don't Ask—Don't Tell: The Secret Practice Of Physician-Assisted Suicide," 44 *Hastings L.J.* 1291 (1993) (examining the frequency of doctor assisted suicide and the reasons behind this phenomenon).

40. Tom Beauchamp, *Suicide in Matters of Life and Death* 97, 116-117 (New York: Random House, 3rd ed. T. Regan, 1991) (reviewing the rationality of suicide decisions).

41. Logue, Last Rights, *supra* note 34, at 130:

> Uncertainty plays a large role in premature death. No one can "count on being lucky enough to have adequate warning of deterioration and enough time in which to deliberate while still free of impairment." No one can count on help being available if he postpones acting. As Percy Bridgman, a Nobel Prize winner in physics wrote in his suicide note at age 80, following his doctor's refusal to help him die: "Probably this is the last day I will be able to do it myself."

42. Bouvia, 225 *Cal.Rptr.* 297 (1986).

43. *Ibid.* at 304-06. Elizabeth Bouvia became a quadriplegic as a result of cerebral palsy. She was denied several requests for permission to starve herself to death, before the California Court of Appeal ruled in her favor. The court noted that the quality of her life was so poor, it had been reduced to utter hopelessness and frustratration. *Ibid.* at 304.

44. Robin Paul Malloy, "Introduction to the Symposium: Law and Economics and the Semiotic Process," 42 *Syracuse L. Rev.* 1, 3 (1991):

> [I]f signs express ideas and exist in relationship to other signs, then power within a society or culture can be analyzed by investigating the relationship between the signifier and the signified. That is, within a society certain people or institutions play roles as signifiers.

45. Robin Paul Malloy, "A Sign of the Times—Law and Semiotics," reviewing Roberta Kevelson, *The Law as a System of Signs* (1988), 65 *Tulane L. Rev.* 211, 215 (1990):

> [B]oth law and economics are dynamic sign systems. While they are often discussed in terms of static "snapshots" of the juridical or economic process, law and economics are in reality best understood as "motion pictures."

46. Fuller, *The Morality of Law* 162, 185 (Yale University, rev. ed., 1969) (discussing the nature of man underlying his vision of legal morality).

47. *Ibid.* at 162-67, 185. Fuller disputed the notion of H.L.A. Hart, espoused in *The Concept of Law* (Oxford Univ Press, rev. ed. 1994), that the proper end of human activity is mere survival. Rather Fuller believed that opening channels of communication is paramount.

48. Nuland, *supra* note 5. See generally Quill, *supra* note 2.

49. Cf. Probert, *supra* note 18, at 90 (examining societal tendencies to obscure meaning through defensive techniques):

> Our society is so firmly entangled with mechanisms for camouflaging, distorting, or hiding-from truthfulness, our culture and its institutions (including politics, but also law) so habituated in hiding behind masks and facades, that the average individual is apprehensive of analyses that seem to tear down these facades ... The result is that we must attempt to communicate as best we can behind these facades. No mere theory will change let alone sweep aside the defensive structures so deeply fortified.

50. Nuland, *supra* note 5.

51. Nuland, *supra* note 5.

52. Wayne LaFave & Austin Scott, *Criminal Law* 609 (St Paul: West Publishing Co, 2d ed 1986). See also Boyle & Grisez, *supra* note 2, at 59-60.

53. Nuland, *supra* note 5, at 123: To be declared legally dead, there must be incontrovertable evidence that the brain has permanently ceased to function. The criteria of brain death currently being used in intensive care and trauma units are very specific. They include such signs as loss of all reflexes, lack of response to external stimuli, and absence of electrical activity as shown by a flat electroencephalogram for a sufficient number of hours.

54. *Browning,* 568 So.2d at 8.

55. David Novak, *Suicide and Morality* (NY: Scholars Studies Press, 1975).

56. *Ibid.* at 48.

57. Laureen M. Crowley, "Parents Demand that School not Revive their Ailing Son," *The Gainesville Sun* (7 February 1994) page 2B.

58. *Ibid.*

59. *Ibid.*

60. Robert Wennberg in his book *Terminal Choices* explains that ending life necessarily involves playing God while extending life does not. Why? Because, he tells us, when we extend life we further God's purpose in creating life, and therefore far from taking matters out of God's hands, we become extensions of his hands." Wennberg, *supra* note 2, at 95. This is a novel answer to the question posed in the text: we are not *playing* God because we actually *become* part of God! By the same token, any extension of life and lives is to be sought, regardless of its lack of quality. And of course the more lives that come into being, the happier God must become! By extension, Bangladesh must become Heaven on earth.

61. Donald J. Murphy, M.D. & David B. Matchar, M.D., "Life Sustaining Therapy: A Model for Appropriate Use," 264 *JAMA* 2103 (31 October 1990).

62. *Ibid.* at 2104-2108.

63. *Ibid.*

64. *Ibid.* at 2104.

65. *Ibid.* at 2104-08.

66. The Roman Catholic Church views this distinction as all important. In 1980 the Church published a "Declaration on Euthanasia," which reads in part:

> Intentionally causing one's own death, or suicide, is therefore equally as wrong as murder; such an action on the part of a person is to be considered as a rejection of God's sovereignty and loving plan. (quoted in Eugenie Anne Gifford, Comment, "Artes Moriendi: Active Euthanasia And The Art Of Dying," 40 *UCLA L. REV.* 1545, 1552 (1993)).

67. Shapiro & Bowermaster, *supra* note 37.

68. *Ibid.*

69. But see Quill, *supra* note 2, at 23 (contradicting this claim):

> [E]nd of life suffering is not exclusively a problem of access to good palliative care. Unfortunately, some patients still experience excruciating deaths in spite of heroic efforts by skilled physicians, nurses, and family members.

70. *Ibid.* at 48-49 (summarizing the limitations of medical care and the tendency of physicians to overestimate the benefits of treatment).

> I believe that physicians tend to overstate the potential adverse consequences of medical interventions in their discussions with patients and their families. We also tend to minimize the severity of a patient's illness and to put the best face on their prognosis, so that the context for making informed decisions is often lacking. *Ibid.* at 49.

71. See *ibid.* at 23 (focusing on limits to pain management):

> [E]nd-of-life suffering is not exclusively a problem of access to good palliative care. Unfortunately, some patients still experience anguishing deaths in spite of heroic efforts by skilled physicians ....

72. Logue, *supra* note 2, at 126-27 (denigrating the notion that reducing pain is an adequate panacea); see also Quill, *supra* note 2, at 106-07 (describing pain and discomfort which can not be alleviated through medication):

> [A] dramatic, at times excruciating lesson comes from the patients with lung or oral cancer who are dying of respiratory failure. These patients struggle to breathe and are often continuously coughing and producing mucous in copious amounts .... [They may] endure a panicked, suffocating struggle just prior to death that is much like drowning .... Some patients can live in an agonizing twilight between suffocation and death because of the ambiguity of our intentions. *Ibid.* at 107.

73. Quill, *supra* note 2, at 106-107 (describing discomforts other than physical pain).

> Some patients are forced to live on the edge of death for weeks or even months

> in semi-concious states .... Such patients must often make very difficult choices on a daily basis between pain and sedation.

Ibid. at 106. He also points out that there is highly significant discomfort other than pain:

> Pain relief is not equivalent to the relief of *suffering*. The latter encompasses psychological phenomena such as the frustration of not being able to do the things one enjoys, hopelessness about the possibility of returning to an acceptable quality of life, and the sense of being a burden to others. Pain medication cannot eradicate these nonphysical forms of suffering.

Ibid. at 107.

74. Diane Ackerman, *A Natural History of Love* (New York: Random House, 2d ed 1994).

75. Christopher Chambers, James Diamond, Robert Perkel, Lori Lasch, "Relationship of Advance Directives to Hospital Charges in a Medicare Population," *Archives of Internal Medicine* 154: 541-547 (March 1994).

76. 42 USC Sec. 1395cc (1991).

77. *Cruzan v. Director, Missouri Dept. of Health*, 110 S.Ct. 2841 (1990). The Court held that states could require clear and convincing proof of an incompetent patient's wishes, before permitting the discontinuation of life sustaining treatment.

78. *Cruzan*, 110 S.Ct. at 2853 (emphasis added). See also *Cruzan v. Harmon* 760 S.W.2d 408, 420 (Mo. 1988) *aff'd sub nom. Cruzan,* 110 S.Ct. 2841 (1990) (articulating the state's interest in an extremely narrow and illogical fashion):

> [S]ome courts find quality of life a convenient focus when justifying the termination of treatment. But the state's interest is not in quality of life. The broad policy statements of the legislature make no such distinction; nor shall we. Were quality of life at issue, persons with all manner of handicaps might find the state seeking to terminate their lives. Instead, the state's interest is in life; that interest is unqualified.

79. David R. Schanker, "Of Suicide Machines, Euthanasia Legislation, and the Health Care Crisis," 68 *Ind. L.J.* 977, 1004-05 (1993).

80. *Ibid.* at 1004.

81. *Ibid.* at 1005.

82. Murphy & Matchar, *supra* note 61, at 2103-08.

83. According to the results of a survey, most older patients are aware of their rights to refuse treatment, "and more than half of those said they learned of [this right] through the newspaper, especially the 'Dear Abby' column." Logue, *supra* note 2, at 89.

84. *Gainesville Sun* (2 May 1994) page 3D.

85. Kohl, *supra* note 35, at 333: "Aside from saints or those who have embraced saintly virtues, it is probably unrealistic to expect health professionals to feel lovingly toward all who come into their purview. It is one thing to experience feelings of love, another to expect humane treatment. However, the latter should not be unrealistic."

86. E.g., Tom L. Beauchamp, "Suicide," in *Matters of Life and Death* 77 (New York: Random House, 3d ed. Tom Regan, 1991).

87. James Rachels, "Euthanasia," in *Matters of Life and Death* 35 (New York: Random House, 3d ed. Tom Regan, 1991).

88. Quill, *supra* note 2. "Somehow we must train physicians to balance their drive to extend life with a mandate to listen and learn from their patients .... *Ibid.* at 42. "In medical training and practice, the prolongation of life is given a much higher value than the lessening of human suffering, even in the care of the dying." *Ibid.* at 49.

> If [the] patient shared his doctor's wish to fight against death no matter what the consequences or the odds, then at least we ... could hang on to the belief that we were granting a dying person his very difficult last wish. Uninformed, however, the patient [becomes] the victim of a brutal medical death ritual. The effect upon health-care providers who have to inflict such torture without being appraised of its purpose or of the patient's personal goals is devastating and demoralizing. The blind fight for life without regard to the specific individual undermines the fundamental values of the profession.

Ibid. at 59.

89. Marvin Kohl, Ph.D., *supra* note 35, at 331 (quoting Mahatma Gandhi in *The Essential Gandhi* 215 (Louis Fisher ed., 1962): "I cannot for a moment bear to see a dog or for that matter any other living being, helplessly suffering the torture of a slow death ... I should kill a dog similarly situated because in its case I am without a remedy. Should my child be attacked with rabies and there was no helpful remedy to relieve his agony, I should consider it my duty to take his life."

Chapter Nine

REPRESENTATIONS of the POLITICAL PRISON: ACTUAL SPACES, VIRTUAL FORMS

Mariana Net

I
Argument

In a recently published article, Ann Rigney refers to fiction as "not always used to create alternative worlds, but to comment critically and yet safely—with impunity, if not secrecy—on ritual states of affairs and the individuals who direct them" (Rigney, 1994:63), whereas, along the same line, a decade and a half ago, M. Heller spoke about "the meaning-producing habits and wishes of the victims" (Heller 1980:243).

Against this background, the present paper will deal with various representations of space in six contemporary Romanian books of political prison memoirs (see *References*). Prison will be considered here as an emblematic space, and the six texts—which, more often than not, are complementary to each other—will be dealt with as *a single, polyphonic macro-discourse*. A fairly ample space will be given to quotations, since these texts are probably unknown to an English-speaking reader.

It should be specified that in communist Romania the great majority of political prisoners belonged to the intelligentsia. Most of them had quite a vast cultural loading; therefore they were quite likely to fictionalize both while experiencing their captivity in jails and in labour camps, and while remembering such an experience and writing it down. An objective perspective is always quite honestly attempted at, but hardly ever achieved. Fiction(alization) is a means of escape. But, just like humor, it is often resorted to for reasons of "decency", discussed above, with a view to ensuring a kind of distance towards the experienced events, in order not to give way to terror and horror, in order not to complain. This is true both as regards the time of the direct experience, and as regards the time of writing.

The lapse of time separating direct experience from its written account, the cultural loading of the Enunciators, as well as their awareness of being involved in a case of book writing enable the researcher to treat these texts as "fictional" texts, no matter how "real" the experience they reflect has been. Like any fiction(alized) world, prison is thus an autonomous, self- consistent universe. As compared to the actual world, prison is an "*identikit*", an "imitation". However, as is well-known, "life imitates art far more than art imitates life," but the opposite view is also possible. Perhaps it is not quite alleatory that Oscar Wilde, the Enunciator of this "witticism" spent two years in prison, too. Consequently, all the representations of space taken into consideration in the following pages are *mental, subjective representations*.

The present study will also deal with various ways of perceiving actuality, when the subject is stongly determined by certain spatial and temporal coordinates. These specific spatial and temporal coordinates are such that, from the very start, they are likely to generate an extreme situation or series of situations.

II
What can Prison be Equivalent to?
Reframing, Metamorphoses.

The most frequent and stereotype comparison to be found in all the books under discussion is between the prison (or the cells of a prison) and a *tomb*. Illustrations of such an equivalence are superfluous. A variant of the tomb is *the cemetery*. Here is an example at random:

> Cell no. 6 is nothing but a poor cemetery, in which a joking death has replaced the usual shrouds by as many uniforms; whitish and greyish striped uniforms look much more proletarian (Constante 1993:67).

It is also common knowledge that, more often than not, the jail is also *an experimental laboratory*. The captives themselves are quite aware of the fact:

> How many medical theories concerning men's physical resistence, as well as their organic possibilities, have not been contradicted by prison evidence, in the course of prison life?! Many other phenomena, in return, have found their medical explanation and confirmation (Ioanid II:35).

Political prison is also *a school*. A complex, intricate school. Every new captive gets explanations from his fellow-prisoners about the way life is organized in jail, about the regulations and about the way they may be infringed, about the significance of noises, etc. But the cell is equally a space in which teaching proper, as discussed above, sharing one's knowledge with one's fellow-prisoners is a means of moral survival, or at least of avoiding madness. Clandestine lessons of foreign languages, physics, history, theology, philosophy are given and taken, fictional books are narrated, personal experience of all kinds is shared with the others. The following quotation in which prison is implicitly equivalent to a *university* has an obvious ludic tinge:

> She is silent. She has understood [my signal]. She was bound to understand [it]. She is one of the *pillars of our jail*. She entered prison at 18 and she is going to leave it at 28, as *a doctor in prison sciences* (Constante 1993:199, my emphasis, M.N.).

Sometimes, prison may be *a law-court*, too. It often happens that some of the inhabitands of a cell—the great majority, in effect—"charge" one of them for having been an accomplice of the administration. Examples are superfluous, for there are only slight, irrelevant variations from one case to another; the "trial" is always an unambiguous, straightforward one.

The beds in a cell are once perceived as *cages*, and the women who live in those cages may resemble as many apes:

> In the evening, when the women were climbing to their beds, and in the morning, while they were getting down, the performance they were unwillingly giving was *a zoological one*. Scores of apes on the right, scores—on the left, were clutching to the iron bars in order *to creep to their cages*, or to glide down on the floor. Occasionally, the claw of one ape was resting on the head of another ape—by mistake (Constante 1993:121-122; my emphasis, M.N.).

In a ludic-pejorative register, the jail is once dubbed *a pub* by a political prisoner who was an academic and a "*bon viveur*".

The prison may be also *a space of imponderability*. Here is just one telling example in this respect:

> Deprived of the iron chains which had been attached to my feet for such a long time, I was first unable to control my movements. I was walking like a spaceman in conditions of imponderability! (Ioanid II:248)

In actual fact, from the point of view of people leading a "normal" life, prison experience is not far from life in outer space; it may seem as fantastic, as remote from "normal", everyday existence.

Since it is, up to a certain point, an autonomous, self-consistent world, prison is also necessarily perceived as *a factory*. Though the narrator's attitude is fairly ironical, the following fragment is only half ludical:

> *My small-scale industry* [of making shirt collars out of used bed linen] was developing more and more. *A new organization* was therefore necessary. [...] In collaboration with X, I devised a new method of getting *raw materials* (Ioanid III :73; my emphasis, M.N.).

Alongside the same line, prison may be also reframed into *an office for trademarks and brands*:

> Y had invented *a camouflage device*; it was he who owned the trademark.[...] The initial brand did not satisfy the inventor, who started to improve it (Ioanid III:79; my emphasis, M.N.).

However, more often than not, prison is *a theatre*. The most obvious example is furnished by a comic performance, actually a "revue," produced, staged, interpreted, and attended to, by the prisoners who share a cell (Ioanid III:259-264). It is quite significant that this performance also includes a parody of prison itself, namely the script of the performance is an adaptation of a well-known comical ballad. It is a *mise-en-abyme* of a special kind, since it is achieved by resorting to fiction proper.

It is often the case that the captives themselves perceive prison as a theatrical space. Thus, during a brief period of relaxation, in which the regulations were rather loose:

> Z pretended that, while he was cleaning the corridor, the loud echo of our discussions gave him the impression that he was in the foyer of a theatre, or in the waiting-room of a railway station (Ioanid III:89).

Since some of the prisoners are occasionally viewed as actors or actresses, it is fairly easy to infer that part of the cell is considered the "stage", whereas the rest of it is the "auditorium":

> But the disputes between A and B were always nothing but a burlesque play. The two women were only two gifted actresses, who performed their parts to our great amusement. Everything looked like an ancient tragedy with A, and like a bouffe comedy with B (Constante 1993:188).

The part of the building in which the official inquests were conducted is also perceived as a "theatre", while the inquest is nothing but a *play*:

> In my opinion, it was a low-quality theatre [where only bad plays were staged] (Banus 1991:52).

All the examples given so far are obvious cases of reframing; theatricalness is a necessary condition thereof. Perhaps the strongest ludically marked example is furnished by one of the narrators while extensively describing "fly-hunting" during another period in which regulations were rather lax. The close relationship between hunting and play is much too obvious to be expanded upon. The prisoners' game was, at that time, to attach a colored string to the flies they caught and then to let them loose on the corridor and in the courtyard, in this way amazing and subsequently frightening their guardians.

> *A series production* of flies with a tail was thus obtained; the captives were rather keen on *the organization of work* and on *the manufacturing process* (Ioanid II:244; my emphasis, M.N.).

Paradoxically enough, it is just *because* the difference between prison and all the institutions it is compared to does exist, that play is made possible. While being momentarily suspended, the difference is actually strengthened. In this way, the prisoners become *accomplices* to this very act of re-inforcing prison. They do it without being aware of it. They are the unwilling collaborators of the administration, which is yet another paradox.

III
Spaces, Destinations, Functions

The investigation of prison memoirs has pointed to the fact that, usually, it is the main *features* and the *destination* of the emblematic space which confer their status to the inhabitands. From this point of view, prison discharges the same function as the stage in a theatre.

Perhaps the most relevant example in this respect is supplied by a guardian who had been shut in a cell by mistake (Ioanid II:362); when he knocks at the door in order to be released, his fellow-guardians take him for a prisoner.

Another text (Ivan 1993:38) describes a scene in which several hundreds of captives are transported from one labor camp to another, shut up in *sealed vans*. The obvious inference is that political prisoners are precious items, "treasures" closely watched by the administration (although, of course, the latter would not have agreed to such an interpretation).

Prison, considered, once again, as an emblematic space, projects its shadow on the outside world. It is the state of mind, the *behavior* of the occupants of a space which confers upon that space a certain status, discussed above, which transforms it into a prison.

Thus, after the narrator of one of these texts learns about the king's sudden abdication, she explains that:

> The two women had come back, too and they were loudly lamenting in the next room. Their lamentation suddenly reminded me of the endless nights spent in prison (Georgescu [1951] 1992:197).

Here, the house, the home is equivalent to a prison. This phenomenon happens because the lamentation is alike in both spaces, and also owing to the fact that the *cause* of the lamentation is much the same, as discussed above, deep sorrow due to a political catastrophe which leaves no hope for the future. That is why both places are reflected in the same way in the narrator's consciousness and in her writing.

When captives have lived in prison for a certain lapse of time, even their *mental* perceptions are altered. Paradise itself may be ironically conceived as yet another prison. The following brief dialogue between two women prisoners (Constante 1993:148) is conclusive to this effect:

> —[...] if we are going to be executed now, we'll meet in heaven.
> —Don't be so sure. There must be quite a big crowd up there. Since people have been going to heaven for seven thousand years now, that place must be even more promiscuous than our jail.

It should be pointed out that in all the examples given so far, as well as in the following ones, the words designating the two compared entities, between which the Enunciator usually establishes an oblique equivalence, have a secondary meaning, quite different from the basic, denotative one. The presence of two dominant features is usually enough for such an equivalence to be established. A narrator who has become a Member of Parliament after 1990 says, for instance, that some of his former fellow-prisoners from the 1950s have become his colleagues in the post-communist Parliament (Ivan 1993:44). There is no suggestion in the text that Parliament could be a prison. However, just like prison, (1) Parliament is a political institution, in which (2) the representatives of the Opposition have quite a limited power. An implicit comparison is made therefore between these two "artificially built" spaces.

IV
The Inside and the Outside: the Implied "Here" and the Expressed "Beyond"

The Prisoners

Different in style, confined to various lapses of time, conceived and written separately, all the prison memoirs stipulate quite clearly that the difference between prison life and everyday life, between the "inside" and the "outside" is, more often than not, irrelevant.

One of the narrators (Banus 1991:89) explains that "while in prison, everybody should mind their own business. Otherwise, they are quite likely to get into trouble." But this is not only a characteristic of prison. It is the same outside, too, both *on this side of the Iron Curtain*, and *on the other side*.

Sometimes, *the inside* and *the outside*, the prison and the country (or the world) are viewed as *concentric circles*; some other times, they are *communicating, permeable spaces*, which can occasionally merge into each other. There are prisons within the prison, as discussed above, prisons *en abyme*. A punishment cell in one of the prisons was once ironically referred to as "the prison of prisons, a kind of Holy of Holies" (Ioanid II:53).

But more often than not, the prison may be said to transcend its own borders and assimilate the whole country, or even a broader space. Usually, the idea of "the country as a prison" or "the socialist system as a prison" is openly stated, whereas the idea of "the world as a prison" is only an indirect suggestion.

Once, while in a labor camp, the prisoners are housed in a wooden cottage, surrounded by barbed wire. The narrator makes the commonplace remark that "it was a smaller prison within the big one" (Ivan 1993:26). The "big prison" may stand here for the political prison as an institution, but also for the whole country or even for the whole "socialist camp", viewed as a macro-prison. The same narrator specifies (Ivan 1993:32) that the members of the administration (as discussed, of the communist country *and* of the political prison, therefore the administration of the political prison as a large-scale institution) are also considering the labor colony, the whole country, *and* the other countries (the world at large) on the same level. The members of the administration stage their scripts for the benefit of all these concentric circles.

Nevertheless, the *center-periphery* question arises here. The closer one is to the center (in this case, the prison), the "freer" those at the periphery seem. Periphery stands here for the world beyond the Iron Curtain, namely for the space conventionally called "the free world." This space is perceived as a "free world" by the people living beyond the Iron Curtain, too, because they know that those people living at *their* periphery (in the socialist camp) are *not* free. Everything is a matter of subjective perception, as well as a matter of distance. The possibility of taking a distance towards the immediate events—no matter how much such events affected them personally—was a privilege of most of the political prisoners referred to in these pages, because they had a vast cultural competence. Culture was a means of salvation.

In actual fact, *the inside* and *the outside* are only conventional spaces. One of the narrators specifies that after listening to several stories told by his fellow-prisoners:

> I'm silent for a moment. The horizon of human tragedies is becoming larger and larger every moment (Banus 1991:91).

But the story he had just listened to also involved some of the people who were still *outside*, not only some of those *inside*. "Human tragedies" are a link between the conventional *inside* and the conventional *outside*.

The relation between these conventional spaces as reflected in the prison memoirs of communist Romania can be much more intricate. Another narrator specifies that "Room no. 6 [in our prison] was the turn-table of all prisons" (Ivan 1993 :25). A cell was the turn-table of all prisons, just as Czechia used to be considered the turn-table of Europe. Microcosm is governed by the same conventions as macrocosm.

Alongside the same line, a narrator (Ioanid II:141) claims "all the paths lead to Jilava" [a famous prison], in this way adapting the ancient saying according to which "all the paths lead to Rome." This particular prison is considered to have the same relevance for the captives as Rome used to have for the ancient world.

An even more complex event is described in an autobiographical "novel" (Banus 1991:93). It speaks of a Romanian restaurant in Rome, where a man is drugged, and while he is still unconscious, he is brought back to Romania and sent to jail. The restaurant functions as a *trap*, and its owner is an accomplice of the secret police, to which he is furnishing fresh victims. Consequently, Rome, which stands for "the free world," is a trap, too. The so-called "free"communist Romania was also a trap. Or rather, people's illusion that Italy, Rome, belonged to a "free world" and their illusion that that particular restaurant was re-creating an *identikit* of "free Romania" are as many traps. In this universe perfused with illusions, it is only the prison and the trap which seem to be "real". The restaurant *is* an *identikit* of Romania, but it is an *identikit* of an *occupied* country, not of a *free* one.

In the same text (Banus 1991:176), the narrator receives a parcel of foodstuffs from home. While examining *the package, the wrapping, the sticker*, he is able "to visualize [his] home, [his] street, [his] friends, [his] free life." The reader is meant to wonder, at this point, whether freedom is only a package, a wrapping, a sticker, whether it is not confined to certain spatial borders only by convention. But stress should be once again laid on the fact that the borders do exist, that they are asserted and strenghthened by the very fact of their being mentally, spiritually abolished.

Yet another oblique reason for establishing an equivalence between *the inside* and *the outside* is the fact that the closed space of the prison does not alter the social hierarchy from the outside. From the peasant prisoners' point of view, the jail is a micro-village (Constante 1993:36). One cannot keep wondering, however, whether it is a characteristic of prison to preserve the hierarchies from the outside, or whether it is a characteristic of rural society to have its rules preserved even in prison. Probably, the latter supposition is closer to the truth: rural civilization, rural society—which is also a closed, self-consistent universe—is stronger than prison.

The Guardians

By the very fact that they move to and fro, the guardians are wavering between the two worlds conventionally represented by the closed space and the outer space. Whether they want it or not, they establish a connection between *the inside* and *the outside*, by the very fact that they stand at the border.

Two scenes rendered in the same book are conclusive. One of them (Ioanid I:36) describes the captives cleaning their cells, while the guardians are cleaning the outside corridor, the captives washing the doors inside, whereas the guardians are washing them outside, and so forth. Comments are superfluous.

The second volume (Ioanid II:38-39) describes a little *ad hoc* "comedy" staged by one of the prisoners, who decided to make fun of his guardians. Through a straw inserted under the door, he manages to suck the soup from the bowls which had been momentarily deposited on the corridor. Once again, the difference between *the inside* and *the outside* is cancelled for a brief interval. Once again, the difference is strengthened while being momentarily suspended. Just because the difference does exist, play is made possible. Paradoxically enough, the prisoners become unwilling accomplices to this very act.

Holes in the Wall

There are always cracks in the doors, holes in the walls; even though scarcely, people circulate even beyond the Iron Curtain, both from West to East, and from East to West. The two mental spaces can occasionally merge into each other.

Once, in 1946, some prisoners open the window of their cell and sing the national hymn. The passers-by, as well as the drivers of some cars and the passengers of a tram stop in front of the open window and do the same (Georgescu [1951] 1992:190). As the national hymn was, at that time, "God Save the King," and Romania was occupied by Soviet troops, who kept the population under terror, singing the national hymn was an act of dissidence by which those who were (still) outside took the risk of being sent to jail.

At a public trial, in spite of all the threats, the accused speak out the truth:

> At that moment, due to our presence there, a valve had been opened, and part of the secrets which had been so carefully preserved have come to the surface and were spread outside (Ioanid II:142).

During the World Youth Festival, which took place in Bucharest in 1953, scraps of paper on which data had been written about the "real" situation in the country were unobtrusively squeezed in the hands of some visitors from Western European countries (Ioanid I:253). Another communicating hole was practiced in the "wall".

Nearly all the books on prison life in communist Romania mention the fact that, sometimes, imported foodstuffs which nobody outside had enough money to buy were sold to the prisoners once they were tainted. The sight of the foreign packages, of the foreign stickers, is said to bring an air of freedom into the cells, as discussed above. But it is important to notice that most of the prisoners had been sentenced just because they had been accused (and sometimes convicted) of having "communication with foreign countries." This is yet another paradox—a tragi-comical one—of which the members of the administration were not aware.

A wide-scale phenomenon which took place in the world outside is equally relevant for this discussion. From time to time, people who had relatives or friends beyond the Iron Curtain used to receive packages of foodstuffs, but also of personal goods: clothes and cosmetics, occasionally a jewel: objects they used to wear, to admire, to be proud of, to sell, or to give to others; objects which immediately drew everybody's attention, which one immediately identified as coming from "a different world"; objects for which, no matter how high or how low their intrinsic value was, the owners were almost unanimously envied. In an epoch when such items were hardly ever imported on the official socialist market and therefore quite a few people were able to "benefit" from them, such stuffs were scarcely called "foreign goods" or "Western goods". Their usual denomination, accepted by everybody, was "goods from *a package* [someone received from abroad]." But the specification written here between square brackets remained nearly always implicit. It was common knowledge what "goods from a package" meant. Just like in prison, some "privileged" people occasionally received a package from an *outside* space. From some "outer space". The package helped them to subsist, to dream, or "to evade". It also strengthened their feeling of constraint. It made them more aware of their oppression.

The texts under discussion also specify that one of the most dreadful punishments the prisoners were threatened with was *the closing of the window*. Some captives even died for lack of fresh air. On a metaphorical plane, the same thing happened *outside* the prison. It is also significant that, in prison, people are shown crowding around the open window or around the cracks in the door, in order "to get a mouthful of fresh air" (Ivan 1993:25). Once again, in a country in which the liberty of circulation and the right to information could hardly be said to exist, much the same phenomenon could be noticed *outside* the prison walls.

The commonplace remark that the difference between *the outside* and *the inside* which seems often cancelled-out can now be nuanced. Sometimes, (Ioanid I:276) prison is an equivalent of the *army*, or of the *hospital*. This happens, for instance, because the bed sheets are once recycled by the captives, within the jail, in the same way that they used to be recycled in the army, or in hospitals. The prisoners give the recycled sheets to a "free" worker employed in the same labor camp, and in exchange, the latter brings them medicine. Through the agency of this worker, *the inside* and certain emblematic spaces *outside* are communicating.

For some of the prisoners it is no longer significant on which side of the bars they are living. Here is a conclusive example:

> His behaviour was so natural, so unsophisticated, that it was obvious he didn't care on which side of the bars he was living (Ioanid II:273).

It may be easily infered that, from this captive's subjective perspective, there was not such a big difference between the two sides of the bars.

Some other prisoners seem even to prefer prison to liberty:

> It is worse outside than it is inside (Georgescu 1992:115).

Outside, there are too many things to worry about, too many anxieties, too much poverty.

The absurd character of prison life has also led to distorted perception. So much so that, occasionally, there are prisoners who "reject" the open space, who refuse a relative liberty:

> I am afraid. I am suffering from a kind of agoraphobia. Whenever I am in the open space, I feel by far more vulnerable (Ioanid I:173).

This feeling can be even ludically led to the absurd. Alongside this line, the same narrator registers a scene of "panache". One of his fellow-prisoners shouts, in French, to a new-comer, hosted in a different cell:

> *—Il vaut mieux rester ici [dedans, que retourner dehors, où un honnête homme ne peut plus boire un verre de bon vin*] (Ioanid II:296).

The ludical aspect is obvious, but the assertion is not entirely devoid of the truth. It also points out, once again, in an indirect way, that prison is a self-consistent, autonomous universe.

During the first day of liberty, the prison is looked back upon as *the only possible shelter* against the evil things taking place outside:

> In the train which brought me home, a strange idea occurred to me. It is quite possible that the prisons and jails spread all over the country were the only shelters against the aggressive expansion of evil. The iron bars had been shielding us from the influence of evil. Common suffering had been a counterpoison against the loss of any moral sense (Constante 1993:219).

V
Means of Projecting Prison

The whole prison literature speaks of the communist administration's design of transforming the whole country into (the equivalent of) a huge prison. Alongside violence, *the absurd* nature of the regulations, as well as the absurd character of everyday life outside the space of prison is one of the main means made use of to this end. Some of the prisoners respond to the *morbid absurd* by a kind of comic, *ludic absurd*. Examples have been already given. But the ludical is also doomed to emprisonment; it is also confined to certain borders—not always metaphorical ones—because the administration are aware that it can "degenerate" into being taken seriously. The ludic must be also checked and cancelled, because it is a possible *salvation*, a possible *evasion*: an evasion from the horrors of jail, and a salvation from psychic destruction. All the prison memoirs bear witness that, in the absurd universe they describe, it is only the fools who are safe. The administration, the jailers, are relatively safe mainly because they are "mad." If a prisoner is mad, too, (s)he is not only safe, but (s)he is also an unwilling accomplice to the administration.

VI
Ways of Escape

Day-dreaming and wishful thinking are among the most favored means of illusory escape from prison:

> I have organized my life. Till 10 a.m., I'm always dreaming. I lean against the wall, and I escape (Banus 1991:119).

Day-dreaming implies the projection of another universe. It is a flat, schematic projection, on an imaginary screen, hung on the wall of a closed space.

Fictionalization of everyday life, within the prison and outside it, is yet another privileged means of escape. In this way, the prison seems no longer "real", though it is real enough. "Evasion" is mainly achieved *through* fiction, and *into* fiction:

> Then, line after line, I attempt to translate the poem into French.
> It was, eventually, an escape. My first.
> [...]
> In this way, for the first time, I left my cell and penetrated into the silver woods (Constante [1990] 1992:24).

This kind of "evasion" into a different space, and therefore into a different universe, is actually similar to any "evasion" from the monotony of everyday life. It is not only a fictional escape, but equally a fictitious one.

In order to escape, momentarily, the constraints of prison, sometimes the captives resort to play. While the women captives are communicating through Morse from one cell to another, the prison becomes "a space of adventure," (Constante 1993:159) for they share a secret, they perform a forbidden activity, they communicate with "distant spaces," as discussed above, the neighboring cells, and in this way, they deceive their guardians.

But first and foremost, it is a kind of *self-deception* they achieve. All the prison memoirs—the few texts chosen to illustrate these considerations are only a representative sample—bear witness to the prisoners' self-deception, be it willing or unwilling.

> This autodisinformation is hard to achieve, but it often works among the general public, particularly when connected to general and fuzzy humanitarian themes repeated again and again (Imbert 1994:45).

In actual fact, I have tried to demonstrate here that self-deception has also characterized "the other side," as discussed above, the members of the administration. The barrier between these two categories is, sometimes, lax. The distinction between them is only seldom a biunivocal one. There are always nuances. Otherwise, none of these wishfully built spaces could ever have existed. "Salvation" would have been impossible, for there is no salvation outside fiction.

WORKS CITED

Banus, Max. *Cei care m-au ucis* [Those Who Have Killed Me]. (Bucuresti: Tinerama, 1991).

Constante, Lena. *L'évasion silencieuse*. (Paris: La Découverte, 1990).

_____. *Evadarea tacuta*. (Bucuresti: Humanitas, 1992).

_____. *Evadarea imposibila* [Impossible Evasion]. (Bucuresti: Editura Fundatiei Culturale Romane, 1993).

Georgescu, Adriana. *Au commencement était la fin*. (Paris: Hachette, 1951).

_____, *La inceput a fost sfirsitul*. (Bucuresti: Humanitas, 1992).

Heller, M. "La desinformation: moyen d'information," *Politique internationale*, 1980, 81, pp. 24-28.

Imbert, Patrick. "Peace and War: Public language, specialized language, and the media," *Semiotica*, 1994, 99—1/2, pp. 29-52.

Ioanid, Ion. *Inchisoarea noastra cea de toate zilele* [Our Daily Jail]. Vols. I—II (1991); III (1993), (Bucuresti: Albatros, 1991-1993).

Ivan, Sabin. *Anchetat, anchetator*. [Cross-examined, Cross-examiner]. (Bucursti: Topaz, 1993).

Rigney, Ann. "Fame and Defamation: Toward A Socio-Pragmatics," *Semiotica*, 1994, 99—1/2, pp. 53-66.

Chapter Ten

SIGNS in the ATTIC: COURTS in MATERIAL LIFE

John Brigham

> Retrospection is a kind of sorcery that imagines, invents, and reinvents those losses that mark survival or that constitute, in its most ancient sense, the image of contemporary identity as person, institution, collectivity, or law.[1]

I
Introduction

Americans began to associate the portico, an architectural feature with columns and a distinctive triangulated shape, with courts during the Greek revival of the 1820s. The triangle is the pediment, a low pitched gable sitting atop the columns and crowning the portico. The shape is part of vernacular architecture in the West.[2] It supports our roofs and shelters our legal processes. With its structural simplicity and its semiotic allusions to Greek temples, the shape claims reverence. It also reflects the triad which legal scholars describe as the basis for judicial authority. In this essay, a triadic quality traditionally associated with adjudication will be discussed in terms of scholarship about courts, their institutional practices, and their architecture. But, like a number of our Founding traditions, this shape didn't materialize in the federal judiciary until 100 years later in a very different social and economic context. The triad has become associated with judicial authority, particularly the Supreme Court, as a civil religion in America and has generated considerable popularity abroad. The triangle is both a symbol commonly mounted on columns and the two dimensional surface for the vernacular space beneath the roof, the attic. The triangle stands as a symbol for the judgment of the court. The three dimensional attic brings people into the picture and delineates a social space. This social or community understanding will be described in terms of institutional practices as we see them in the Supreme Court and on television.

Local courts employ bureaucratic practices while being supported by the myth of ultimate appeal to the high courts which I call the mythology of adjudication. The triadic form links the Supreme Court and vernacular images of adjudication while reappearing in our houses and other institutions like the New York Stock Exchange. The triad is less evident in local courts where there is also relatively little adjudication. To consider the meaning of this development we look to the Midtown Community Court, around the corner from the Ed Sullivan Theater, newly refurbished home of the David Letterman show in the Times Square area of Manhattan. The move away from adjudication claims to be a reform offering more efficient "dispute processing" institutions.

When we get behind the facade, into the attic, we have an appropriate metaphor for the relationship between courts, communities, and material life. Our thoughts and our memories have been in the attic space as the bureaucratic reality of modern courts developed. How this is linked to past claims for adjudicatory authority will be explored by moving from the video monitors so indicative of the modernity of the Midtown Community Court to the television set through which the inside of the courthouse has become increasingly familiar. The concluding proposition is that the portico is now a symbol in the video frame and that this electronic frame has taken the place of the Marble Temple as the place of justice.

II
From Triangle to Triad

Ancient Greece fascinated western culture when the United States was founded. George Peet and Gabrielle Keller (1984), authors of a photo essay on courthouses in Massachusetts, describe the "discovery" of Greece in the federal period by the new science of archaeology. The archaeologists depended on the prior "invention" of history, one of many contributions the Enlightenment passed on to the American Founders. Ancient Greece represented a time, "simpler and more direct; nobler and truer than Rome," with lessons for a new democratic political culture. The key feature of that Greek past in 1800, as it is still in the late 20th century, was the buildings. The buildings and the statutes that adorned them were "just then coming to light and being popularized by the exhibition of the Parthenon's sculptures in Britain by Lord Elgin" (Peet and Keller 1984:92-99). The result was that "The citizens of New England came to live in Greek houses, worship in Greek churches, shop in Greek markets, and keep money in Greek banks. ... [T]he devotion to reform and ancient Greece took root and flowered to such an extent that colonial and Federal New England was remade in a new, white, and monumental way." The end of this style as a symbol of egalitarian democracy when Greek architecture came in the middle of the 19th century when it was linked to the American South.[3] "[T]he Greek Revival ends with sectional conflict, loss of faith. The white temple sailed away west on the grassy sea or faded into a humid dream amidst the Spanish moss" (Peet and Keller 1984, pp. 92-99). That remained largely true at the local level where the simple Greek lines were replaced by the Victorian and Romanesque, but the temple reappeared at the national level in the 20th century and took its grandest form when the forces in Washington decided the United States Supreme Court needed a fitting home.

Through construction of the Supreme Court under the stewardship of William Howard Taft, the triad became a ubiquitous representation of judicial institutions in the late 1930s. Former President William Howard Taft chafed at the notion that the Supreme Court should share Congress' building and formulated a plan for a new building that would better express the independent nature of the judicial branch. The Supreme Court, completed in 1936, was built to appeal to a collective consciousness. The building had just been completed when President Franklin Roosevelt took on the Court over its reaction to his New Deal policies.

Today, national law broadcasts regularly invoke the triangular image drawn from the portico of the Supreme Court building. The evolution of that symbolism provides a perspective on contemporary courts in America and other cultures where the American model of courts is in practice. The configuration of social forces that brought the institutional vision of the Greek Temple to prominence has been on the wane in judicial practice for some time. Rather than making courts and law more awesome, these institutions seem to be diminishing as alternatives to courts gain increasing attention. But, the images of justice vary by the significance of the courts and those who use them. The irony is that the United States Supreme Court adopted the attic form and became its most important expression at the point when the traditional temple was least expressive of what courts in America were doing.

III
The Attic

The pediment atop marble columns that represents courts as temples or shrines also frames the attic. Attic, originally a Roman reference to one from Athens,[4] came to indicate someone or something from Greece and, more broadly, the space under our roofs. In the vernacular, the attic is a space where we store old stuff. Above the places where we live and beneath the roof is a space that has some of the evocative qualities of the madeleine, the common little cookie that did so much for Proust.[5] When we bring forth, for instance, something long hidden, an old doll, a yearbook, as out of our past, we are likely as not to be bringing it from the attic.[6]

Justice in America has often been understood in social terms where the image presented by the institution was an aspect of the social value to be obtained (Merry 1990). We have seen how the triad framing the attic suggests an institutional array where two disputants are equally balanced and a case is heard or adjudicated. This is the picture we get of the Supreme Court where a flurry of media activity accompanies oral argument and the justices are expected to be learned and thoughtful. Adjudication, the model of trial, is also still the picture most commonly associated with courts at the local level. This image is highly subjective and reasoned adjudication is rarely seen on a visit to courts in America.

Institutions like the Supreme Court amount to ways of acting. In America, the steps to the "marble temple" behind the Capitol Building are the ultimate symbols of having gone "all the way," and when robed men (and two women) give opinions from the Temple, those opinions have authority sufficient to reprieve the convicted and compel that the rejected be accepted. Because institutions give action authority, they require more reflective scholarly attention than they have been given. We need to think about how institutional authority works.

Like Justice Potter Stewart's response in another context, we may have trouble defining an institution, but we know one when we see it. We know the Court, or most of us do, so when the Marble Temple serves as background for a picture of a robed person we know something of the place that person has. We are encouraged to be in awe when we take in the building, the courtroom, or even a wrinkled old man, if he is a Justice of the Supreme Court. The symbols that constitute the High Court as the ultimate judicial body give the institution interpretive authority and much of the authority of law in America is keyed to the authority of the Court. Various practices, like wearing robes, listening to "argument," and meeting in secret at the Supreme Court or in chambers in lower courts, define the setting as a place of justice and the end of the legal line in America. The link between the Court and the Constitution is a central institutional practice for the Supreme Court.

Practices draw on public perceptions of the institution, from journalists, scholars, lawyers, and citizens. Judicial commentary and commentary on the justices in all its forms, from opinions to personality profiles, is a special source for the treatment. Pursuing the "cult" of the Court resists the pull of authorized material or official opinion from the bench. In addition, the effort to portray the cult around the institution provides a framework for interpreting a variety of Court-related materials. Cases, history, and commentary on the institution are a key to the possibilities around which institutional politics is conducted.

For some time, communities have been linked to relativism and political opportunity rather than to essentialism and political constraint. Robert Cover exhorted his colleagues to tell tales, spin yarns, and create a legal order grounded in new practices. Cover's call is "to stop circumscribing the nomos ... to invite new worlds" (1983). This is more difficult for those of us who operate outside the great law schools or do not have access to the appellate bench. The institutional life of the community of law professors makes their yarns particularly important. Thus, when we say that there are social foundations to law and office, we mean that the nomos is constituted by convention. The community of the Supreme Court is "law's empire." In the work of Yngvesson (1993) and Merry (1990), the community is provincial, but arguably part of the empire.

The concept of practice situates courts in the interpretive communities that give them significance. An institution like the Supreme Court is constituted by the communities familiar with it. This means knowledgeable groups or even entire societies where they are accepted. Traditionally these groups know something others don't. We say of a text, in the case of law, of a court, in the case of office, that its social foundation is the group or community that can interpret the text or understand the court. The special sociological contribution of an investigation into the practices making up an institution comes from identifying the ways of operating and the social relations behind them that give the elements of law and office their significance.

The extent to which a practice constitutes the Court will be a matter of interpretation. For instance, the assertion of judicial review by John Marshall in *Marbury v. Madison* (1803) reiterated a possibility that had been mentioned by others, most notably Alexander Hamilton in *Federalist 78* and *81*, but judicial review was certainly not conventional wisdom or an undisputed understanding, much less constitutive of the institution at that time. Marshall articulated the possibility for the Supreme Court as a strategic move that drew on conventions such as the supporting claims in Blackstone's *Commentaries*, the *Federalist Papers*, and the written constitution. The practice should be considered constitutive of the institution sometime in this century, probably around the time the building was constructed (Brigham 1987:22-24).

At every level, the constitutive practices of courts are a function of material interests. We see this symbolically at the national level in the similarity between the architecture of the Supreme Court, the New York Stock Exchange. In local courts, the architecture of efficiency has taken over for the architecture of justice. In addition, in many localities the detention facility, once in the basement, has come to rival the courts of justice in physical terms.[7] For instance, the Sonoma County Hall of Justice and Jail, a model of modern court architecture built in 1962 presents a detention facility across a courtyard that is every bit as large as the facilities for justice. Of course much of the imprisonment is at the state level and thus removed from comparison with the courts, but in places like California, where county government remains strong, detention is clearly a large part of the activity. Here, rather than taking the anti-essentialist position on culture discussed widely at this time in the communities of law and society (Abu-Lughod 1993; Lazarus-Black and Hirsch 1994), we suggest that constitutive practices are indeed determinants of law and action which become material in texts, courthouses, constitutions and clerks.

Court processes in America have been predominantly public. The processes are hard to understand, and the public interest may fade as it did during the complex debates over suppression of evidence in the preliminary hearing on the O.J. Simpson case. But, we have rights of confrontation and expectations of public proceedings. To most Americans, Kafka's vision should seem foreign, and "The Trial" a poor symbol for law, albeit popular for critical intellectuals (Bonsignore 1992; Derrida 1985). Television in court and television about court has become critical for the public authority of law.

While few developments in the law move explicitly toward opening the processes up, developments in news broadcasting and in entertainment are producing more public presentation and greater familiarity with legal processes (Williams 1974). One of the most important recent practices for courts is visual access to them through television. The institutional homes of adjudication are now experienced visually and vicariously far more widely than they used to be. One of those developments, Court TV, appears to be an alternative to the traditional semiotics of marble and concrete. Therefore we need to consider what television means for how we see adjudication.

Television makes law public, yet some fear that the nature of the account provided by TV does a disservice to popular understandings of justice (Harris 1993). For David Simon, "More than anything else, it's the cathode-ray tube—not the prosecutor, not the defense attorney, certainly not the evidence—that gives a Baltimore juror his mindset. Television ensures that jurors are empaneled with ridiculous expectations" (Simon 1990). While we believe that professionals have a procedural understanding of law, we expect something different from TV, where through news and drama, most individuals get their understanding of courts.

In the very optimistic view of one informed observer, David A. Harris,

> Court TV ... allows the public to observe the entire judicial process. No television producer selects a thirty second slice of the day's proceedings, based on the potential to entertain or boost ratings. The viewer can 'attend' the whole trial. Thus Court TV makes the criminal courts accessible to virtually anyone with cable television. The network also presents experts to interpret events. Presumably, this may make for exactly the informed accountability our democracy needs, and will also encourage and enrich the public debate on the broader issues raised by the trials presented. This addition of Court TV to popular culture might mean, if nothing else, that the appearance of justice would more closely resemble reality (Harris 1993:787).

On the other hand, as Harris points out, most court time is not trial time and the image of courts that is publically conceptualized through the video screen is largely of courts at trial. Here we are developing an experience that maintains the cult of the court in another form and fails as a reflection of the practice of adjudication.

Even when the presentation includes more than the actual trial, as it has done recently with the proceedings against O.J. Simpson, the form of television packages the legal culture and presents it as a seamless expression of real life. This presentation, popularized by Raymond Williams (1974) as "flow," along with the expert commentary that accompanies television presentations, has become the new authority for courts. Joining with the promises of efficiency that are so often linked to video monitors, the new architecture of courts is the television set.

IV
The Monitors of Justice

Ties between functional and semiotic considerations are required for institutions to wield power successfully. We have suggested this in the shift from the triad to the attic, from surface symbol to its constitutive qualities in the beliefs and understandings of people. In contemporary America, the symbolic promise of courts is less and less about adjudication and more and more about bureaucracy. That is, there has been a shift in emphasis from the wisdom of the judgments symbolized by the triad to processing and resolution that is "satisfactory" and efficient. The by-words are informal, modern, and efficient. These changes have been reflected in the architecture of courts for at least thirty years.

We can see them in such structures as the "Halls of Justice" building in Grand Rapids, Michigan built in 1966, and the Sonoma County Hall of Justice built a few years earlier. Like the schools built in California at the same time, the buildings are "modern." That is without either rounded lines or much in the way of ornamentation. The straight lines, flat roofs, and boxy windows do little to suggest that what goes on inside is an elevated practice. The architectural presentation is informal in that the only public signs are functional. They direct traffic, identify buildings. The most impressive structure is the Sheriff's Department communication tower. The result is authority that reflects contemporary jurisprudence.[8] In contemporary courts, as evident most notably in states that have developed recently, like Florida, Arizona and California (Nash 1992), the move for efficiency is driven by the specter of pressure on scarce judicial resources and is evident in the lack of artifice and the visibility of computers (Neal 1992). Computers are everyman's tool now and the familiar screen is becoming a reassuring symbol of up to date processes and accurate handling of information.

It remains paradoxical that these moves have been associated with "friendlier courts" (Hoffman 1993). This is especially true in the context of ADR where popular eagerness for access to justice (Merry 1990) appears as a model for future institutional sites. The paradox is in the interpretations that emphasize the formal and imposing qualities of the older Neo-classical and Victorian structures. The judge is elevated, the symbolic forms (Greek gods, Latin phrases) are high culture, and those who stand before the bench are presumably diminished in stature. In the modern court, the judge is closer to the witnesses and the symbolism is minimal. In the nationally publicized Los Angeles courtroom where the Simpson Pre-hearing was held, the only traditional text in the interior design is the seal of the state of California. In the increasingly familiar television presentations, the authority is in the commentary and in the audience where the victims family is prominently shown.[9]

In one widely publicized experiment in local justice we can see the key elements of modern jurisprudence, informality, and efficiency, coming together as institutional reform. This is the Midtown Community Court in Manhattan. For the Midtown Community Court the terrain is the social and economic fabric of the "middle West Side." Critics from the other, poorer city courts, all housed inadequately "downtown" is the extent to which vast sums of money are being lavished on a very visible institution in a particularly visible part of town. The community eager for this particular reform and able to pull it off is the midtown community of *The New York Times*, *The Letterman Show*, and the Broadway Theaters.

The court, located at 314 West 54th Street, opened in September of 1993 in a building that once housed the Magistrates Court and the Eleventh District Court. The building is next to the Midtown North police precinct headquarters. Operating 9-5, five days a week, the court handles non-felony cases and is presided over most of the time by Judge Judith Krantz. 35% of the cases are for "theft of service" (or fare beating—sneaking on to the subway), 20% Petit Larceny, 11% Unlicensed Peddling, 10% Prostitution, and 9% low level drug charges. This is only minor criminality but the presence of the institution as a court in the neighborhood is the most significant aspect.

In the court's advertising material, computer screens take the place of references to Greek democracy and the promise of "the latest technology" includes "graphical screen interfaces" as attractive features of the new institution. Editorials from local papers tout the hi-tech aspects of the institution, employing the familiar "windows" framework that has become indicative of our age. The advertising tells us the sort of thing once communicated by the Greek symbols and Latin inscriptions on the buildings of another era and the institution appears user friendly. Electronic processes move the defendants through the system with the efficiency government institutions are expected to aspire to in contemporary America. Monitors that depict the cases to be called reflect the monitors on the desks of court officers, making the overall impression one of modernity as well as access and intimacy.

One of the special reform aspects of the court is the use of alternative sentences combining treatment, education, and prevention with a strong impulse to direct the sentences back to the community through service. The former includes drug treatment, health, housing, and employment counseling and the latter includes a variety of services such as sweeping the streets, cleaning the bus station, feeding the homeless, and local beautification projects. Rather than the traditional punishment which may affirm the authority of the court but do little for the population, these forms are highly focused on visible benefits to the population. Yet, in this way, the benefit to state authority may be greater.

All of this was produced at a time when cutbacks in public services were widespread. The city provided $1 million for renovation and $475,000 for annual operating expenses, with $600,000 from corporate and foundation support which is coordinated by the Fund for the City of New York. In an editorial on 4 April 1992, *The New York Times* supported the plan, citing the basic advantages as "proximity and efficiency along with social services and punishments that benefit the neighborhood." Six months before, *The Times* heralded the effort as one that "stirs the imagination" and also saves the city the expense of taking prisoners downtown for arraignment and often holding them overnight. Originally scheduled for the Longacre Theater, which was to be donated for the purpose, the court ended up in a city-owned building when theater groups and neighbors objected to the original plan.

This attention to midtown and "Times Square" may have been a result of the influence that city fathers wield in the neighborhood. As the headquarters for *The New York Times*, part of the central business district, and a prominent tourist attraction, Midtown had the clout and the incentive to rid its streets of unlicensed peddlers, prostitutes, petty thieves and the homeless even before David Letterman began to feature the streets of that part of town on TV's most popular late night show.[10]

V
Conclusion

One of the things that motivated me to write *The Cult of the Court* was the question of how practices make a building into a court. That book traced the evolution of an institution through careful analysis of its practices, particularly the ones that gave the Supreme Court the power to authoritatively interpret the Constitution. That inquiry is expanded here to consider a very different manifestation of legal power in the cultural presence of courts more generally. We see new developments which take the place of adjudication in contemporary society. These developments may not be courts in the traditional sense at all and when they are compared both functionally and semiotically with the place courts held in the society, much less the promise of the cult of the Supreme Court, the results are sobering.

Heydebrand and Seron concluded their discussion of the increasing rationalization of justice with the observation that "... what is squeezed out of the traditional form of law is a locale for a moral vision and political debate" (1990:184). In processing cases, the courts nurture an environment dominated by technical expertise with few links to the discursive practices of the culture more generally. Although we hear appeals to the grand tradition, in the closing statement by O.J. Simpson's lawyer in his challenge to the warrantless search of the pitchman's house, for instance, they ring hollow in the context of process where informality and efficiency are the operative concepts.[11]

ENDNOTES

1. Peter Goodrich, 1994, "Doctor Duxbury's Cure: Or, A Note on Legal Historiography," *Cardozo Law Review* 15:1567-1589, 1568.

2. The tympanum is the face of the pediment which often contains sculptures. On the United States Supreme Court, the tympanum is a single 250 ton slab of Vermont marble sculpted by James Earle Fraser after the theme "Contemplation of Justice." The tympanum is surrounded by the cornice.

3. Apart from the natural desire for stylistic change, the end of the Greek Revival in the North was brought about in part by its acceptance in the South. Southern "Greek Apologists" like Calhoun claimed legitimacy for the institution of human bondage by trumpeting the fact that the ancient democratic Greek city-states had been a slaveholding society ... plantation homes, set behind verandas nestled in a screen of enormous white columns at the end of a mile-long driveway ... (Peet and Keller 1984, pp. 92-99).

4. Cicero's letters to Atticus were to the Roman who lived among the Greeks and they remain of some interest due to their attention to the cultural variations between the two regions.

5. Having spent some time in my own attic, I can comment from experience. In any season, my attic would represent the extreme, hot in summer and cold in winter. In the elements, I was surrounded by memories (old baby toys, camping gear now little used, and clothes no longer in fashion). Mixed with the memories were aspirations (another baby, a camping trip). This is stuff from which we build and the cultural attic is much the same.

6. This was the case in an article in *The New York Times*, 3 July 1994:H1, entitled "Out of the Attic and Asylum and Into the Camera's Eye," by Maria Laurino, about the new prominence of retarded or less mobile people in contemporary movies.

7. Given the prevalence of the plea bargain it would be interesting to see if the halls where so much of this bargaining takes place have grown at all in size.

8. The Sonoma County facility has housed the accused killer of Polly Klaas, the little California girl who has come to represent the victim in the contemporary focus on victims as a basis for much of what goes on in criminal courts.

9. In the Simpson hearings, the families of Nicole Brown Simpson and Ronald Goldman sit directly behind the podium from which both prosecution and defense conduct their questioning of witnesses.

10. One recent story in the *Times* (Martin 1994) described the success of Business Improvement Districts (B.I.D.'s), private organizations created by property owners, which indicated the influence of these districts in city government. The Midtown Community Court is in the Times Square District.

11. See transcript of preliminary hearing, Los Angeles, California, 6 July 1994.

WORKS CITED

Abu-Lughod, Lila. *Writing Women's Worlds*, (Berkeley: University of California Press, 1993).

Bonsignore, John, et. al. *Before the Law*, (Boston: Houghton-Mifflin, 1992).

Brigham, John. *The Cult of the Court*, (Philadelpia: Temple University Press, 1987).

Cover, Robert. "The Supreme Court, 1982 Term - Foreword: Nomos and Narrative," *Harvard Law Review*, 1983, 97:4.

Derrida, Jacques. "*Prejuges Devant La Loi*," *La Faculte de Juger*, (Paris: Editions de Minuit, 1985).

Garapon, M. Antoine. *L'Ane Portant des Reliques*, (Paris: editions du Centurion, 1987).

Goodrich, Peter. "Doctor Duxbury's Cure: Or, A Note on Legal Historiography," *Cardozo Law Review*, 1994, 15: pp. 1567-1589, 1568.

Goodsell, Charles T. *The Social Meaning of Civic Space: Studying Political Authority through Architecture*, (Lawrence: University Press of Kansas, 1988).

Handler, Benjamin, Project Director. The American Courthouse: Planning and Design for the Judicial Process, ABA and AIA.

Harris, David A. "The Appearance of Justice: Court TV, Conventional Television, and Public Understanding of the Criminal Justice System," 35 *Arizona Law Review*, 1993, 785.

Heydebrand, Wolf and Carroll Seron. *Rationalizing Justice: The Political Economy of Federal District Courts*, (Albany: SUNY Press, 1990).

Hoffman, Jan, "A user-friendly experiment in justice; community court aims at saving time and money in dealing with minor offenses," *The New York Times* Oct. 1; "A Manhattan court explores service-oriented sentencing," *The New York Times* 27 November 1993.

King, Anthony D., ed. *Buildings and Society: Essays on the Social Development of the Built Environment*, (London: Routledge and Kegan Paul, 1980).

Laurino, Maria. "Out of the Attic and Asylum and Into the Camera's Eye," *The New York Times* 3 July 1994: H1.

Lazarus-Black, Mindie and Susan F. Hirsch. *Contested States: Law, Hegemony and Resistance*, (New York: Routledge, 1994).

Martin, Douglas. "Districts to Improve Business Proliferate," *The New York Times*, 25 March 1994.

Merry, Sally Engle. *Getting Justice and Getting Even*, (Chicago: University of Chicago Press, 1990).

Nash, Jim. "Autoclerk PC kiosks enlisted as LA's very own 'robocop' team," *Computerworld*, 1992, pp. 26:53.

Neal, Carol M. "Courts Enter the Computer Age, but Slowly," *National Law Journal*, 1992, pp. 14:7.

Peet, George and Gabrielle Keller. *Courthouses of the Commonwealth*, (Amherst: The University of Massachusetts Press, 1984).

Simon, David. *Homicide*, (Boston: Houghton-Mifflin, 1990).

Williams, Raymond. *Television: Technology and Cultural Form*, (Hanover: Wesleyan University Press, 1974).

Yngvesson, Barbara. *Virtuous Citizens, Disruptive Subjects*, (New York: Routledge Press, 1993).

PART IV

Chapter Eleven

LAW at the BORDER

Roberta Kevelson

I
Blurring Limits of Meaning

In my monograph, *Inlaws/Outlaws: A Semiotics of Systemic Interaction*, I introduced legal semiotics and based this branch of general semiotics on Peirce's philosophy and theory of signs. Here I focus attention on dynamic, evolving relations between two terms or universes of discourse which move from relations of equilibrium to various stages of dissociation or opposition, and may cross and recross like an intertwining caduceus, perhaps, or like parallel lines from a noneuclidean perspective. The discourses I used to illustrate and begin to explain this critical process of the Peircean Quest of Quests—the establishing of new, complex sign-relations between sign-systems—were the respective discourses of English law prior to the Norman conquest and the French law which came into relation with it as a result of the conquest. The emergent conquest of English commonlaw is the consequent of interaction, a conflictual interaction, between two sign systems as two systems of law (Kevelson 1977).

The strategies of sign interaction were described with reference to Perelman's views, as presented especially in *The New Rhetoric* (1971 edition English translation). I had especially wanted to show analogies and other similarities between Perelman's unparalleled study of rhetorical tactics and Peirce's regard of Rhetoric, "Pure Rhetoric," as equivalent in meaning with his own understanding of the method of semiotics: Methodology or the *Method of Methods* (Kevelson 1987). In this early study of legal semiotics I indicated that in Peirce's work it is the logic of discovery rather than the logic of justification which describes "... the laws by which in every scientific intelligence one sign gives birth to another, and especially one thought brings forth another" (Peirce cited in the Buchler 1955 edition of selected papers, p. 55; see detailed discussion in Kevelson 1977:84-89).

My decision to use law as a means of explicating Peirce and, reciprocally, to use Peirce's semiotics as a way of opening up otherwise inaccessible problems in law has been for me an evolving idea. This early concern with conflicts between legal systems has remained an ever-deepening area for investigating both law and Peirce as related in this focus.

For example, I discuss the changing concept of the idea of law, in as short a period of time as a few centuries: in the 18th century law was in the main described as a mediating principle for referent axiomatic reasons which lie "behind" the law. In the early 19th century the predominant interpretation of the general meaning of the idea of law was that the reason behind the law was itself produced by referent popular custom that represented social practices based on socio-economic modes of trade and transactions of goods and values. In the late 19th century the idea of the law had come to be regarded, in large measure, as an instrument for indicating relations between leading principles deeply embedded in the legal discourse and current disputes arising between people in a jural state. By the middle of the 20th century, following the influence of Holmes and the Realists, law as idea represented a complex conflict of legal subsystems in any given society. This ideal sign-system of law came to be characterized as dynamical and dramatistic (Kevelson 1987:76).

In *The Law as a System of Signs* (Kevelson 1988) I continue exploring and describing the Peircean *quest of quests*, by means of the "method of methods." I suggest here that the problems designated as problems of conflicts of law are especially important in getting an understanding of the relation between logics of discovery and paradox and the evolving of complex, open-ended (or "free") sign-systems. In this book, in a concluding section, I note that the "problem of conflicts of law may be seen as the type of problem of paradoxical structures as a whole and thus may provide insight into the process whereby codes of conflicting reference become transformed and new values emerge as a result of mediating, transforming semiosis" (Kevelson 1988:294).

A subsequent book on this topic, *Peirce, Paradox, Praxis: The Image, the Conflict, and the Law*, investigates issues in law and semiotics directly related to the intersystemic relationships between sign systems or universes of discourse. The Austinean notion of "competing analogies" is taken up, as are changing interpretations and redefinitions of conflicts of law and also of conflicts in law, as Bentham's "repugnancy" signifies (Kevelson 1990). This complex issue of semiotics in general, central to the problem of law and the making of value-signs as an aesthetic process, is of paramount importance in Peirce

(Kevelson 1993). This study is followed by work on codes and complexity (Kevelson 1994a and 1994b).

In our present, transforming world this problem thickens. The idea of accounting for transdiscursive relations is so far from an academic problem that it has, indeed, brought Peirce's pragmatism out from the seminar, and even out of the laboratory (in Fisch's sense 1958) onto the open arena of global intersystemic conflict where law plays a kind of thematically doubling role: of *Law versus Law*. Especially do we find this conflict between legal systems in the arguments for self-determination or aboriginal peoples (Kevelson 1994c). We find it also in societies where transnational corporations assume the function of virtual legal systems in third-world countries. Also, the erosion of the value of property in the self-proclaimed democracies of the world, in the name of Equality and its congeneric value-signs, brings law into conflict with itself everywhere in the areas of commonlaw countries. But perhaps nowhere has this contest between legal systems been so critically appraised as in those countries which until very recently were called communist states (brought to attention by Grazin 1993).

I present his view of the problem before going on to related instances of "law at the border," that is, on the edge of itself as defined *by itself*.

II
Differentiation as Process

Grazin notes that "Although the natural law idea has prevailed in developed and advanced democratic countries, the situation in post-communist countries is principally different. In other words, while judges in the United States must adhere to certain professional skills and ethical standards in deciding questions of law, judges in the former communist countries are not bound by these stable ethical standards; nor, for the judges, do these principles even exist" (Grazin 1993:719).

Grazin is assuming, or presupposing for the sake of his argument, a stability in commonlaw countries that is perhaps ideal but nonexistent. Still, there are implicit principles that are not separable from these competing commonlaw subsystems, (in Friedman's sense, 1975) such as Property. Indeed, all the relational "rights"—civil, as opposed to "human" rights—described in the Bill of Rights of the U.S. Constitution, are in point. But I will return to the changing function of value principles which results from an evolving, changing concept of the idea in focus as a general idea, such as is Law in this case.

Grazin further explains, with respect to the crisis perceived in former communist countries regarding law, that in those countries the old pre-communist assumption that institutions are man-made, and that such "organizations and man-made laws are extinct, or have become so unstable that in searching for justification," today, in post-communist societies, all that remains is zero remnants of the pre-communist notion of postivist institutions. Among the rubble is only, in his words, "God, Man, Nature, and societies ... (for which) ... whole relationships must be rebuilt" (Grazin 1993:720). It must be emphasized that Grazin points out that in the wake of communism, in its collapse, it is not the case that only "lawless societies" survive. Rather, the materials remain but the structures or forms into which they had been organized are no longer existent. Yet, he says, "the situation has raised the possibility of choice: Which law, and what kind of legal order?" (Grazin, above).

The devolution of an idea, a complex and relationally-significant idea, is not equivalent with its demise but is rather a confrontation with a conflict of possibilities. It is not an opposition between the determined or defined and the vague. *It is an opposition between vague and vague, or hypothesis versus hypothesis.* This opens up a very new and anomalous concept in the vast literature of legal semiotics, and of general semiotics as well, since it presents the opportunity for choice between free-floating or value-free objectives. Nothing is anchored, in other words. Yet this is far from the structuralist problem of signifiers with no signified, since the semiotic action or process is one of interaction or conflict: the drama is improvisational in a whole new sense. This is the sense, I suggest, of self-organizing principles that the theorists of complex systems variously explore and discuss and which have been brilliantly described by Joseph Earley for one (Earley 1989, 1994).

This is, indeed, the crux of the problem for investigation by legal semioticians, and made observable in the situation presented so clearly and poignantly by Igor Grazin, to whom I return briefly here: Grazin states that "every idea of law is a development of leading principles (to use Peirce's term) and the law as institution" tied to "morality," "states" and aspects of "bourgeois society" (Grazin 1993:720). The question raised by communism is; Is the State "above positive law? or, If positive law is man-made, is the State to be subordinate to the machinations of mere people?" The paradox confronting post-communist countries today is, in Grazin's words, "that the principle of legality itself can be eliminated with positive law" (Grazin 1993:720).

Ironically, it is natural law that is in contrast to positive law. On the one hand, natural law is associated in some vague manner with holy, theological works and abstract, scholarly arguments, political propagandist papers and other rhetorical modes of discourse (using rhetorical in an everyday way). These intertwinings of natural law are also connected, on the other hand, with the commonlaw principles of Consent, Contract and especially Private Law; it assumes that social institutions such as law and economics are also, *as positive law also assumes*, man-made human inventions and artifices as is the Humean justice (Kevelson 1993). Now, as Grazin explains, communist ideology replaced this complex sign-system of natural law replete with its own internal inconsistencies and contradictions. *One discourse was,* he suggests, *substituted for another*.

The question he raises is whether Natural Law in some form can once again be inserted into that slot now vacated by communist ideology. What Grazin does not confront is the fact that the grid is not stable, and the process of one idea-system replacing another in dominance is not a substitute process but is, as Peirce observes in his criticism of 19th century economic theory, a permutative and transformational process (see Kevelson on this point in 1988, referring to Peirce's critique of Stanley Jevons).

III
Two Discourses in Relation

Above I noted that we have before us a problem without precedent with respect to the fact that it has not been explicitly defined and/or represented. It appears to be a conflict between two new open, or undefined idea-systems which are grown from, but are not extensively deduced from, a stable referent concept. When, for example, we find ourselves agreeing with Dietze and others (Dietze 1963) that the evolution of democratic principles has tended, in its process, to destroy the once constituent idea of private property, we need to look at the terms, Democracy, Property, Natural Law, Positive Law, Human Invention or sign-making, and propose new meanings to these counters or terms. If, indeed, the referent frames continue to be changed as an entire process of thought evolves and meaning becomes cumulative as a result of the transformation and revision of frames of reference, how do we have referent principles that both *are* and *are not*? That is, the *references are then of the nature of fictions in motion, where stability or states of ideas are frozen and false representations*. It is more than the problem as Peirce noted, that all our arguments are at bottom fallible, but rather that the continuous, dynamical shift of references in the process of "signifiers" in conflict with one another without a referree, as it were a point outside which traditional analogical relations used to find in the noting of an idea, confronts us with a new kind of problem.

The situation with respect to semiotics of law, especially as we focus on conflicts of law and international law in general, is, as Antony Carty has remarked: The idea of international law, as it has been understood by mainstream international lawyers since the 19th century, rests upon generally accepted methods of inquiry. These methods of inquiry—the doing of a universe of discourse in other words—themselves are based upon and representative of certain presuppositions of "thought-patterns." These referent patterns may be faulty and flawed, or simply not adequate to the situation for which they are made to serve.

To invent an instrument for more accurate inquiry from which explanation both more complete and more elegant may be derived is as important for our understanding of the complexity of human organization, as at a different level is invention of "super strings" that provides more comprehensive access to multidimensional, complex relations of forces in the universe than did the earlier quantum theory or still earlier theories from which quantum cosmology derived. It may be the case that the more sophisticated super strings do not themselves create new networks of interaction in the actual world. But they do permit such representation that gives rise to new hypotheses and to the creation of new ideas and complex thought-systems or ideologies. For this purpose it is critical to begin to understand how the meaning of complex ideas happens, and how inquiry is an integral part of such complexity. Further, if an idea is meaningful it will produce consequences for the actual world, since it is that world, and not only the world of ideas, that ideas interpret and interact with. *It is the method of inquiry that provides a mediating instrument for linking us to dimensions of our world that could not otherwise be observed.*

To refer again to Carty's interesting paper, which raises the question as to whether 19th century consensual theory as a "frame of meaning resting on the State"—the then defined notion of State—is still, a century later, "appropriate for the analysis and normative governance of international relations" (Carty 1986:vii). Professor Carty's concern invites semiotic attention, for he is indeed talking about legal and other related institutions as fraying around the edges, as decaying and devolving from some moment of historical ripeness. Carty correctly takes the issue of the decay of international law as seriously as it needs to be taken, *but not as far as it should be taken*. What is wanted, I suggest, is a comparative methodological approach which would bring the allegedly decaying system of international legal theory into a relationship with whatever it is or might be competing, even if the latter is a hypothesis only, that is, a conceivable dimension of a comprehensive notion of international law that provides us with the bigger picture. Carty correctly notes that the imminent danger to international law as defined at present can be seen as a "crisis of method in international law, in terms of the role of legal doctrine in the creation and fundamental concepts of that law" (Carty 1986:vii).

Here is another point of view on the core problem Grazin discusses above, and also widely prevalent in the dual legal systems of emergent nations and in the assertion for self-determination of aboriginal peoples, for example, Amerindian law vs. Constitutional law (Kevelson 1993, 1994a, 1994b, 1994c).

IV
Individual As Archaism

While Grazin and others, in particular some leading spokespersons for Critical Legal Theory, seem to want to replace the gap left by the Communist state with a version of Natural Law, others equally fortified/ resist a return to a Natural Law replete with mythic substructures. Instead, the latter advocate a development in new directions, in the light of evolved global human values, of a man-made law (Kevelson 1995). Such man-made law, for culture-specific and national-specific human organizations as well as for an over-arching system of international law would seem to smack, on the surface, of what has been broadly defined as Positive Law. It is Positivism that has had such a "bad name" throughout all the various developments of special branches of semiotics, in the course of this 20th century growth. Positivism has been linked with a reduction of individual human beings and has been tied to a mathematical map from which the individual features and contours of intersubjective human relations are effaced.

At its worst this is indeed a positivism that has earned the impassioned response from humanists of the 20th century that it has received. In the early work of Habermas, for example, *The Legitimation Crisis,* Peirce is criticized as a Positivist, and is wrongly opposed to the very intersubjectivity Habermas argues for. Habermas has since came to know Peirce better and revises early judgments based on inadequate access to the bulk of Peirce's work. Even dedicated Peirce scholars such as Richard Bernstein are still critical of the tendency of pragmatism to blunt fine details of human societies, to be indifferent to nuances of value in pragmatically-dominated social institutions, for example, Peirce-derived legal pragmatism, including the Realism indebted to Holmes, and legal semiotics which follows Peirce's theory (Bernstein 1990).

And surely, whatever was meant in the 19th century as the "Method of Science" is not the same idea as has been evolved into these last years of the 20th century. Yet this concept of a "method of science"—the pragmatic method of Peirce—is an idea which grows *as it is inquired into*. As it is continously interpreted it becomes, *as an idea*, more complex; the process it denotes is proportionally increasing in complexity just as the process-as-idea becomes, connotatively, more complex as well. The idea of the Individual at the heart of the myth of Natural law remains among the rejects, as autonomous Individual and sustains its function in pragmatism now, as in Peirce's own day, as a relate in a relational social structure (Peirce's definition of Individual as indeterminate term, in Baldwin I, 537-38). The term individual, from this point of view of pragmatism, is no less a function of a relation than are the terms Father, Student, Citizen, Child, Partner, Agent, Object. Thus the relationship is Individual *with* Individual; the basic social unit is a relation and not an autonomous context-free and relation-free atom. This is the same sense Peirce holds with respect to the position that a statement is but the response part of a relation which requires a link with a question: the basic logic of discovery is erotetic, a relation of question and answer (Kevelson 1977, 1987, 1990, 1993).

V
Stretching Boundaries and Nonfinite Property

An overview of the development of legal semiotics since the 1970's when I first indtroduced it, at a time when it was also introduced as a ramification of Saussurean, structural linguistic approaches to semiotics by Greimas and Landowski (1976), would show that the mythology of the Lockean-based natural law is seen to be falling apart, just as the underlying mythology for civil law is seen to be disintegrating (J. Van

Doren, "Things Fall Apart, or Modern Legal Mythology in the Civil Law Tradition," in *Widener Journal of Public Law* 2 1993:447-489). Van Doren presents an interesting discussion of code ideology, and he contrasts Civil Law Codes with Common Law Systems (Van Doren, above, 459-460; see also the collection of papers from the perspective of modern legal semiotics in Kevelson, *Codes and Customs,* 1994; Cungi and Pieck, in particular, discuss the special problems involved when a society shifts from one legal culture to another, with special focus on modern Italy's legal culture, in Kevelson 1994 at pp. 45-76.

Van Doren also presents a useful critique of legal positivism. He suggests that the very nature of the positivist approach is a-moral: "Positivists have little to say about what values should be implemented. Positivism may be morally neutral as to what 'commands' are carried out ... The acceptance of positivism, however, is not morally neutral ..." (Van Doren, at 462 and following). In other words, the moral structures may not be explicitly written into a legal system, but the informing value is an active force, by implication. It is an active, ethical force and referent, I might add, in precisely the way that a system of reasoning carries ethical value if it is an appropriate choice of a method of reasoning for the purpose at hand, Peirce says (Kevelson 1988, 1990).

While it has become usual to treat the idea of morality as if were synonymous with the idea of ethics, as derived from a value code, Peirce would relegate morality to the frame of theological canon and would, by contrast, distinguish ethics as an index for social transactions which derives from Esthetics regarded as the Science of Value (Kevelson 1993). I keep this distinction, and emphasize that the establishing of an equivalence between morals and ethics is nothing but the result of rhetorical force or the *use* of strategies of argument. Further, every discourse style conveys its own conventionalized and symbolic connotations of value. Stylistic types, including types of notational systems, become paradigmatic or symbolic representations for referent esthetic value. The very notion of the esthetic function in the creating of social values would seem to suggest that values are indeed artifices, artworks and man-made inventions. This brings us to the edge of the "black-holes" of legal systems, where the force of values are most dense and grave, and hence to the question of whether revolutions in law, as revolutions in science, invite counter-revolutions in both law and in science since what is in conflict in this continual unstable and living world are values themselves as motivating forces, *evolving*.

In following general semiotic assumptions derived from Peirce's theory of signs, an idea is regarded as a network of cross-referential sign-functions, that is, a sign-system. An ideology, in apolitical and neutral sense of the terms, is a complex system of signs. Ideas increase in their complexity as they evolve so that the network of meaning becomes dense and at the same time larger, such that the increase of "meaningful area" becomes *more* with respect to the number of objects denoted within the defined boundaries of a term while the connotative system becomes *more deeply layered*: implicated and imbricated (Bohm 1978, 1989; also Levi-Strauss on "imbrication": Kevelson 1990, 1993).

What we see as a social institution is a representation of a complex, evolving sign-system, or ideology (Kevelson 1988). Again, Peirce observes and explains how ideas as Interpretants interpret one another and advance/evolve meaning from provisional "definites" to possible "vagues" and hence to new relational, general symbolic sign-functions.

With the creation of each new layer or dimension of an evolving general idea there is an interim of stability, or *apparent* stability, which acts as quasi-constant referent and frame of reference until it becomes destabilized by "some surprising fact" which opens fresh inquiry on the idea in question.

Ideas which do not appear to cross categorial boundaries may seem merely to be extending properties, adding on attributes while maintaining a kind of specific, semantic "order." But the imposition of frames of reference, that is, semantic categories, one upon another, seems to violate the very laws of thought and reason. Two universes of discourse, as it were, appear to occupy the same "space" and to produce incongruities such as "wavicles" and "duckrabbits" and other similar absurdities. These superimpositions are not paradoxes in an authentic sense of the paradox, but are con-fusions of idea-systems. When these confusions are brought about by intention of semiotic questors the result is, in Peirce's view, the objective of the semiotic Quest of Quests which is to bring together two ideologies or universes of discouse into a more comprehensive relation, *a new generality* (Kevelson 1987, 1990). The marriage of civil and common law represents such a con-fusion in the dynamical process of the complex system of signs called The Law, as it evolves, and develops. From the point of view of each relate—of civil law and of common law—what seems unclear is the definition of each, or the boundaries that open so that each idea penetrates the other in a kind of ideological conflict of law, or *border war*. For our purposes here we may substitute for the term, civil law, legal positivism, and for the term, common law we may use the term natural law. I am not suggesting that these are equivalent or closely synonymous substitutes. But for our further discussion we may use the analogy, that civil law is to positive law as common law is to natural law, and not concern ourselves further at this time with other, correct distinctions between terms *here* placed in the same general camp.

Property, as an indispensable aspect of Common Law, is described as an ethical value by Dietze for example, in *In Defense of Property* (Dietze 1963/1975) since it is an idea which mediates in social relations as a code and channel in such exchanges of goods and values, he suggests (1975:57-64). Further he contrasts the rise in the value of democratization—synonymous here with the general concept of "distributive justice" or utility—with decline in the value imputed to private property. Dietze says "... the distinction between property rights and so-called "civil rights" and the assertion that the latter are entitled to greater protection because they are more necessary for the working of democracy, are unwarranted not only because they misconceive the nature of freedom, disregard the nature of man, and do not take into account the experience of ages, but also because they were rejected by the very people that are usually quoted in their support, namely, by the founders of modern democracy" (Dietze, above p. 64).

From a similar point of view Hayek speaks of the spontaneous order in law and in economic institutions as a representation of *freedom as value* which has survived by evolving through the preference and choices of members in free transactional relations. These "spontaneously grown institutions" are dynamical, self-organizing and cybernetical organizations. The multidimensional forces of which they are composed interact in ways we have yet to discover and to make clear. We need to construct, Hayek would suggest, some "super string" theory of explanation to permit us to hypothesize of that which we cannot observe. Positivism, as may be presently defined, he says, is limited and inadequate since while it may show us the coherence and combinations of forces interacting in any given slice of the market system, it does not enable us to "predict the precise results which any particular change will have" (Hayek 1952/1952:74-75).

Thus, to adapt Hayek's understanding of a positivistic limitation to the notion of man-made law, versus prioristic "given" natural law—the systems here regarded as semiotic systems of law in conflict—positive law is not *sufficiently man-made*, since it is not a representation of a fully-intended, projected meaning of an idea. Rather, the positivistic theory has gaps of meaning, empty spaces or meaning-ellipses (to be distinguished from the gaps in law of Kantorowicz, 1958, in degree only). Hayek equates modern positivism with what he calls, "scientism" —an "abuse of reason"—and contrasts it with its antagonist, modern socialism. Both—that is, the conflict of which both ideologies are relates—evolved to a gordian knot in which the entangled ropes of ideas are distinguishable but the dis-entangling of the knot still needs an herculean approach: the one side is that which represents the liberalism of Kant, Adam Smith, Hume, for example, and the other side represents the totalitarianism of Hegel, Marx, Comte (Hayek, above p. 399).

Hayek speaks of the infiltration of positivism, or scientism, as a kind of counter-espionage, such that a counter-revolution is an illicit betrayal of a confidence and informational trust rather than as a stage in purposeful evolution, in law and/or economics and in all the sciences.

Finally, in regarding social institutions as complex sign-systems and representations of complex ideas of ideologies I am merely providing illustrations of the Peircean semiosis in a less abstract, more practicable manner. What Peirce's theory provides for is an instrumental handle on a process of inquiry and explanation which permits description of aspects of social, human (and non-human organizations) that are not otherwise explainable. For example, the exciting, interesting group of intellectuals who have come to constellate around the Santa Fe Institute for Studies in the Science of Complexity are genuinely interdisciplinary but are still in search of a theory or set of theories to use as a frame of general reference. Peirce seems to offer such a working basis (Kevelson 1993); but he has not been brought in to a position of centrality at this point, although scholars of the stature of Bohm, Prigogine, and others, important to but not part of this group, have taken Peirce as a great influence upon this new work.

The late Nobel Laureate Hayek has also cited Peirce's work and his own indebtedness to Peirce as indispensable for his own positions on law and economics, including the principle of informational decentralization in game-theory of Economics. This game-theoretic approach to trading and the double auction market is not my focus here, but I mention it in passing since it grows out of an earlier attempt, by the Institute, to define the idea of ecomonics as an evolving, complex system, that is, a sign-system (1988 in P.W. Anderson, K. J. Arrow, D. Pines).

The link between law and economics, from the perspective of semiotics, has been largely the work of Robin Paul Malloy, for example, *The Symposium on Law and Economics and the Semiotic Process* (in *The Syracuse Review*, 42 1 1991). This symposium builds on general semiotic theory and thus indirectly on Peirce (Kevelson 1977, 1988, 1990.)

In summary, in this present paper I regard two systems of law in conflict as representing Peirce's notion of the development of an idea from less to more complex. The point of departure is a critical situation that is occurring in postcommunist countries today, where the question is open as to which legal system is to fit into the place left open under the heading, "rule of law." Is it a place appropriate for Natural Law or for Positive Law? This is the problem posed and discussed by Grazin, in his insightful and provocative paper in the *John Marshall Law Review* (26 1993:719-737). This crisis shares several significant aspects with what Hayek has much earlier described as *The Counter-Revolution of Science* (1952/1979). Here Hayek argues, in a Peircean sense, that we begin with our predilections, our inclinations, and our prejudices in our constructions of models to represent and build upon what Austin had referred to as conflicting and "competing analogies" (Hayek, above pp. 41-60).

Conflicts of law and of competing analogies in the development of a complex ideology we call The Law may begin to explain how an institution, as a complex network of meaning, evolves and grows.

WORKS CITED

Earley, Joseph. "Recent Development in Science Important for Legal Scholarship." in R. Kevelson, ed., *Codes and Customs*, (New York and Berne: Peter Lang, 1994), pp. 77-92.

Fisch, Max H. "Introduction" in M.H. Fisch, ed., *Classic American Philosophers*. (New York: Appleton-Century-Crofts, 1951).

Friedman, Lawrence M. *A History of American Law*. (New York: Simon & Schuster, 1973).

Grazin, Igor "The Rules of Law: But of Which Law?" *John Marshall Law Review* 26 (1993):719-737.

Kevelson, Roberta *The Law as a System of Signs*. (New York: Plenum, 1988).

_____. *Peirce, Paradox, Praxis*. (Amsterdam: Mouton de Gruyter, 1990).

_____. "Peirce at the Millennium" in R. Kevelson, ed., *Codes & Customs*. (New York and Berne: Peter Lang, 1994) pp. 173-176.

_____. *Peirce, Science, Signs*. (New York and Berne: Peter Lang, 1995).

Peirce, Charles Sanders. *Collected Papers*, 8 Vols., C. Hartshorne, P. Weiss, A. Burks, eds. (Cambridge: Harvard University Press, 1931-1935;1958).

_____. Microfilm Edition of Manuscripts with annotated catalogue, by R. Robins. (Amherst: University of Massachusetts Press, 1958).

Chapter Twelve

THE PARADOX of JURISPRUDENCE

Joel Levin

I
Introduction

There is a central problem with legal theory. Past legal events are studied for existence conditions—when do actions and statements constitute a binding contract, what are the necessary and sufficient conditions for a legal system—and then, after observation, analysis, and synthesis, a theory is constructed which tells us how to categorize and label legal objects. An accepted offer, consideration, mutuality, and the technical niceties appear: *voila*, a contract. Primary and secondary rules are spotted in the vicinity of a rule of recognition: poof, we have a legal system. Legal theory seems to be just some descriptive sociology or history, tightly repackaged, and made ready to serve as a set of criteria to judge future pretenders to legal status.

There is, of course, a serious problem for this straight-forward description: legal ontology differs radically from that of natural science in its basic contingency. Law need not exist, doesn't everywhere exist, and exists and is shaped through the unpredictable behavior of different societies. That contracts once had to be under seal, or that all (known) societies once were led by a conqueror, strongman, or hereditary ruling class might be interesting legal facts. The question is, what use are they? Any legal theory of the Middle Ages deciding contracts or assessing legal systems would incorporate these facts as significant. Today, seals and the aristocracy are neither reasonable nor relevant. Should legal theory have predicted this? Is imagination or aspiration important here?

Moreover, in this way—observing and synthesizing the past—legal theory cannot help but be profoundly conservative and often intolerant, at least to new ideas. The conservativism might be desirable. It may dampen excesses or curb the unethical behavior of those who typically reject wholesale past legal process. But as an exercise in theorizing, is it of any value to characterize law?

We might step back and look, very generally, at the purpose of theorizing. No catalogue of purposes could be complete here, (nor would it be useful). However, in natural science we look to theories to explain and predict natural phenomena, in order to understand why, for example, a certain mixture of chemicals explodes, when particular cells turn malignant, how computers can be constructed to be faster and more efficient, or when the universe began. A good theory should have predictive power, and explain what we see. Clearly, legal theory is not quite like that. Law is more than a prediction of police or court actions, and many legal issues, in fact, only incidentally concern the courts. Moreover, it is comprehensible to think of scientific theory as locating some sort of objective truth, a claim difficult to make for legal theory. Law is a human invention, and has an irreducibly human component, unlike, for instance, rocks, molecules, and planets.

Legal theory might be thought to be more like theory in mathematics, with its aspect of human invention and its search for formal proofs; or like ethics, with its construction of a normative system and its search for what is right or good or virtuous. But these areas, too, are quite unlike law. Very little admits of proof in law, and to formalize is already to remove most of what is important and interesting. The exciting and unexpected results of elegant mathematical proofs seem foreign and remote from legal reasoning, even good legal reasoning. As for the ethical theorist's hope to know right from wrong conduct: the activities of autocrats don't count, while the imperative of a consistent theory is all important. Looked at in terms of purpose: mathematical and ethical theory solve potential problems for the practitioner. They allow the enterprise to continue by offering new information.

This does not mean that other types of theories are not suggestive of how legal theory works. One activity which shares much with the lawyer's is that of the historian, or at least the historian of human history. In the areas of both history and law, individuals have created a contingent activity, but neither historians nor legal theorists are personally responsible for the creation. Historians do not just naively find or locate history. They must examine situations where there is often, at once, too little and too much information. They may have (depending on somewhat arbitrary counting criteria) five or ten million economic, military and social facts about the French Revolution before them, yet have only scant information about the personal lives of certain of the *sans culottes*, or the motivations of those who stormed the Bastille. Which information should be used in a book setting out a theory of the events, which should be read, what should count as the beginning or end of the Revolution, how should events with little information be considered, what theory of human behavior should be used to filter the actions of eighteenth-century peasants, burghers, soldiers, and members of the *ancien regime*: answering these questions turns the archivist into a philosopher of history. The historian's activities here—of looking at data for choice and selection, of using a theory of human behavior, of having a pre-theoretic methodological paradigm for deciding what to consider, of filling in gaps in what seems clear and of deciding how to treat outcomes which do not possess diminished certainty—all involve the creation and use of a philosophy of (doing) history.

Regardless of the appropriateness and heuristic value of comparisons with other types of theory, it is clear that lawyers commonly use at least some minimal, legal theory. Legal theory is used to identify legal objects, and, in that sense, imparts knowledge to the practitioner. For example, among the set of putative contracts—agreements, promises, bids, rewards, predictions, orders, pacts, compacts, casual words, and vows—we need a theory to tell us which are valid, binding, and legally enforceable. How would one construct a theory to answer such a question? Historical criteria have the limitations suggested earlier: they tell what was, but without any guarantee of validity in the future. Societies once enforced marriage contracts and religious vows; now, generally, they don't. The social, family, occupational and religious orientation of individuals has changed, and that reorientation took the law with it.

A theorist might respond that he or she could give an explanation of what has counted as a valid contract. Things change, facts and lives are ephemeral, and that can be no concern of theirs. But if I think that vows are contractually binding and you don't, what does the theory tell us in such a case, and does that theory matter?

Any general theory of jurisprudence presents an even more elliptical problem. Legal systems may have always behaved in a certain way (or those things we have called legal systems have traditionally shared certain features), but we may be more than happy to change our criteria if social and political reality changes. The theory, though, can in no way take account of how the reality changes. Why, do it (that is, do theory) then, or better yet, why have we done it?

I want to suggest that we do it because it must be done in order to carry out law: that is, one must be a theorist to be a lawyer. Law can only be understood through theory. That said, the reason we see theory as failing, and the reason it so often does fail, is that law is mistaken for a social rather than individual construction. The centrality of legal notions to the human experience causes particular views of the law to be tied to individual notions. This calculus of individual theories forms the legal fabric and explains, without contradiction or paradox, legal change.

Let us return then to the initial claim here: namely, that in order to understand and practice law, one needs to engage in legal theory. To return to the contract example: suppose we notice that individuals are engaging in frequent and various putative contract behavior. They say things such as "I'll give you $500 for that bicycle," "Let's meet for lunch at 12:30 p.m.," "You're hired," "Give me your money or your life," "I'll take 21 gallons of hi-test," or "I will marry you." Suppose we wish to know which of these types of utterance, located in the social context in which they are stated, constitutes contractual behavior. The only way of making sense, of discovering the meaning, of understanding the signs and language and performance conditions of such utterances would be to construct a theory which tells us what happens when such utterances fail, what remedies there are, what sanctions might be taken against a breaching party, what incentives there are to perform, what conditions would count as ameliorating or excusing performance, and the various other elements and concepts common to understanding the law of contracts. One might not think of oneself as a contract theorist, nor think that to be necessary, in order to make sense of what counts as enforceable agreements; but one, in fact, needs to engage in contract theory even to understand the meaning of such language. Today, our normal discourse of exchange and trade—whether we bring a gallon of milk to a convenience-store counter or ask for a room in a hotel—is given meaning by the type of theory we construct to make sense of contractual behavior. We understand that an actor playing Shylock does not make a binding agreement when exacting the promise that a contract breach shall be remedied by a pound of flesh, just as we understand that predictions ("it will rain tomorrow" said on the evening news) are also not enforceable promises. We cannot put together the various past enforceable agreements—whether marriage contracts, real estate sales, promises to ship box cars of coal, or personal service contracts—without constructing some theory to make sense of them.

II
On Legal Complexities

That said, we notice that one of the puzzling features of law is that the number of hard cases continually increases rather than diminishes. One might think, given the notion that there are a certain number of difficult or unsettled cases, and that the courts are in the business of deciding those cases that, over time, at least within a given area, the number of difficult or hard cases would diminish. To use the example of both Holmes and Hart, a turn-of-the-century rule that vehicles are not allowed in the park might come under some scrutiny as motorized wheelchairs, skateboards or golf carts used by the minimally-ambulatory come racing by. However, at some point, not all that many new vehicles exist, or rather any new vehicles are at best minor improvements over what has already been categorized and settled, with rules generally having been crafted which give dispositive guidance to virtually every possible case. Thus, the number of difficult cases ought to diminish. However, even the most casual look at what goes on in law courts and society reveals that, in areas as diverse as tort, contract, criminal law, securities, probate, and family law, the number of fierce disputes and filed cases reaching the appellate courts has increased; the number of dissents and contradictory opinions has grown; and, more interesting yet, what was once-settled law has increasingly become less settled rather than more certain.

The reason this is puzzling is that the way legal theory is often done and the claims of theorists themselves misconstrue what the basic legal enterprise is about, and additionally, how important it is to its participants and its bystanders.

Initially, the category mistake of confusing law with a set of cases, statutes, and constitutions on one hand, or rules, principles, and miscellaneous standards on the other, needs to be put to one side. These objects alone are insufficient to constitute a legal system. It is, rather, their acceptance which allows a system to exist, which is why Roman law is studied everywhere but adhered to nowhere in the world today. The acceptance includes an important mental component, a component which in turn involves not only beliefs (which may be truth-conditional, although that is not always clear) but attitudes, which clearly have political, emotional, and, in general, value-laden elements.

If legal theory is, then, considered as a mental construction by participants in legal systems who select the correct set of legal propositions, then, given the number of contenders for inclusion in the proper set, and given the competition for weight and place within that set, theory is crucial in order to understand law. That said, the theory must be individually based.

Individual beliefs and attitudes sift the legal debris and allow sense to be made of various contenders for true legal propositions in particular and for a complete picturing of the legal landscape in general. Particular notions of what should be included in the set of legal propositions, the criteria for choosing that set, and the notion of the role of various (formal) players in the legal community might, *in toto*, be called an individual legal view. Because legal views are often similar, many are lulled into the belief that law is constituted by shared views, and that some consensus must exist of similar views, with the consensus constituting the law. Certainly, there are those many instances when this cannot be the case, although such societists (as we might call them) dismiss such instances as peripheral. Thus, revolutions, civil wars, and *coups d'etat*; societies run by warlords, pirates, and rebels; and colonial, religious and sectarian disruptions are legally marginalized. Given the chaos of the modern world, and given much of the chaos of world history, the societist risks trivializing his or her own theory by eliminating much of what needs to be explained.

However, even if such societies are put to one side, there is no reason to believe that consensus exists, even in western, (so-called) well-ordered societies. In fact, given the emotional and attitudinal components to judicial views, and given that the truth conditions for legal beliefs are controversial at best and (at worse) perhaps considered by many to be irrelevant, it would be surprising if consensus occurred. Rather, in fact, human beings living in a particular society often happen to agree on many things, but the fact that they do disagree on particular issues should not count as evidence either that, where there is disagreement, law fails to exist or that there is a mistake being made. Rather, one needs to look at the fundamental distinction between convergence and consensus. Where there is a convergence of views, individuals reach the same conclusions but not necessarily for the same reasons. On the other hand, where there is consensus, there is agreement not only on final conclusions but the reasons for those conclusions. We see convergence, for example, where there is agreement on the validity of a precedent but not on its relevance, use, or extension, or where all concede the existence of a given right, but not on its scope, weight, or exceptions.

Convergence is common, and in fact, there would be civil war everywhere if it did not occur. Consensus is much rarer, and might often indicate that the issues held in common are either well-settled or trivial.

Let us look at an example from both legal doctrine and general theory. Certainly, specific doctrine and general theory do not need to run parallel as to their ontological features: the specifics of legal problems may shape individual rules in a way that does not govern or circumscribe theory. The growth, for instance, of justifications and excuses due to mental incapacity as defenses to charges of criminal conduct—whether this incapacity is seen as heat of passion, mental disease, intoxication, hormonal imbalance, neurological anomaly or trauma affecting basic moral judgment—might be thought to be governed by factors far removed from the general concerns of jurisprudential theory. These factors involve changes in perceptions about criminal conduct, increased knowledge about the human brain, new awareness about the effects of intoxication and addiction, as well as other reactions to crime on one hand, and the place of freedom and determinism in individual conduct on the other. The evolution of criminal law doctrine can only be accounted for by looking at such factors in explaining changes in defenses to criminal charges. The factors appear to be of a different nature than the factors which shape general theory: the construction of a legal theory through an examination of societies and an analysis of normative systems and structure.

Nevertheless, the process turns out to be virtually the same. Individual perceptions, beliefs and attitudes vary concerning the weight, place and validity of various criminal law justifications and excuses. Often individual differences are disguised by broad agreement that wrong-doers should be punished, that the mentally impaired do not understand they have done wrong and should not (in anything like the same way) be punished, and that line drawing concerning individual conduct is difficult. But there is no necessary, agreed, single, right answer as what counts as a good (sufficient) defense. Particular persons each have their own answers as they choose which factors amount to legal doctrine. You or I may have a view, and be able to justify it, as to whether, for example, the law allows that intoxication blurs judgment sufficiently to excuse statutory rape where the fact of minority of the victim was made less clear. But our views, while similar to others, differ from competing views, which may also be justifiable.

This irreducible singularity leads to a legal pluralism in doctrine. The same forces which create such micro-pluralism operate at the level of general theory. General theorists all recognize that any theory must account, in a central way, for certain examples of legal behavior (statutes and judicial decisions), the role of bench and bar, the place of morality, and the dynamics of authority. Most theories agree on most matters, and convergence of outcome among parts of different theories is likely. However, the basic beliefs underlying each theory are individual, and no canonical test for judging a theory's validity or testing its verisimilitude is possible.

All of this is disguised because of the fact that most views of doctrine and theory are, not surprisingly, very similar. Moreover, a second, related reason concerns the complexity of individual's view.

Logicians call this phenomenon "over-determination." Put simply, any of a number of reasons would be sufficient to support a particular conclusion. For example, many reasons support stopping at a stop sign: prudence, safety concerns, good driving habits, a well-ingrained fear of a traffic citation, setting an example for others. Seeming agreement may fall apart in situations of medical emergency or pursuit by criminals. This does not mean that social agreement really existed, only that individual theorizing is tested, and the language of law has, as odd as it might appear, a profoundly democratic component.

How does this delimit the ontological range of empirically possible legal objects sufficiently to do legal theory (or, less pretentiously, as human creativity and insanity seem to place no limits on what gets included in legal systems, how can we tell in advance what we need to account for)? Theocracies and democracies, republics and oligarchies, slave states and (American) Indian nations, governments led by Hitler, Kahn, and Amin or by Jefferson, Cincinnatus, or Brandt: what theory of law accounts for this?

The answer is that the theorizing, once removed from the requirements of accounting for social consensus, recreates as it recapitulates past legal (empirical) reality, gives a basis for deciding what counts as law in the future, and conflates, irreducibly, both a value and predictive account of law. Verisimilitude in theory replaces truth as to a particular fact, and matters of degree (or a logic of vagueness) explains how we measure and value various accounts. The question of when a *coup d'etat* changes a legal system is not tested by seeing (only) how a theory gets right the reality "out there": the process of finding law reconstructs empirical events through the individual filter of beliefs and values deciding what counts as an adequate account.

III
Some Interim Conclusions

One might think by way of metaphor, if not analogy, of Hume's problem with finding causation from the simple aggregation of past events. Constant conjunction does not imply causation at an empirical level, most often, because of the unreliability of the constancy. We can scoff at simple mistakes of primitive peoples—drawing astrological or meteorological conclusions which are easy to falsify—but ought to remain modest even as to the claims made for our own, more sophisticated, empirical methods. In any case, the Humean argument is that a theory is necessary to make the logical move from correlation to causation, and past events alone don't get us where we want to be.

Even at the level of pure abstraction, theory is necessary. Wittgenstein's point in his philosophy of mathematics that no unique answer can be found for the unknown next number in any series (*e.g.*,—if 2, 4, 6, 8, 10, 12, 14, then ? If the numbers represent driving competency in a jurisdiction which does not allow seniors privileges, the next number, representing the driving-disqualified population, might be "70") is instructive. A coherent picture is more than past, concatenated dates summed. Beliefs, purposes, attitudes and a larger theory are necessary to complete or clarify the picture.

Where does all of this lead us? First, we might dismiss any simple notion of legal objectivity from the basis of some rational and uninvolved observer. Participation is an essential component in understanding how to do law. Second, the paradox of finding general answers to what constitutes a legal system—a paradox drawn from the fact that legal systems and law can in theory take any form, thus leaving the theorist with no grounds for justifying any particular theory—cannot be overcome when law is reified, or worse yet, anthropomorphized. Third, we might be better off thinking of law as an attitude rather than an authority, and figuring a way to allow those beliefs and attitudes shared among various legal view holders to be used to solve rather than contribute to future legal problems and concerns.

Editor's Note: Editorial liberty, for the sake of stylistic conformity with other chapters, permitted me to append subsections and subheadings, but always with deference to author's original stylistic preference.

Chapter Thirteen

LAW, REASON and JUSTICE: QUESTIONING the MODERN TRIAD

José de Sousa e Brito

I
Modern Questioning about Law and Justice: Hume and Bentham

The tradition of western thought considers the conceptions of law and justice as being interconnected. The language itself invites to that: in German, the word *Gerechtigkeit* comes from *Recht*, as well as, for instance, in Greek *dikaiosune* from *dikaion*, and in Latin *iustitia* from *ius*. In English—or in French—there is no etymological relation between "justice"—or "justice"—and "law" or "right"—or *droit*—, which is very modern; but those who—as the neo-thomist philosopher Villey—love to think in Latin, replace the word *droit* (which is translated by "law" or by "right," according to context) by the word *juste* ("just")[1] when what really matters is to think clearly. Beyond words, the traditional definition of justice as virtue, or disposition or permanent, will to give each one his right (*constans et perfecta voluntas ius suum unicuique tribuere*)[2] leads to right.

Modern questioning separates the question of law from the question of justice. It was always well-known that laws as well as court decisions can be unjust, and Sophocles' *Antigone* and the platonic Socrates have deeply reflected on this. It is typically modern to present the problem in relation with two theses: that *is* and *ought* are to be separated and that reason has to do with theoretical truth. "The difference between the way one lives and the way one should live"[3] was clearly for Machiavelli: the methodical base for scientific politics which abstains from questioning about the ideal republic. Already Galilei has deduced audaciously from the modern conception of science "that there is no truth nor falsity in the law,"[4] but he did not explain it further. However it was no one but Hume who knitted both theses and formulated it decisively.[5] "No ought from an is," this is Hume's law, where the good moral theories separate from the bad ones, that commit such a logical fault—like, for instance, the theory of natural law. On the other hand, the moral distinctions, such as good or bad, just or unjust, are not derivable from practical reason, that is, from true sentences, but they are determined by passions. Thus the domain of justice lies outside of being and therefore also outside of reason. Hume is consequently the spiritual father of legal positivism. We will see how—after Hume—legal positivism argued about the three concepts law, justice, and reason. We shall concentrate on the two greatest legal positivists who consciously followed Hume: Bentham and Kelsen. We shall then study the most important attempt of refutation of legal positivism in today's philosophy of law, namely the one of Dworkin. At the end, I shall offer my own interpretation.

Bentham applied Hume's law insofar as he admitted an essential difference between law as it is and law as it ought to be. The arguments about this in his first published work, the *Fragment on Government*, of 1776, show most clearly in the terminology and world of ideas the derivation from Hume: "to the province of the **Expositor** it belongs to explain to us what, as he supposes, the Law **is**: to that of the **Censor**, to observe to us what he thinks it **ought to be**. The former, therefore, is principally occupied in stating, or in enquiring after **facts**: the latter, in discussing **reasons**. The **Expositor**, keeping within his sphere, has no concern with any other faculties of the mind than the **apprehension**, the **memory** and the **judgment**: the latter, in virtue of those sentiments of pleasure or displeasure which he finds occasion to annex to the objects under his review, holds some intercourse with the **affections**."[6] Law is accordingly a fact which must be described and belongs therefore to another sphere than the one of justice, of the law as it ought to be, of morals. Naturally it remains to explain what kind of fact law is. Bentham further says in a foot-note of the above text "The establishment of a Law may be spoken of as a **fact**, at least for the purpose of distinguishing from any consideration that may be offered as a **reason** for such **law**."

But in the doctrine of reason Bentham dissociates himself from Hume. An essential contribution of Bentham to the history of philosophy is precisely the recuperation of practical reason as a science, which he calls utilitarianism. Besides, in "Of Laws in General," Bentham has developed a logic of will as a kind of deontic logic (of command, prohibition, and permission) which he discovered independently of Leibniz (the deontic logic of Leibniz hasn't been published before in this century).[7] The methodical separation between *is* and *ought* inspired

Bentham anew when he distinguished within the utilitarian reason an expository and a deontological (or "censorial") principle. By the first one it is determined how everyone behaves according to the conception of his individual interest. By the second one it is determined how one ought to behave in such a way that his behavior leads to the highest degree of well-being of those sensitive beings on which well-being it exercises any influence.[8] The expository principle would show how the legal obligation is to be defined, as a probability of a pain caused by a legal sanction in case one doesn't act in a certain manner. Later, Bentham developed a finer theory of legal obligation, according to which there is a legal obligation whenever the legislator commands or forbids a certain action. The facts of applying sanctions are essential ones for the description of the legislator as a political superior and thus, as the particular person or set of persons to have the power of applying coercive sanctions. The actual positivists would be closer to this last explanation. They dispose, however, with Hart to a better theory of the sources of law: of the recognition by the organs or subjects of adjudication, preferred than the possibility of drawing attention to a sovereign armed with sanctions. The expository principle would also explain which sanctions are capable of obtaining a conformity of personal interest with legal obligation.

It is by means of the deontological principle that one determinates which contents the law should have in order to maximize general well-being. According to such a principle of reason we would also know when it conforms to general well-being to render obedience to the law or to refuse it, the latter when avoiding the law, offering resistance or making a revolution correspond more to the interests of all.

II
Kelsen or the Abolition of Reason in Law

Kelsen didn't start from Hume; he approached Hume more and more during his life.

For Kelsen law does not belong to the sphere of being (where Bentham places it), but to the sphere of ought, because law consists of norms. Thus law as a system of norms can only differ from the normative system of justice, as two systems of norms can differ. What makes one system of norms differ from another is the respective basic norm. It is necessary to explain this shortly. According to Kelsen "ought" is the subjective sense of a person's act of will intentionally directed to the conduct of another one. "But not every such an act has also objectively this sense. Only when it has also objectively the sense of ought, ought is designated as 'norm'."[9] "This is the case ..., when this act is authorized by a norm which is therefore considered as a higher norm. A gangster's command to give him a certain sum of money has the same subjective sense as a tax-officer's command, that is the sense that the individual to whom the command is directed ought to pay a certain sum of money. But only the tax-officer's command, not the command of the gangster, has the sense of a valid norm, binding the addressee of such a norm; only one, not the other is an act setting a norm: because the tax-officer's act is authorized by a tax law, while the gangster's act is not based on a norm authorizing him."[10]

So Kelsen comes to his construction by steps of the legal order which has in the constitution the highest norm, as the sense of the act which authorizes all other law giving authorities to make laws. But there is no norm authorizing the constitution because there is no corresponding act of will of an authority standing above the constitution. Nevertheless the authorizing norm must be presumed, in order to allow the constitutional assembly to be thought as competent and the constitution itself as valid. Kelsen calls it "basic norm." If justice is thought as a valid system of norms, this has to presuppose also a basic norm and a highest normative authority, that is God. But, according to Kelsen, two systems of norms cannot be thought as simultaneously valid. So, if law is valid, justice cannot be an objective ought.

These consequences are for Kelsen all the more unavoidable, as for him there are no logical relations between norms. Two norms can be contradictory and also both maybe valid. No norm is derivable from other norms. Indeed Kelsen has developed this theory only relatively late, mainly in his *Allgemeine Theorie der Normen* of 1965-73.[11] In the second edition of *Reine Rechtslehre* of 1960, Kelsen still wrote:

> Since legal norms as prescriptions, that is as commands, permissions, authorizations, can be neither true nor untrue, follows the question how logical principles, especially the principle of contradiction and the rules of reasoning can apply to the relations between legal norms (such as the pure theory of law used to do at all times), when according to traditional conception these principles cannot apply but to statements which can be true or untrue. The answer to this question is: that logical principles may apply to legal

norms, if not directly at least indirectly, provided that they are applicable to the legal sentences describing these legal norms, which can be true or untrue. Two legal norms are contradictory and thus cannot be affirmed valid at the same time, if the two legal sentences which describe them are contradictory; and a norm can be deduced from another one, when the legal sentences describing them can enter into a logical syllogism.[12]

But this is clearly wrong. The legal sentence which describes the norm forbidding the communist party does not contradict the legal sentence describing the norm which allows the communist party, and yet both norms cannot be thought of as valid at the same time. Just the contrary is to be affirmed of Kelsen's former as well as later theses: there are contradictory norms and a logic of norms, but the corresponding legal sentences are not contradictory of one another.

With his later denial of logic in law, Kelsen approaches Hume mostly. And Kelsen knows why: "With regard to the relation between is and ought Hume is more consequent than Kant. For him there is no practical reason."[13]

III
Regaining Justice by Legal Principles According to Dworkin

Ronald Dworkin based a vast attack against legal positivism on the main argument, that it reduces law to rules (Kelsen would prefer to say "to norms"). However this model of rules neglects the fact that in law there are also principles and policies having another logic than the rules. In fact principles have another relation to the counter-examples which can be stated against their formulation than the rules. A counter-example to a rule implies a contrary rule, which comprises the counter-example, and thus a rule conflict. This conflict only can be solved by transforming one of the rules, which will include an **exception** to it, or by invalidating one of the rules. But a principle can give way to another principle or to a rule in the case of a counter-example without becoming therefore invalid or having to be transformed. This becomes understandable by a specific dimension of a principle, its **weight**, which can be **weighed** compared with other principles or rules. Let us take a simple example: the rule "it is forbidden to kill a person" is only compatible with self-defense, if it includes an exception for cases of self-defense. On the other hand, the principles usually valid in cases of necessity for weighing values in a situation of self-defense (in case of a present and illegal attack) cede to the prior principle "right does not have to cede to wrong."

In principle we should agree with Dworkin when he refers to the logic of legal principles.[14] But this is not an argument against legal positivism: at most, it is against the doctrines of legal positivism which misunderstand principles and their own logic. So Hart can, for example, integrate the principles in his theory of law, what he actually did in his answer to Dworkin.[15]

What the legal positivism cannot accept is the rational use of legal principles as described by Dworkin. While for the legal positivists only the principles formulated in the sources of law or derivable from the phrases expressing the legal sources are to be accepted as law, for Dworkin all the principles giving the best possible foundation for the solutions existing in the sources of law are immanent in the law.[16] So not only the principles of reason in law (the principles of justice), but also the rational norms (the norms "consistent with the best possible interpretation of the general practice of deciding hard cases"), which allow to decide the "**hard cases**," become a component part of the existing law, that is, of the law which the judge has to take into account when he decides. Therefore the difference between the application of the law and jurisprudence is only due to the abstract character of the latter. "Jurisprudence"—Dworkin says—"is the general part of adjudication."[17] General theories "try to show legal practice as a whole in the best light it can bear. So no firm line divides jurisprudence from adjudication or any other aspect of legal practice."[18]

How can we then distinguish law from rational law, jurisprudence from theory of justice? Here Dworkin accepts a limitation, which he calls **"fit"** dimension. Each step of the interpretative work of jurisprudence and adjudication has to "fit" to the former whole of the law. This is why jurisprudence and adjudication proceed by interpretation, therefore by a hermeneutic method. The interpretation tries to show the whole law in the best possible light. But what, when it cannot be avoided that the law still remains dark, when each interpretation that still fits shows the law of the community in its bad aspect, that is, when any interpretation leads to an unjust result? Then, says Dworkin, the limitation of **fit** is only one among others in the interpretation and it may be surmounted: "the constraint fit imposes on substance, in any working theory, is therefore the constraint of one type of political conviction on another in the overall judgement which interpretation makes a political record the best it can be overall, everything taken in account."[19] Therefore a just decision which does no more fit the antecedent law as a whole remains, according to Dworkin, within the law.

IV
The Just Limitation of Justice in Law

Hume's law is still an unshakeable rock on which any ethical theory should rest. It remains valid independently of the weakness of the main argument which it was intended to support—namely the proof that there is no practical reason. This does not mean to ignore the fact that there are institutions, such as the law, that link to certain facts, such as acts of Parliament or customs, the validity of norms. This happens by means of constitutive norms of these institutions, such as the norms concerning legal sources, which are certainly compatible with Hume's law. The state of the theory of meaning until the late work of Wittgenstein and the philosophy of language of the Oxford school helps to explain how difficult it was for the legal positivists before Hart to apply Hume's law to law and jurisprudence. In the same way what must be explained is the incapacity to find inspiration for the analysis of the meaning of the sentences of legal language from Hume's fine remarks about the meaning of the sentences of morals. Hume already distinguished the reference to the conduct intended to be influenced, from the moral point of view of such influence, the point of view of "humanity." This could lead to consider that the same sentence, such as "you shall not murder," has different senses, if it is uttered by the prophet Moses or by the legislator or by a lawyer or by a philosopher.

So Bentham correctly maintained the distinction between *is* and *ought* in spite of having rejected the restrictive sense of reason of modern philosophy and of having investigated the rules of practical reason that apply to law. What he then says about the "fact" of a law and about the meaning of a law and of the sentences of jurisprudence shows that he didn't take to heart Hume's remark that a sentence seeking to influence the conduct of others cannot be a statement of fact. Bentham misrepresents the meaning of the sentences of law since he takes them to be statements of the existence of psychic facts, namely of acts of will of the legislator.

When the legislator says "you shall not murder," he does not make a statement of his mental acts. A prohibition says nothing about the state of mind of the person who prohibits. Bentham even explains this in the case of permission: it may co-exist with three different states of mind of the legislator: the case in which he has never so much as contemplated the conduct; the case in which he has contemplated it yet he has made no choice whether the subject shall or shall not have his choice as to the performing it, and the case where he has positively chosen that the subject shall have his choice.[20] It may be said that the expression of an imperative implies conversationally (following Grice) a certain will of the speaker, though there is no contradiction, when the act of speech is affirmed and the corresponding will is denied, as in the case in which a Belgian public prosecutor accused for abortion in order to politically promote the abolition of the abortion law.

A similar criticism applies to any form of reduction of legal rules or principles to assertions (for example, of the probability of sanctions, thus Bentham,[21] or of future court decisions—so Alf Ross).[22]

By saying so I do not mean that the statement that there is a descriptive science of law, like the historical science of Roman law or Hart's concept of law intended to be, is false. This statement doesn't depend on a philosophy of language which reduces imperatives to assertions. So Kelsen distinguishes between the legal norm which is the sense of an act of will, which can be neither true nor false, and the legal sentence, which states or denies the existence of legal norms, and which is true or false. I do not know exactly what Kelsen understands by a statement about the existence of a norm. I would think that to state that there is a norm is not different from saying that it is valid, and this is equivalent to the expression of the norm itself, which is not an assertion.

In a second-order statement one can naturally state of a certain norm that it consists of an hypothesis and a legal consequence, and such a statement is true or false. By stating it one does not mean what one generally means by norms—that is, the law—, but the sentences expressing the law. I agree with some interpreters of Kelsen,[23] that the distinction between "meaning" and "use" may be applied to legal norms, but I don't think that Kelsen has ever intended to make such a distinction.

The sentences of jurisprudence, in its usual meaning of legal doctrine, are sentences which intend to formulate the rules of each case and to ascertain the meaning of concepts, principles and rules which allow the rule in each case to be found in a systematic way.[24] Such sentences say how legal subjects and officials have to behave if they wish to behave in accordance with the law. They don't say it in an authoritative manner, that is, from a position of authority implying that they are to be followed because the lawyer says them, but they are to be followed because they are a component of the law. The lawyer intends to influence the conduct of others according to the law, as a counsellor (***iurisconsultus***). The typical sentences of jurisprudence are therefore one species of those speech acts which Kenny denominates **fiats**.[25]

Let's consider now the role of reason and therefore of justice in law. I shall not discuss the rational foundations and content of the theory of justice.

As already mentioned, to Bentham goes the merit of having reenlarged the restrictive concept of reason and of science typical of modernity. His theory of practical reason, which he called utilitarianism was so much successful that it legitimated until today classical political economy as a science, even partially as a normative science. He restricted, however, too much the role of reason in law. I shall begin by pointing out two other aspects of the rationality of law.

Firstly, the law is only a part of a broader practice of the legislator and of each of us. The creation, alteration, derogation and also the application and non-application of the law by courts and the legal subjects are part of a more general practice of each of these persons: statutes, contracts, court decisions are intended to be means to other ends and can therefore be understood only by reasoning from premises which are not part of the law. Therefore a general theory of the practical argumentation should explain the relations between the practice of law in a broad sense and the other domains of social action and of human practice in general, including the special ideal practice of morals as the subject of the philosophical ethics. In this paper this must remain a ***desideratum***.

Secondly, the general principles of international law and most constitutions (which often include declarations of human rights) and at least the greater part of private law and of the general part of criminal law (by reference to culpability) include not only explicit (by general clauses referring to reason or to good faith, for example) references to rationality but they intend to be the work of reason, so that if some consequence proves to be irrational it cannot be said to be legal in these fields.

I am not implying that I could follow Dworkin in his own path, which leads to integrate jurisprudence in the theory of justice, with the methodical constraint imposed by the dimension of "fit." I think that the fit-dimension is more than a politically relevant point of view among others in the decision-making process of the judge or of the lawyer, leading in last resort to a political decision. The fit-dimension constitutes one of the peculiarities of the practice of law, which separates it from the philosophical practice of ethics and so gives to the **ought** of legal norms a specific sense, that distinguishes them from the norms of ethics. In this way should the law of a democratic constitutional state be conceived as a rational limitation of justice.

There are, however, several limits to rationality in law so that the overall picture is much more complicated. One source of complexity comes from the fact that it is rational to adopt procedures of decision-making which limit the number of sentences which are admitted in legal reasoning. In a procedure before the court, for instance, only some persons are allowed to argue on only some occasions and their arguments must be compatible with some given sources of law—mainly statutes and judicial decisions.

These limits are an essential characteristic of the role of reason in the law. Law is limited practical reason. There are not several kinds of institutional reason, otherwise it would indeed not be possible to criticize internally the institutions including the law. But I think that there is a criticism of the law, which acquires validity within the law and leads to the corrective of the law. And this is, in opposition to the opinion of the legal positivists and therefore of Bentham, the greatest of them, legal and not moral criticism. The rules of this legal criticism are those of practical philosophy in general with some reasonable limitations. But as these limitations are dictated from practical reason itself, they also are rationally limited in the case of legal disobedience, legal resistance and revolution (as revolution of reason). Thus, law is rationally limited reason. And jurisprudence should be thought of as an application of ethics, thus as legal philosophy at work.

ENDNOTES

1. M. Villey, *Questions de Saint Thomas sur le droit et la politique*, 1987, p. 114.

2. *Dig.*, 1.1.10.

3. N. Machiavelli, *Il Principe*, c. XV (ed. B. Richardson), 1979, p. 44.

4. *Dialogo dei massimi sistemi,* in *Le opere* (ed. nazionale), VII, p. 78.

5. D. Hume, *A Treatise of Human Nature*, III, I, I (ed. Selby-Bigge, p. 455 ff.).

6. J. Bentham, *A Comment on the Commentaries and A Fragment on Government*, (ed. J.H. Burns, H.L.A. Hart), 1977, p. 397.

7. J. Brito, On this my article "Relire Bentham," *Archives de philosophie du droit*, 17, 1972, p. 458 ff.

8. Bentham MSS, Library of the University College, London, U.C. XVIII, 172-175. See my article "Praktische Vernunft und Utilitarismus," *Archiv für Rechts- und Sozialphilosophie*, Beiheft 51, 1993, p. 90 ff, with full quotations.

9. H. Kelsen, *Reine Rechtslehre*, 2nd ed., 1960, p. 7.

10. a.a.O., p. 7-8.

11. H. Kelsen, ed. by K. Ringhofen and R. Walter, 1979, p. 166 ff.

12. P. 77.

13. H. Kelsen, *Allgemeine Theorie der Normen*, p. 68.

14. Ronald Dworkin, *Taking Rights Seriously*, 1977, p. 22 ff.

15. H.L.A. Hart, "El nuevo desafio al positivismo juridico," *Sistema*, 36, 1980, p. 3-18. See Hart's new postscript to the 2nd edition of *The Conceipt of Law*, 1994, p.259 ff.

16. Ronald Dworkin, *Law's Empire*, 1986, p. 225 ff.

17. R. Dworkin, "Legal Theory and the Problem of Sense" in *Issues in Contemporary Legal Philosophy*, ed. Ruth Gavison, 1987, p. 15.

18. *Ibid.*, p. 14.

19. R. Dworkin, *Laws Empire*, p. 257.

20. J. Bentham, *Of Laws in General*, ed. H.L.A. Hart, 1970, p. 98.

21. J. Bentham, *Fragment on Government*, p. 429-30; *Chrestomatia*, (ed. M.J. Smith/W.H. Burston), 1983, p. 202.

22. A. Ross, On Law and Justice, 1958, p. 40.

23. M.P. Golding, "Kelsen and the Concept of Legal System," *Archiv für Rechts- und Sozialphilosophie*, 47, 1961, p. 355 ff.

24. Philip Heck, *Grundriss des Schuldrechts*, 1929, p. 471 ff.

25. A. Kenny, *Will, Freedom and Power*, 1975, p. 39, following A. Hofstädter, J.C.C. McKinsey "On the Logic of Imperatives," *Philosophy of Science*, 6, 1937, p. 446 ff.

WORKS CITED

Bentham, Jeremy, *Commentaries and A Fragment on Government*, ed. J.H. Burns, H.L.A. Hart, (London, Athlone Press, 1970.)

_____, *Of Laws in General*, ed. H.L.A. Hart, (London, Athlone Press, 1970).

_____, *Fragment on Government*; *Chrestomatia*, ed. M.J. Smith/W.H. Burston, (London Athlone Press, 1983).

Brito, José de Sousa e, "*Relire* Bentham," *Archives de philosophie du droit*, 1972 17: pp. 451-472.

_____, "Praktische Vernunft und Utilitarismus," *Archiv für Rechts- und Sozialphilosophie*, Beiheft 1993 51: pp. 87-101.

Dworkin, Ronald, *Taking Rights Seriously*, (Cambridge, Massachussets, Harvard University Press, 1977).

_____, *Laws Empire*, (London, Fontana Press, 1986).

_____, "Legal Theory and the Problem of Sense," ed. Ruth Garisson, *Issues in Contemporary Legal Philosophy*, 1987 9-20, Oxford, Clarendon Press.

Galilei, Galileo, *Dialogo dei massimi sistemi*, in *Le opere*, Edizione nazionale, a cura di Antonio Favaro, VII, (Firenze, Barbera, 1897).

Golding, M.P., "Kelsen and the Concept of Legal System," *Archiv für Rechts- und Sozialphilosophie*, 1961 47: p. 355.

Hart, H.L.A, "El nuevo desafio al positivismo juridico," *Sistema*, 1980 36: pp. 3-18.

_____, *The Concept of Law*, 2nd edition, (Oxford, Clarendon Press, 1994).

Heck, Philip, *Grundriss des Schuldrechts*, (Tübingen, J.C.B. Mohr, 1929).

Hofstädter, A., J.C.C. McKinsey, "On the Logic of Imperatives," *Philosophy of Science*, 1939 6: pp. 446-457.

Hume, David, *A Treatise of Human Nature*, eds. L.A. Selby-Bigge, 2nd ed. by P.H. Nidditch, III, I, I, (Oxford, Clarendon Press, 1978).

Kelsen, Hans, *Reine Rechtslehre*, 2nd ed., Wien, Franz Deuticke, 1960.

_____, *Allgemeine Theorie der Normen*, eds. K. Ringhofen and R. Walter, (Wien, Manzsche Verlags-und Universitätsbuchhandlung, 1979).

Kenny, Anthony, *Will, Freedom and Power*, Oxford, Blackwell, Villey, Michel, 1975).

Machiavelli, Niccolò, *Il Principe (De principatibus)*, edited by Brian Richardson, (Manchester, Manchester University Press, 1979).

Ross, Alf, *On Law and Justice*, (London, Stevens & Sons, 1958).

Villey, Michel, *Questions de Saint Thomas sur le droit et la politique*, (Paris, Presses Universitaires de France, 1987).

Chapter Fourteen

NOTES for a SKETCH of a PEIRCEAN THEORY of the UNCONSCIOUS[1]

Vincent Colapietro

I
Introduction

While C. S. Peirce clearly acknowledged the reality of the unconscious, he himself did not explore in a systematic or sustained way this dimension of mind. Nor did he (as far as I have been able to discover) draw upon his general theory of signs to illuminate, even in the sketchiest fashion, the particular range of phenomena customarily subsumed under the rubric of the unconscious. As a result, there is at least a fourfold task imposed upon anyone undertaking a study of what would have been Peirce's approach to the unconscious, had he investigated this topic in the manner he explored, say, inquiry or inference or even consciousness. Such a scholar must (1) collate Peirce's own scattered remarks about the unconscious and various allied topics such as rationalization, self-delusion, and hypnosis; (2) suggest fruitful ways in which Peirce's most important doctrines (above all others, his doctrine of categories and theory of signs) might be used to articulate a distinctively Peircean approach to the unconscious; (3) develop in an explicit form a semiotic interpretation of the unconscious; and (4) compare this approach to the unconscious with the approaches encountered in Sigmund Freud, Carl Jung, Jacques Lacan, Julia Kristeva and others. I am a long way from completing any one of these tasks, but I am sufficiently far along in my research to present my notes for how to sketch a Peircean theory of the unconscious. In this essay, I will address myself to parts of the first two tasks. In the spirit of Peirce himself, the justification for presenting these notes is *heuristic*: they might serve to guide and goad the inquiry of other scholars into an important but neglected area of research. More immediately, responses to my sketch will assist me in carrying on my own investigation.

The mention of Lacan a moment ago invites the observation that, within the Saussurean tradition of semiology there is a full-blown theory of the unconscious, while within the Peircean tradition we do not find anything comparable. It may indeed be the case (as Lacan contends) that the unconscious is structured like a language (Lacan 1977); the meaning of this assertion, however, depends entirely on how one conceives the structure of language itself (Shapiro 1963; Pharies 1985). In particular, language conceived as a system of purely formal differences is one thing, whereas language understood as a nexus of concretely embodied habits is quite another (Colapietro 1980, 1991; de Lauretis 1984, 1994). This and other differences will bear directly and in some cases deeply upon how Peirce—in contrast to Lacan—would construe the claim that the unconscious is structured like a language. But, before either instructive comparisons can be made or constructive disagreements can be enacted, the Peircean perspective needs to be articulated in its own right.

Even before presenting this perspective, however, two final points of a preliminary nature are in order. First, in a recent article, Lucia Santaella Braga (1993), explores the most serious difficulties in and the most fruitful strategies for applying Peirce's semiotics. In my own efforts, I have tried to follow her hermeneutical and heuristic strictures, above all, her counsel "to avoid the intellectual feebleness that is common when his [Peirce's] definitions and classifications are isolated from the interconnectivity which gives them portent" (Braga 405; Freud 1930:110). We increase the likelihood of avoiding such feebleness when we trace in detail the formal and dynamic relations generated by a conscientious reliance upon Peirce's categoreal scheme (407-408; Savan 1987-88; also Shapiro 1983). Second, it seems appropriate to note here, even if only in passing, an important similarity between Peirce and Freud (in fact, but one striking similarity among numerous others). As Richard Wollheim notes, "Freud relied on two heuristic principles .... The first was a conviction of the meaningfulness or significance of human action. 'A gain in meaning is a perfectly justifiable ground for going beyond the limits of direct experience' (Wollheim xiv, 167). Secondly, Freud respected any postulation that resulted in an increase in generality; and he was suspicious of any supposition to the extent to which it seemed *ad hoc* or to result in loss of generality" (Wollheim 1971:195-196). Of course, Peirce's own thought drives in the direction of both meaningfulness and generality, of construing generously the domain of significant phenomena and of pursuing rigorously the implications of his own categoreal commitments. But, like Freud, generality is for Peirce not to be purchased at the price of specificity. He insists that: "Thought must live and grow in incessant[ly] new and higher translations, or it proves itself not to be genuine thought" (CP 5.594). But he immediately notes that "the mind loses itself in such general questions and seems to be floating in a limitless vacuity" (CP 5.595). In order to avoid this and at the same time to avoid blocking the road of inquiry (by erecting walls between areas of inquiry, that is, by restricting the momentum of generality), it is crucial for us to realize that the very essence of thought and purpose drives toward specificity and concreteness, "just as truly as it is of the essence of either that it should be general" and (presumably) also vague (CP 5.594; for distinction between generality and vagueness, see CP 5.450; CP 5.05ff). In addition, generously construing the boundaries of significant phenomena does not mean irresponsibly discarding any and all criteria by which the relative merits of competing interpretations might be assessed: while anything is potentially significant, not every interpretation is equally valid (Eco 1992:144). Fantastic overinterpretation is not more desirable than limitless vacuity (Eco 1992). We see an exemplification of both heuristic principles in Peirce's explicit treatments of consciousness and, I would contend, also in his largely implicit conception of the unconscious.

II
Peirce on Mind and Consciousness

"Most of us are in the habit of thinking that consciousness and psychic life are the same thing and otherwise [we] greatly overrate the functions of consciousness" (CP 6.489). In opposition to these two tendencies, Peirce carefully distinguished consciousness from mind and, moreover, persistently ascribed only a modest role to our conscious selves. Let us, accordingly, consider both points in some detail.

In 1902 Peirce claimed that "[Eduard] Von Hartmann, as long ago as 1869 [1868?], proved conclusively that unconscious mind exists" (CP 7.366). Peirce insistently argued that it was a mistake to define psychology as the study of consciousness: "For if psychology were restricted to phenomena of consciousness, the establishment of mental associations, the taking of habits, which is the very market-place of psychology, would be outside its boulevards. To say of such departments of psychology,—from every point of view, the most essential parts of it,—that they are studies of phenomena of consciousness, is as if an ichthyologist were to define his science as a study of water" (CP 7.367). One way to interpret this metaphor is to take consciousness as the *medium* in which habits are formed. But however we interpret this trope the thrust of Peirce's text is plain: the chief business of experimental psychologists concerns not processes and states of consciousness, but the formation and functioning of habits.

In this context, habit encompasses instincts (for example, CP 5.504) since the latter are, as Peirce himself suggests, either innate dispositions or innate tendencies for the acquisition of more or less specific dispositions: "An animal instinct is a natural disposition, or inborn determination of the individual's Nature (his 'nature' being that within him which causes his behavior such as it is), manifested by a certain unity of quasi-purpose in his behaviour" (CP 7.381, note 19). (For one of Peirce's more elaborate classifications of instincts, see ms 1343.) Peirce goes on to claim that, in humans, this instinctually determined behavior is hardly ever spasmodic and virtually always conscious. More than that, unless the human organism is under some extraordinary stress, "the behaviour is always partially controlled by the deliberate exercise of imagination and reflexion," so much so that the action appears to the organism itself "to be entirely rational" (CP 7.381, note 19). Though the self-image of being in rational control of its spontaneous impulses is on the part of the organism a gross exaggeration, it nonetheless has a basis in fact: rational control is not a complete delusion.

The highest quality of mind involves readiness to take and to lose habits (CP 6.614), mind itself being a multilayered system of intricately related habits. More narrowly, the rational mind, "precisely because of its childlike character," is "an Unmatured Instinctive Mind" which can evolve in the direction of greater self-consciousness and self-critique and, by means of these reflexive tendencies, of greater self-control (CP 7.381). In short, immaturity is a necessary condition for rationality in Peirce's sense (CP 5.440; CP 5.419-419). It is just because human instincts are either entirely or overwhelmingly weak, uncertain tendencies that they become "infinitely plastic"; this plasticity precludes them ever reaching an ultimate state beyond the possibility of further refinement (CP 7.381). To put the matter paradoxically, complete maturity would entail nothing less than arrested development. To push the matter beyond where Peirce himself appears to have felt it, allow me to suggest that instinctive mind is *at once* a prematurely matured and an invincibly immature set of complex tendencies, in some respects mutually supportive and in others inherently opposed. Thus, the cultural encoding of our instinctive tendencies is simultaneously the fissuring of prematurely determined tendencies and the directing of wildly immature impulses. Human instincts exhibit neither rigid fixity nor complete plasticity: their character and especially their force implicate them in a long biological history, whereas their development and integration with one another show them to be vital forces in a relatively short yet deeply transformative cultural history.

The instincts—the habits with which we are born—significantly facilitate the acquisition of other habits. If my hypothesis is correct, the acquisition of these other habits involves something like the breaking of established habits *and* the directing of inchoate tendencies. Yet, leaving instinctual dispositions aside, this much can be safely asserted: in general, the disruption of established habits enlivens consciousness, whereas the acquisition of new habits quells consciousness. In Peirce's own words, "consciousness subsides as habit becomes established, and is excited again at the breaking up of habit" (CP 6.614). Yet, in some contexts, the acquisition of habits itself depends partly on the presence of consciousness. In one of its principal manifestations, consciousness is, in the etymological sense, a dis-ease engendered by dysfunction. It is in effect just this manifestation of consciousness on which Peirce himself focused in his early pragmatic essays (most obviously, "The Fixation of Belief" and "How to Make Our Ideas Clear") and also in his later pragmaticist pieces. This dis-ease, experienced by the agent as doubt, is taken as a signal that something is amiss. The interpretation of this and countless other clues, somatic as well as environmental, by the human organism is required if that organism is to maintain its foothold in an ineluctably precarious world. This means that human well-being and human sign-use are inseparably linked, but only because human existence and human semiosis are of a piece.

The claim that the acquisition of habits lessens the degree of consciousness, however, needs to be qualified.[2] The qualification is important for it suggests a more nuanced comprehension of the relationship between habituation and awareness; moreover, it secures a more accurate depiction of Peirce's actual views, fully considered. Not only does the acquisition of habits require in some contexts the presence of consciousness, but the effect of certain habits is in some respects nothing less than the likelihood of focused attentiveness. For example, the habitually solicitous person is one who, *as a matter of habit*, is attentive to the feelings, thoughts, concerns, etc. of others. So, habit in this case does not quell but rather enlivens awareness. Yet, even here, one might argue that as the patterns of attentiveness become engrained they work against attaining as full and fine an attentiveness as any concrete situation truly demands. Hence, even regarding those habits which prompt and facilitate attentiveness, there are respects in which they also quell consciousness.

The attempt to describe and explain human conduct in terms of the interplay of consciousness and habituation is part and parcel of psychology, at least according to Peirce's understanding of this science. In turn, the attempt to describe and illuminate consciousness and habituation themselves in semiotic terms (for example, to interpret our everyday, practical consciousness as a complexly concatenated sequence of indexical signs (CP 5.493) or to interpret our evolved, evolving habits as the interpretants of affective, energetic, and cognitive processes (CP 5.487ff) is, of course, indicative of his experiment to view everything whatsoever *sub specie semiotica* (Hardwick 1977 (ed.), 85-86; Eco 1976:27).

As one would readily expect, then, psychology and semeiotic are, for Peirce, intimately connected. The idioscopic study of habit-taking on the part of sentient organisms and the coenoscopic study of sign-functioning on the part of virtually anything whatsoever (from geological formations to theological myths, from fossils and physical displacements to metaphors and literary allusions) depend upon one another, though unequally. "Of course, psychologists ought to make, as in point of fact they are making, their own invaluable studies of the sign-making and sign-using functions,—invaluable, I call them, in spite of the fact that they cannot possibly come to their final conclusions, until some more elementary studies [of signs] have come to their first harvest" (ms 675; quoted in Fisch 1986:340). In order to approximate its objectives most efficiently, the experimental investigation of mind (that is, of habit-systems) must wait upon the general study of semiosis or sign-processes, even though this experimental study might in the meantime make its own distinctive contributions to our comprehension of a specific order of semiosis.

Yet centuries before humans ever established the experimental study of mind, they relied on what Peirce did not hesitate to call an instinctive psychology. Nor is this a useless vestige of a primitive past, for we ourselves inescapably rely on such a psychology. Moreover, it is appropriate for us to do so: "We ought to give high authority to natural, instinctive conceptions of the mind, so far as they are of any practical utility" (CP 7.409; 5.511). This "natural psychology" is one that "grows up nearly the same in all men as the natural result of similar experiences acting upon similar understandings" (CP 7.421). Peirce explicitly concedes that: "There is not the smallest reason for supposing that that natural psychology is at all accurately true; on the contrary, it probably involves great errors." Nonetheless, "its authority must be allowed to be very high indeed in regard to all features which are of importance in the conduct of life; for, on the whole, man [that is, *Homo Sapiens*] has prospered under such beliefs."

Peirce also held that: "We have the naive idea that our beliefs are principally determined by the exercise of our *conscious* intellect; but it is not so" (CP 7.456; emphasis added). "Our daily life is," according to him, "full of involuntary determinations of belief. It is the egotism of the ego, or [the conscious] field of [our voluntary] attention, which imposes upon [us] with its High German modest conviction that whatever is known is known through it. It is [however simply] not so" (CP 7.447). It is plausible to suppose that this naive belief is in some measure an instinctive belief, for the assumption of control of one's conduct and consciousness is arguably a biological imperative as well as a cultural ideal. Moreover, it is instructive to juxtapose to this text a famous passage from Freud's *General Introduction to Psycho-analysis*:

> [P]resent-day psychological research ... is endeavoring to prove to the 'ego' of each of us that he is not even master in his own house, but that he must remain content with the veriest scraps of information about what is going on unconsciously in his own mind. We psychoanalysts were neither the first nor the only ones to propose to mankind that they should look inward; but it appears to be our lot to advocate it most insistently and to support it by empirical evidence which touches every man closely. This is the kernel of the universal revolt against our science ... and the liberation of opposition from all the restraints of impartial logic (Freud 1920:296).

But, for Peirce, the degree to which the "I" is not even master of its own house cannot be so great as to preclude any and all possibility of self-control (Colapietro 1989). So, too, the degree to which unconscious mind is other than consciousness cannot be so great as to seal hermetically the one from the other. Indeed, given Peirce's commitment to synechism (that is, to the principle of continuity), he refused to draw an absolutely sharp distinction between the conscious and unconscious dimensions of the human psyche. The one shades into the other. "We naturally make all our distinctions too absolute" (CP 7.438), including the distinction between consciousness and the unconscious (Wollheim 1971:180).

III
The Unconscious in Contradistinction from the Preconscious

Here it is appropriate to recall Peirce's inclination to think of human consciousness "as a bottomless lake, whose waters seem transparent, yet into which we can clearly see but a little way" (CP 7.547; CP 7.553; CP 7.554). But this raises a question regarding the possibility of equivocation, for (in Freud's terms) we need to distinguish not only consciousness from the unconscious but also the unconscious from the preconscious. Does Peirce recognize the unconscious in its strict Freudian sense or merely the preconscious? While this is a thorny terminological issue (especially since Freud's own usage shifted), there are texts in which Peirce clearly acknowledges the unconscious as opposed to the preconscious. For example, he asserts that: "Reason is of its very nature egotistical .... Men many times fancy that they act from reason when, in point of fact, the reasons they attribute to themselves are nothing but excuses which unconscious instinct invents to satisfy the teasing 'whys' of the *ego*. The extent of this self-delusion is such as to render philosophical rationalism a farce" (CP 1.631). This text seems to point toward the unconscious, not the preconscious. Freud revealed: "We obtain our concept of the unconscious from the theory of repression" (Freud, *Standard Works* XIX, 15). The sort of self-delusion to which Peirce refers here seems closely allied to the kind of mechanism by which ideas, images, wishes and incidents are according to Freud repressed. In short, it suggests the unconscious in the strict sense.

Even so, the other text just quoted—the one in which Peirce offers the metaphor for human consciousness of a bottomless lake—continues in a manner that points in a different direction; for he elaborates his trope by suggesting that, in the waters of this lake, "there are countless objects at different depths; and certain influences will give certain kinds of those objects an upward impulse which may be intense enough and continue long enough to bring them into the upper visible layer" (CP 7.547). On the one hand, there is a ubiquitous downward force exerted on all mental objects, forcing them to sink toward oblivion (CP 7.553). On the other, there is a selective upward force exerted on some objects, pushing (and, in some cases, perhaps luring) objects toward the surface of consciousness. Thus, what is not conscious appears to be at most preconscious in Freud's sense, something outside of immediate awareness but within easy reach: it is not marked by resistance to conscious articulation in an undisguised form. But this appearance is deceiving, for Peirce's outlook makes room for the unconscious in the strict Freudian sense.

In addition to a ubiquitous downward force or set of forces (consider, for example, his remarks regarding fatigue (CP 1.390; CP 7.552; mss 318, 1107, 00018), Peirce could readily admit without contradiction or contortion the presence of other, more selective forces (such as repression or censorship in its Freudian sense). In fact, CP 1.631 (the text quoted above) implies Peirce's rather acute awareness of such a selective force. Hence, there is more to Peirce's notion of the unconscious than the preconscious. In a fuller treatment of Peirce's understanding of the unconscious, the explanation of our mental life in terms of the interplay of forces and the underlying conception of force would have to be explored in detail. Again, similarities and differences between him and Freud are likely to be instructive. In particular, the question of the degree and ways in which Freud's theoretical commitments to a thoroughgoing determinism and to the human psyche as a homeostatic system undermine his own hermeneutic (and, thus, semiotic) approach is of course crucial here.

In this connection, it is illuminating to recall Dewey's observations in *The Public and Its Problems*: "Combined activity happens among human beings; but when nothing else happens it passes as inevitably into some other mode of interconnected activity as does the interplay of iron and the oxygen of water. What takes place [we may add: within as well as among human agents] is wholly describable in terms of energy, or, as we say in the case of human interactions, of force" (LW 2:330). But this is of course not the end of the story, for signs and symbols radically alter the interplay of intra- and interpersonal forces (even on the assumption that such forces are always already in some manner and measure themselves semiotic phenomena). "Only when there exist *signs* and *symbols* of activities and of their outcome[s] can the flux be viewed as from without, be arrested for consideration and esteem, and be regulated. Lightning strikes and rives a tree or rock, and the resulting fragments take up and continue the process of interaction, and so on and on. But when phases of the process are represented by signs [and symbols, as they always are for human witnesses and participants], a new medium is interposed. As symbols are related to one another, the important relations of a course of events are recorded and are preserved as meanings. Recollection and foresight are possible ..." (LW 2:330-331). "A community thus presents an order of energies transmuted into one of meanings which are appreciated and mutually referred by each other on the part of those engaged in combined action" (LW 2: 331). So too is the self such an ongoing transmutation of an order of forces into one of symbols. On this account, "'[f]orce' is not eliminated but is transformed in use and direction by ideas and sentiments made possible by means of symbols" (LW 2: 331). What Dewey outlines here is a semiotic approach closely akin to that of Peirce and somewhat distant from that of Freud (for Freud's mechanistic and hermeneutic sides are, given his theoretical commitments and controlling models, less easily brought into harmony with one another).

IV
The Preconscious: The Characteristic Awareness of Competent Agents

But the preconscious itself does not deserve to be slighted, especially given Peirce's emphasis on habits and his insistence that the smooth functioning of habits generally means a minimal degree of consciousness. For instance, we are in the process of opening a door largely unaware of the doorknob unless, contrary to expectations, it resists the deeply engrained and finely coordinated habits of hand, arm, eye, etc. The effectiveness and rapidity with which we realize our humbler purposes insure that human semiosis is characteristically a preconscious process. This is truly remarkable, for the realization of these purposes depends on interpreting with instantaneous facility the truly kaleidoscopic patterns of immediately impinging signals. Because of such facility, we are ordinarily not aware, but could readily become conscious, of the doorknobs we turn, the buttons we push, the laces we tie, etc.

This simple observation prompts me to propose what might seem to some a bold hypothesis. Not only do we need an account of how ideas become operative in the unconscious but inaccessible to consciousness (in a word, how ideas become repressed), we also need to comprehend how preconscious ideas become conscious. Given the effectiveness and thus fluidity of our habits, most of our ideas are preconscious. Semiotically speaking, the overwhelming majority of the signs we interpret are not focal objects of a heightened awareness; and, to an even greater extent, this is true of the processes by which we interpret these signs. The slight hitches inevitably punctuating any sustained endeavor invite us to be more attentive than we were just prior to the felt resistances; they signify the absence of a perfect attunement between the habits constitutive of our embodied agency and the habits ingredient in encountered objects. In addition, the complex array of animating purposes by which human endeavor is initiated, sustained, modified and of course frequently abandoned is such that it has itself engrained habits of attentiveness. For example, the musician walking through the woods is likely to hear the musical quality of the random sounds emanating from countless directions. My guess is that these two factors—the absence of perfect attunement and the presence of habituated attentiveness—go a long way toward explaining how preconscious ideas move in the direction of explicit attention, though the majority of them never reach that level of attention. In most of our everyday undertakings, we are perhaps far more like somnambulists than we imagine. Even so, in the course of our routines, we experience slight jarrings far more often than rude awakenings. These jarrings and our habits of attentiveness work together as an upward impulse; they act as a selective force by which certain objects are brought toward the visible surface of that bottomless lake called human consciousness. These objects are for the most part below, often *just* below, the surface of consciousness.

The fluidity experienced as the result of a finely nuanced and deftly flexible attunement, such as our embodied agency affords us in countless circumstances, could be called the firstness of thirdness. It is the qualitative aspect of an effective habit and, as such, is like the felt qualitative integrity of a melody in which one phrase melts into another. The utter arrest of a habit is painful (though depending on the circumstances perhaps only slightly so); to characterize such an experience as painful means, for Peirce, that it is marked by a struggle toward *quietus* (CP 5.113). In contrast, the fluent exercise of a habit is pleasurable; and, in turn, pleasure lies "in a peculiar mode of consciousness allied to the consciousness of *making a generalization*, in which not Feeling, but rather Cognition is the principal constituent" (CP 5.113). Hence, neither pain nor pleasure is a phenomenon in which firstness is predominant. Pain is predominantly a Second, whereas pleasure is principally a Third. Even so, the thirdness definitive of pleasure is such that the inherent delight of artful execution, no matter how rudimentary or even instinctive the art, propels and guides the execution itself; it is thirdness at one with both its own inner momentum and fortuitous circumstances.

Such attunement to inherent dynamism and environing factors can be so thoroughgoing as to encompass secondness only as a spur to ever more satisfying mediations (the way dissonance can serve in a musical composition to foster ever more melodic resolutions). In this case, secondness facilitates the flow of thirdness in a manner effacing its defining trait—its brute otherness. In it, the *fluidity* of habit can manifest the *firstness* of thirdness to a degree approximating primisense, that mode of consciousness in which qualitative immediacy and unbroken integrity distinguish it from altersense and medisense (CP 7.551).

Primisense or consciousness as firstness—as pure spontaneity, undifferentiated suchness, absolute ineffability, etcetera—is so far removed from how we ordinarily attend to bodily and worldly events and objects (from what we customarily call awareness or consciousness) that one *might* say to Peirce what Peirce himself said to James regarding the Jamesian use of "pure experience": "What you call 'pure experience' is not experience at all and certainly ought to have a name. It is downright bad morals so to misuse words, for it prevents philosophy from becoming a science" (CP 7.301). But, in truth, such a retort would not be just; for as Peirce takes pains to show (among other places, in various letters to William James), the equation of consciousness with feeling is firmly established, and, in addition, one of the meanings of "feeling" supports Peirce's own usage. With the appearance of each one of us and, presumably, also of organisms similar to us, it is as though an evolving world burst upon the scene out of "a chaos of unpersonalized feeling"—and did so in just the fashion Peirce described at the conclusion of "The Architecture of Theories" (CP 6.33)—only to confront a world already in place (albeit also an evolving world). It is not that idea-signs are first conscious and, then, by either a ubiquitous or special force exiled from consciousness; but rather that initially such signs are conscious only in a most attenuated form (that is, as primisense) (CP 7.551). They need to be brought to the level of what we most readily understand by consciousness, a sense of awareness in which both the otherness and significance of objects are immediately ingredient.

In actuality, our everyday awareness results from a continuous vacillation between, on the one hand, fluently functioning habits in which the otherness and significance of objects and events is more or less muted and, on the other, unexpectedly thwarted exertions in which this otherness and significance stands out to some extent. Alternately put, it vacillates for the most part between the firstness of thirdness (a completely unobstructed enactment of purpose) and a thirdness in which secondness and thirdness jostle for position with neither getting the upper hand. Purposeful endeavor, the very fabric of our everyday experience, is accordingly truly a tapestry woven of fulfillment and frustration, of deft execution and blind stumbling.

Experiences of marked secondness (for example, that of stubbing one's toe) are brutally punctuated exclamation points that, in the first instance, prompt immediate action (sometimes simply stopping what we are doing or, in the case of the stubbed toe, hopping on one foot and cursing the fates!) and, for reflective persons at least, invite an accounting of the self to itself. In the course of deliberation, the exclamation point is transformed into a series of question marks: Do I know what I am doing? Do I know where I am? In the midst of what sort of objects am I pursuing my purposes? Do I not care adequately for my safety? But, to repeat, everyday awareness is largely *not* a series of jolting frustrations; it is a shifting field in which now the feeling of unhindered process is predominant, now a delicate balance between resistant forces and facilitating clues (most characteristically, between an altersense relative to purposeful exertions and a medisense calling on interpretive ingenuity).

For Peirce, human beings are more or less competent actors, the everyday awareness described above being just the practical consciousness of competent agents (Giddens 1984; Colapietro 1994). To say this about humans is, of course, to imply that in some measure we are unwitting dupes. But the extent to which we are the playthings of forces beyond our consciousness and thus beyond our control ought not to be exaggerated. Indeed, given Peirce's commitment to agency (Colapietro 1991:141-143; 152-155; 1992), he refused to reduce consciousness to an epiphenomenon. While conscious agency plays only a modest role in the actual determination of present conduct and an even more modest part in the formation of our habits, such agency truly does exert an influence over how we are about to act and, beyond this, how we are disposed. But such agency is thwarted in its attempts to assist in the often precarious processes of evolving "normal interpretants" (Savan 1987-88:61-2). The more or less law-like ways in which the evolution of such interpretants is arrested are, upon my interpretation, the mechanisms of repression, the strategies by which the unconscious disrupts and undermines the ability of the self to develop more finely attuned, appropriately flexible, and effectively nuanced patterns of cognition, affection, and volition.

Above we noted that the extent of our self-delusion "is such to render philosophical rationalism a farce" (CP 1.631). In opposition to philosophical rationalism, Peirce explicitly defends philosophical sentimentalism. This defense is based on the conviction that the sentiments make the substance of the soul while cognition is only the surface (CP 1.628). Conscious reason, the agency by which cognitions are formally articulated, analyzed, and inferred from other cognitions, is but a superficial part of the human psyche. Moreover, reason "appeals to sentiment in the last resort. Sentiment on its side feels itself to be the man (or the woman to whom the appeal is being made). That is my simple apology for philosophical sentimentalism" (CP 1.632). In the text from which we have been quoting, Peirce does not hesitate to speak of sentiment and instinct in the same breath (for example, CP 1.628). He also asserts that "[i]nstinct is capable of development and growth" (CP 1.648). But the growth of instinct and sentiment takes place only by a slow process of largely unconscious percolation, the results of which "gradually reach the very core of one's being" (CP 1.648). On my reading, this core is the cluster of one's habits of affection and disgust, of sympathy and antipathy—the habits of feeling ultimately underlying our habits of both outward exertion and imaginative deliberation (that is, of action and thought).

In sum, then, mind is at once wider and deeper than consciousness. For Peirce, there are three forms of consciousness: the feeling of qualitative immediacy, the experience of brute opposition, and the awareness of ongoing mediation. One of the best discussions of these forms is still Nathan Houser's article entitled "Peirce's General Taxonomy of Consciousness," published in 1983 in the *Transactions of the Charles S. Peirce Society*. But what we ordinarily designate as everyday consciousness is, in fact, a complex affair in which the firstness of feeling, the secondness of opposition, and the thirdness of mediation are continuously interwoven to generate ever shifting patterns. The characteristic level of consciousness on which competent actors move and live is, in the strict sense, a preconscious level. But the disruption of our endeavors is of course due not only to unanticipated environmental obstacles but also to unacknowledged psychic burdens; we can be at odds with ourselves as well as with our environments. This suggests the need to come to terms with the unconscious. Analogous to Peirce's analysis of consciousness into three modes, it seems plausible (especially given his triadomania! (CP 1.568), to assume that for him there are three aspects of the unconscious as well.

V
The Unconscious in Light of Peirce's Categories

As noted earlier, only a conscientious reliance upon Peirce's categoreal scheme holds out the possibility that theoretical feebleness and facile eclecticism will be avoided. More positively, such reliance empowers us to trace the formal and dynamic relationships so crucial for the successful conduct of theoretical inquiry. Moreover, such reliance alone equips us to explore the unconscious from a truly Peircean perspective; for even though the unconscious clearly demands a semiotic interpretation, in its turn such a semiotic interpretation presupposes categoreal analyses at various levels of generality, ranging from the coenoscopic level of phenomenology itself to the idioscopic level of experimental psychology. In the words of David Savan, "While Peirce's three categories play an important role in every aspect of his thought, they are absolutely vital to his semeiotic. Peirce's first published papers on the categories presented them simply as the most basic part of his theory of signs. Semeiotic in all its definitions, divisions, trichotomies, branchings, and combinations is entirely governed, according to Peirce, by categorial theory" (Savan 1987-88:15; Shapiro 1983). Accordingly, what would be valuable at this point is to suggest a categoreal description of the unconscious.

Wollheim suggests that, for Freud, "the unconscious falls into two parts, that which was 'innately present originally' and that which 'was acquired in the course of the ego's development'" (Wollheim 1971:183; quotations from XXIII, 165). In contrast, Peirce's categories goad us into experimenting with the conceptual possibility that the unconscious falls into *three* parts. But just what might these be? Allow me to suggest, albeit very tentatively, the following. Somewhat paradoxically, the unconscious is itself a phenomenon in Peirce's sense. In fact, anything whatsoever is not only potentially a sign but also—again, at least potentially—a phenomenon. "That which underlies a phenomenon and determines it, thereby is, itself, in a measure, a phenomenon" (CP 7.569). The unconscious mind as that which underlies and determines the immediately or easily accessible regions of psychic life both conceals itself behind masks and reveals itself in its complex disguises and deceptions. In short, it is, "itself, in a measure, a phenomenon"—something which appears in some manner and measure and context(s), if only observers are skillful interpreters (CP 1.35) and in turn if interpreters are categoreal theorists. Of course, it might be objected that such interpreters and theorists patently fabricate the phenomena they allegedly observe; but such an objection can only be sustained by supposing that interpretive and theoretical schemes play no role whatsoever in defining what counts, in a given context, as a phenomenon (Short 1988). Such a supposition is, however, untenable.

If the unconscious is a phenomenon, even if only in an attenuated and indeed problematic sense, it must exhibit in its own unique way the ubiquitous features of any phenomenon whatsoever. But, to repeat, just what might these be? First, the unconscious as a phenomenon in which firstness is predominant would be the mind in its irrepressible spontaneity, its ineliminable wantonness, and its inexhaustible fecundity as (above all) iconic resource and symbolic possibility. Second, the unconscious as other, as second, would be that which stands over against consciousness, its irrepressible spontaneity operating precisely as a disruptive force, as an anarchical impulse.

Against the claim of Elisabeth Saporiti made in the discussion following the presentation of the original version of this paper, this emphasis does not bespeak merely a concern with the early Freud to the neglect of the later developments in his psychoanalytic theory (Wollheim 1971). To be sure, however, the distinctive form of otherness between ego and superego (or, to use the terms suggested by Bettleheim, between the I and over-I) would need to be explored along with the otherness of the unconscious itself.

Two points regarding the otherness of the unconscious might help to clarify what the distinctive shape of Peircean theory would be. First, Peirce is explicit that "we have an occult nature of which and of its contents we can only judge by the conduct that it determines, and by phenomena of that conduct" (CP 5.440). He supposes that: "All will assent to that (or all but the extreme nominalist), but the anti-synechistic thinkers wind themselves up in a factitious snarl by falsifying the phenomena in representing consciousness to be, as it were, a skin, a separate tissue, overlying an unconscious region of the occult nature, mind, soul, or physiological basis" (CP 5.440). In contrast a synechist will avoid such snarls by adhering to the view that "the difference is only relative and the demarcation not precise" (CP 5.440).

Second, Peirce's distinction between two grades of existence might help to clarify, on the one hand, the otherness between the unconscious and consciousness, and on the other, that between the I and the over-I. Peirce suggests that there are two grades of existence, namely, "a lower kind, approximating to the inner being of a simple quality, yet existential, instead of being merely potential, consisting in the action of a thing upon itself, a sort of embryonic self-consciousness; and a higher grade consisting in the action of a thing upon all other things of the same universe, and measuring by its intensity its remoteness from each of them" (CP 6.346). Peirce notes that: "A whole universe of such existents can only have the lower, or internal grade of existence" (CP 6.346). While the otherness between I and over-I is best conceived in terms of the lower grade of existence, that between a conscious agent and its actual world is best construed as the higher grade of existence. Finally, the otherness existing between the unconscious and consciousness is an otherness approximating that between self and world, though of course not an absolute or thoroughgoing otherness.

But brute tyranny is a wholly destructive affair, thus one guaranteeing its own annihilation. Thus, the surreptitious tyranny of unacknowledged symbols and repressed narratives far better serves the hegemony of the unconscious. Yet the moment we introduce symbols and narratives we have the unconscious as a phenomenon in which thirdness is predominant (disguised thirdness being an even more complex form of mediation than straightforward symbolization, since it is dependent upon but not reducible to such symbolization). In other words, we have the unconscious itself as *that which mediates* between our (pre)conscious agency and the shifting scenes of our various engagements. Frequently if not characteristically (Dewey 1925: 227-228; 239), the unconscious mediates in such a way as to render our responses infantile or, at most, far from subtle and nuanced. While John J. McDermott (1976) is certainly correct in asserting that the pragmatists did not develop in much detail a theory of repression, there are perhaps greater resources in this philosophical tradition than even most of its sympathetic interpreters fully realize. What I have attempted to accomplish here with respect to Peirce, Bruce Wilshire has in effect also tried recently to do with respect to Dewey—namely, to open a field of inquiry in which the texts of the pragmatists are brought into fruitful contact with influential articulations of the psychoanalytic perspective. See his "Body-Mind and Subconsciousness: Tragedy in Dewey's Life and Work" (Wilshire 1993). Note well: the unconscious so conceived is as much (if not more) *between* ourselves and our world as it is behind or beneath the conscious regions of our own psychic life.

VI
Conclusion

From a detailed categoreal description of the unconscious (of course, one far more detailed than my all too quick sketch), we would need to move toward an equally detailed semiotic description in which habit as interpretant would play a, if not *the*, central role (de Lauretis 1984, 1994). But, alas, what is at once so exhilarating and yet so frustrating is the tremendous amount of time and energy required simply to catch up to where Peirce was, especially, in the last decade or so of his life. This practically means that we must continuously begin anew in thinking about (among other matters) the unconscious. Even if, as Teresa de Lauretis argues in her most recent book, we need to read Freud with Peirce (1994, chapter 7; 1984, chapter 6) we also need to read Peirce with Freud and, no doubt, with Jung, Lacan, Kristeva, and others. We need to read the unconscious in light of Peircean categories and semeiotic, no less than the man and philosopher in light of psychoanalytic theories (Colapietro 1994). My modest hope is that, in assembling these notes for a sketch of a Peircean theory of the unconscious, I not only have rendered some of these suggestions somewhat plausible but also have offered helpful clues for how to execute an exciting but arduous task.

ENDNOTES

1. This paper grew out of a presentation (University of California, Berkeley; June 13, 1994) at the Fifth Congress of the International Association for Semiotic Studies—Association Internationale de Semiotique (IASS-AIS). A number of people were helpful in commenting on earlier drafts of this essay, but above all Robert Ashmore, Anne Freadman, Josephine Glorie, Wojciech Kalaga, Elisabeth Saporiti, and Kory Sorrell.

2. I am indebted to Robert Ashmore for helping me see the need to qualify this claim. On the ways and degree to which habits can prompt and facilitate attention or awareness, Dewey is especially illuminating (MW 14). Much more than James and even more than Peirce, he is alive to this possibility *inherent in* some types of habituation.

WORKS CITED

Braga, Lucia Santaella. "Difficulties and Strategies in Applying Peirce's Semiotics." *Semiotica* 1993 97-3/4: pp. 401-410.

Brent, Joseph. *Charles Sanders Peirce: A Life*. (Bloomington: Indiana University Press, 1993).

Colapietro, Vincent. *Peirce's Approach to the Self: A Semiotic Perspective on Human Subjectivity*. (Albany: SUNY Press, 1989).

_____. "Two Rival Conceptions of the Semiological Ideal: Peirce versus Saussure." *Face - Revista de semiótica e comunicação*, número especial - 1 (agosto 1991): pp. 135-158.

_____. "Purpose, Power, and Agency." *The Monist* (October 1992), volume 75, number 4: pp. 423-444.

_____. "Philosophical Biography: Preliminary Reflections on a Distinctive Form of Historical Inquiry." 1995 *Semiotics 1993*, eds. Robert Corrington and John Deely, Lanham: University Press of America.

Davidson, Donald. "Paradoxes of Irrationality," eds. Wollheim and Hopkins, 1982.

de Lauretis, Teresa. *Alice Doesn't: Feminism, Semiotics, Cinema*. (Bloomington: Indiana University Press, 1984).

_____. *The Practice of Love: Lesbian Sexuality and Perverse Desire*. (Bloomington: Indiana University Press, 1994).

Dewey, John. *Human Nature and Conduct*. (New York: Henry Holt & Co., 1992). All references in this paper are to *The Middle Works of John Dewey, 1899-1924*, volume 14 Carbondale: Southern Illinois University Press, 1983. Cited in the paper as MW 14.

_____. *The Public and Its Problems*. (New York: Henry Holt and Company, 1927). All references are to the *Later Works of John Dewey, 1925-1953*, volume 2, (Carbondale: SIU Press, 1988). Cited in the paper as LW 2.

Eco, Umberto. *A Theory of Semiotics*. (Bloomington: Indiana Unversity Press, 1976).

Fisch, Max H. *Peirce, Semeiotic, and Pragmatism*, eds. Kenneth Laine Ketner and Christian J. W. Kloesel, (Bloomington: Indiana University Press, 1986).

Freud, Sigmund. *General Introduction to Psycho-Analysis*. (Liverright: New York, 1920/1924).

_____. *Das Ich und das Es*. (Leipzig, Vienna, & Zurich: Internationaler Psychoanalytischer Verlag, 1923). All references in this paper are to *The Ego and the*

Id, translated by Joan Riviere and revised by James Strachey (New York: W. W. Norton & Company, 1960).

_____. *Das Unbehagen in Der Kultur*. (Vienna Internationaler Psychoanalytischer Verlag, 1930). All references in this paper are to *Civilization and Its Discontents*, the English translation by James Strachey, (New York: W. W. Norton & Co., 1989).

Gardner, Sebastian. *Irrationality and the Philosophy of Psychoanalysis*. (Cambridge: Cambridge University Press, 1993).

Grosz, Elizabeth. *Jacques Lacan: A Feminist Introduction*. (London: Routledge, 1990).

Harwick, Charles S., ed., *Semiotic and Significs: The Correspondence Between Charles S. Peirce and Victoria Lady Welby*. (Bloomington: Indiana University Press, 1977).

Hartmann, Eduard von. *Die Philosophie des Unbewussten*. (Berlin, 1868). *The Philosophy of the Unconscious*.

Houser, Nathan. "Peirce's General Taxonomy of Consciousness." *Transactions of the Charles S. Peirce Society*, 1983 volume XIX: pp. 331-359.

Kaufmann, Walter. *Discovering the Mind: Freud versus Adler and Jung*. (New York: McGraw-Hill, 1980).

Lacan, Jacques. *Écrits: A Selection*, translated by Alan Sheridan. (New York: W. W. Norton & Company, 1977).

MacIntyre, Alasdair. *The Unconscious: A Conceptual Analysis*. (Atlantic Highlands: Humanities Press, 1958).

McDermott, John J. *The Culture of Experience*. (New York: NYU Press, 1976).

Nietzzsche, Friedrich. *Jenseits von Gut und Böse*. Leipzig: Druck und Vrelag von C. G. Naumann, 1886. All refereences in this paper are to *Beyond Good and Evil*, the English translation by Walter Kaufmann, (New York: Random House, 1966).

Peirce, C. S. *Collected Papers of Charles Sanders Peirce*, volumes I-VI, eds. Charles Hartshorne and Paul Weiss. (Cambridge, Massachusetts Belknap Press of Harvard University Press, 1931-).

_____. *Collected Papers of Charles Sanders Peirce*, volumes VII & VIII eds. Arthur W. Burks. (Cambridge, Massachusetts: Belknap Press of Harvard University Press, 1957).

Pharies, David A. *Charles S. Peirce and the Linguistic Sign*. (Benjamins North America, 1985).

Ragland-Sullivan, Ellie. *Jacques Lacan and the Philosophy of Psychoanalysis*. (Urbana: University of Illinois Press, 1986).

Rorty, Richard. "Freud and Moral Reflection" in *Philosophical Papers*, volume 2. (Cambridge: Cambridge University Press, 1991).

Savan, David. *An Introduction to C. S. Peirce's Full System of Semeiotic*. (Toronto: Toronto Semiotic Circle, 1987-88).

Shapiro, Michael. *The Sense of Grammar: Language as Semeiotic*. (Bloomington: Indiana University Press, 1983).

Sheriff, John K. *The Fate of Meaning: Charles Peirce, Structuralism, and Literature*. (Princeton: Princeton University Press, 1989).

Short, T. L. "The Growth of Symbols." *Cruzeiro Semiotio*, numero 8 (janeiro 1988): 81-87.

Stephens, G. Lynn. "Noumenal Qualia: C. S. Peirce on Our Epistemic Access to Feelings." *Transactions of the Charles S. Peirce Society*, 1985 XXI: 95-108.

Trilling, Lionel. *Freud and the Crisis of Our Culture*. (Boston: Beacon Press, 1955).

Wilshire, Bruce. "Body-Mind and Subconsciousness: Tragedy in Dewey's Life and Work" in *Philosophy and the Reconstruction of Culture*, edited by John J. Stuhr (Albany: SUNY Press, 1993).

Wittgenstein, Ludwig. "Conversations on Freud" in *Lectures and Conversations*, ed. Cyril Barrett. (Berkeley: University of California Press, 1972).

Wollheim, Richard. *Sigmund Freud*. (Cambridge: Cambridge University Press, 1971).

Wollheim, Richard and James Hopkins, eds., *Philosophical Essays on Freud*. (Cambridge: Cambridge University Press, 1982).

BIOGRAPHICAL NOTES

Joseph Brent is Professor Emeritus at the University of the District of Columbia and author of *Charles Sanders Peirce: A Life* (Bloomington: Indiana University Press). He is currently working on an interpretive history of crime in the United States, a perceptual model of human interaction, and, as a three to five year project, a comprehensive biography of C.S. Peirce.

John Brigham is Professor of Political Science at the University of Massachusetts, Amherst. His books include *Property and the Politics of Entitlement (1990), The Cult of the Court (1987), Civil Liberties and American Democracy (1984), Constitutional Language (1978), Making Public Policy (1977).* He is former Chair of the Law and Courts Section of the American Political Science Association and Trustee of the Law and Society Association. He is currently studying the manifestations of law on the Lower East Side of Manhattan (with Diana Gordon) and other ways law contributes to the constitution of social life.

José de Sousa e Brito is a distinguished judge in Lisbon, Portugal, and well-known for his work on Kelsen's theories of law. He has published in the *Archives de philosophie du droit*, in the *International Journal for Semiotics of Law*, and has presented papers at IVR, at the IASL and at the Round Table on Law and Semiotics. At present he is working on aspects of comparative constitutional law and pragmatism.

Vincent M. Colapietro, Professor of Philosophy at Fordham University, is the author of *Peirce's Approach to the Self* and *Glossary of Semiotics*. At present, he is exploring (along with other topics) a distinctively Peircean approach to psychoanalytic theory and practice. His contribution to *Spaces and Significations* is part of this ongoing project. In addition, he is investigating the implications of Peirce's claim to be "a convinced Pragmaticist in Semeiotic."

Marcel Danesi is Professor of Italian Studies at the University of Toronto where he also directs the Semiotics Research Unit. He is one of the principals in the International Summer Institute for Semiotic Studies, in collaboration with the University of Helsinki. His extensive publications on Vico, and on the semiotics of music are widely respected as major texts. He is the principal organizer for an important interdisciplinary symposium on semiotics as a bridge for the sciences.

Ingo J. Hueck is a Doctor of Law, teaching at the Department of Law at the University of Bielefeld. He has published extensively on issues in Public International Law and International Economics. He has presented papers at international meetings of colloquia on law and semiotics. His present project in legal philosophy deals with the works of Walter Jellinek.

Roberta Kevelson, Distinguished Professor of Philosophy at Penn State, directs the Center for Semiotics of Law, Government and Economics. Her fifth, most recent book on Peirce, *Peirce, Science, Signs*, 1995 Rodopi, links the previous book on *Peirce's Esthetics*, 1993 P. Lang, with *Peirce's Pragmatism*, in process.

Joel Levin practices law in Cleveland, and teaches on aspects of jurisprudence at Case Western Reserve University. His publications include book-length studies on problems in Natural Law as well as recent papers on semiotics of law: "The Action in the Transaction: Life around the Contractual Edges," ed. R. Kevelson, *Flux, Complexity and Illusion*, 1993, and "Lear's Final Argument ..." in ed. R. Kevelson, *The Eyes of Justice*, 1994.

Robert C.L. Moffat is Professor of Law at the University of Florida. He is also the Executive Director of AMINTAPHIL, the American branch of the International Association for Philosophy of Law and Social Philosophy, (IVR); Editor in Chief, *Southwestern Law Journal*; and recipient of the Lon Fuller Prize in Jurisprudence, 1987.

Mariana Net is Senior Researcher at the Institute of Linguistics in Bucharest, Romania and is Associate Professor in the English Department at that same university. She has published extensively in the fields of linguistics, semiotics, poetics, philosophy of language and spectacology. Her recent books include *Poetics of Atmosphere*, 1989; *The Metalanguage of the Literary Text*, 1989; and a forthcoming work on Alexander Dumas. Her book in progress concerns relationships "between semiotics and mentalities."

William Pencak, Professor of History, Penn State, has belonged to the Center for Semiotic Research since its inception. He is the author of *History, Signing In; Studies in History and Semiotics* (Peter Lang, 1993) and *The Conflict of Law and Justice in the Icelandic Sagas* (forthcoming from Rodopi in 1995) in addition to nine other books he has written and edited. He edits the journal *Pennsylvania History*.

Norma Procopiow teaches Legal Writing at the University of Maryland. Her main area of research has been the semiotic systems underlying rhetoric as diachronic cultural communication. She is currently working on an article which questions the oppositional narratives in the O.J. Simpson Case as constructs of evidence which have traditionally been considered "legally autonomous." She has published widely on cultural semiotics, including work on film, graffiti, and the politicization of the art museum.

W.T. Scott is Professor of Language and Media at Caledonian University where he heads the Department. His important works on language and semiotics of law include the well-known book, *The Possibility of Communication*, 1990, Mouton de Gruyter and also many contributions to the publications of the Center for Semiotic Research at Penn State: "In Search of the Truly Fake," 1988, Plenum; "Codification," 1992, P. Lang, and "The Literary Fraud," 1995, P. Lang.

SUBJECT INDEX